"*This Jade World* is beautifully candid, funny, and heartbreaking, a startling meditation on intimacy and marriage, family history and legacy, and the strangeness of how relationships change."
—Beth (Bich Minh) Nguyen, author of *Stealing Buddha's Dinner*

"In *This Jade World* Sukrungruang offers us a prayer and a meditation on the beginnings and endings of love. The love of parents and their children. The love among men and women. The love between the skin we live in and the memories we house. In this rare and beautiful offering, we experience a man undone by love and his journey to salvage hope in the face of incredible loneliness and doubt, a search for salvation found first in a dream."
—Kao Kalia Yang, author of *Somewhere in the Unknown World* and *The Latehomecomer: A Hmong Family Memoir*

"It is a truth, universally acknowledged, that when seemingly happy couples break up we all wonder what the hell happened. In Ira Sukrungruang's affecting and vulnerable memoir, *This Jade World*, he narrates the dissolution of one marriage and the burgeoning of another as a double love story, laced with wonder, grief, downward spirals, and mature reinventions. Set in both Thailand and the U.S., examined against an epic web of family, domestic strife, and rearrangement, this gorgeously written book illuminates the necessity and complexity of intimate joy."
—Barrie Jean Borich, author of *Body Geographic* and *Apocalypse, Darling*

"*This Jade World* is compulsively readable—its short chapters are polished stones, each delightful by itself while leading us on to another, another, until we've walked the road through the author's divorce and into his new life and love. Mostly set during his yearly visits to his family, Sukrungruang offers a keenly observed Thailand—the monks slipping their cellphones into their robes, the tattoo artist praying before pushing his needle into the author's back. And throughout we have the deepest pleasure—that of language charged with imagery, leavened with humor, and pierced with insight."
—Beth Ann Fennelly, author of *Heating and Cooling: 52 Micro-Memoirs*

THIS JADE WORLD

AMERICAN LIVES

Series editor: Tobias Wolff

This Jade World

World   *Ira Sukrungruang*

University of Nebraska Press

LINCOLN

Earlier versions of the following essays were previously
published: "The First" as "The First Transgression"
in *Midwestern Gothic*, no. 19 (Fall 2015); "What I
Want" as "On Wanting" in the *McNeese Review*
(April 2015); "Touch" in the *Los Angeles Review*,
no. 21 (June 2017); "Okay" as "OK" in *Stone Canoe*,
no. 11 (2017); and "Invisible Partners" and "After
the Hysterectomy" in *Brevity*, no. 49 (May 2015)
and no. 56 (September 2017), respectively.

Library of Congress Cataloging-in-Publication Data
Names: Sukrungruang, Ira, author.
Title: This jade world / Ira Sukrungruang.
Description: Lincoln: University of Nebraska
Press, [2021] | Series: American lives
Identifiers: LCCN 2020057439
ISBN 9781496226013 (paperback)
ISBN 9781496228840 (epub)
ISBN 9781496228857 (pdf)
Subjects: LCSH: Sukrungruang, Ira—Travel—
Thailand—Chiang Mai. | Sukrungruang,
Ira—Family. | Chiang Mai (Thailand)—Description
and travel. | Chiang Mai (Thailand)—Social life
and customs—21st century. | Thai Americans—
Thailand—Chiang Mai—Biography. | Tampa
(Fla.)—Biography. | Man-woman relationships—
Florida. | Man-woman relationships—Illinois.
Classification: LCC DS589.C5 S84 2021 |
DDC 305.8959/11073092 [B]—dc23
LC record available at https://lccn.loc.gov/2020057439

Set in Ehrhardt by Mikala R. Kolander.
Designed by N. Putens.

for Aunty Sue (1935–2017)
for my father (1934–2017)
for Bodhi

Contents

Acknowledgments

This Jade World began as a travel blog of my annual trip to Thailand, but soon after writing the first post it became so much more. That's the magic of writing: the discovery that a word can open up a world and that world is dark and light. Every day, for six weeks, I sat on my mother's porch in Chiang Mai, writing in a gray hoodie even though the temperature was hot, even though I sweated and suffered. I am grateful for that hoodie. I am grateful to that porch and the fan aimed at my legs to chase the mosquitoes away. I could not have written a draft of this book anywhere else but there. There, as Thailand was trying to find herself (again). There in the heat of the rainy season. There with my family ever present: Aunty Sue, whose existence on this earth was a gift; my father, Montri, whose laughter I can still hear; and my mother, who sat and watched me write every morning without saying a word, who answered questions about Thai history and the nuances of the Thai language, who simply, then and now, watched over me.

I am indebted to the thousands of students I've taught over the years; your energy propels me to the page, reminding me of the necessity of art and why it matters. Thank you to Brush Creek Foundation for the Arts and the Ragdale Foundation for providing me time to sit and think and read and be. I am forever grateful to the editors and magazines who published some chapters of this book in different versions: *Brevity*, the *McNeese Review*, the *Los Angeles Review*, *Stone Canoe*, and *Midwestern Gothic*.

This was not an easy book to write, so I'm sure it wasn't an easy book to read for those closest to me, my forever friends, who took the time to sift through multiple drafts: K. C. Wolfe—your love for language enlightened these pages; Alysia Sawchyn—you found the shape of the memoir with your meticulous read; Jon Chopan—your keen eye sharpened the direction of this book and your honesty cut through some of the bs in those early drafts and, most importantly, your friendship got me through that year.

To Katie Rigel, thank you for shaping the writer I am. I value our friendship in ways I can't articulate. You and your family were and are so essential in my life. Thank you for letting me write my version of our story.

To the folks at University of Nebraska Press who saw something other than lots of whining in this book. I am honored to be part of the American Lives Series, honored to be among some outstanding writers.

Dee—you saved me.

Bo—you are my heart.

THIS JADE WORLD

The First

You meet a woman you've seen online in a motel room. The door of the motel is off-white, the number of the room bleeding rust. Imagine standing outside that door, looking back to where you came from, at the car parked at the very edge of an empty lot, at the neon sign of a strip club next door, advertising no cover, at the dark, shadowy flats of Florida beyond. You think about driving home to where your wife is packing to leave for Illinois, the end of a marriage. Maybe you can tell her to stay. Don't go. Maybe you can apologize for what you have done in the marriage, the distance you put between you and her. Apologize for failing to give her what she wants and needs and deserves. But the door opens. A woman says hello in a shaky voice. You don't remember what color her hair is because the lights are dim, and the planet seems suddenly absent of color. You aren't in the right state of mind to remember much of anything, only that you have walked in and closed the door behind you, only that you have crossed a threshold and there is no going back. Your insides shake. Blood races through your extremities, blood surging like the hot gush of a geyser, making you feel light on your feet and light in the head, so you brace yourself on a round table. The woman sits on the bed, cross-legged, in jeans. She does not look like her picture online, where she wears only a black bra and smiles coyly with vivid red lips and pale skin. *Looking for adventure*, her tagline reads. *Can you deliver?* Here, in the dark, in this room that smells of stale cigarettes, she is even more beautiful, shy, as if this might be her first time, like you. You want to think this. You want to believe that perhaps she is here because her life has not fulfilled its promises, and at home there is a husband watching the Rays game on television, not knowing his wife has ducked out to come to a dirty motel to meet a man, just as lonely, just as desperate as she is. You want this to be true to alleviate the rock of guilt in your stomach. You want to believe you are not alone in this, not as dirty as you feel. She takes off her blue blouse—or is it gray?—one button at a time, not like a stripper, but like someone figuring out for the first time what buttons are for. You remember her bra, plain and white with a curious bow in the middle. Your eyes shoot up toward the ceiling because you haven't seen another naked woman in fifteen years. Not someone who isn't your wife. Not someone who sits a few feet from you. She asks if you are going to take off your clothes, and you suddenly suck in your stomach as far as it can go, suck it in so deeply that your breath gets stuck and you cough. She laughs, and you laugh. She says it's okay, the lights can be off, and if it's more comfortable for you she'll turn around. You shake your head and walk over to the bed and sit next to her, the heat from her body on your shoulder. And then she pushes you down while carefully sliding your shirt off. You lie there like a child, your hands on either side of your head, and she moves down and slips off your shorts. As she does this, her fingers graze your legs, your thighs, your ankles. She asks if it's okay to kiss you and you nod and her lips finds yours and her tongue dances in your mouth and she tastes like white Tic Tacs, like the ones your wife always keeps in her purse. You pull her into you and she moans in your mouth. Your hands travel the length of her back and she startles just a bit, but before you can say anything, before you can apologize for the rough calluses, the sharp edges of skin, she says it's okay, it's okay okay okay, and she's onto your neck with soft kisses. You slide your hands under the waistline of her jeans, squeezing her bottom. She rises and straddles you, her jeans grinding slowly in circles. She asks if this is okay, a whisper, and you nod. A nodding machine, you think, a stupid nodding machine. Her breaths quicken, her hands on your chest, and she seems to be looking at the ceiling, the water stain just above you, and you seem to be trying to look at what she's looking at because you can't look at her, her in her little bow bra, her and her breasts, which are heavy, which, when she presses her arms together, form a dark canyon between them. She asks if it's okay to touch you and you nod. So she feels underneath your underwear and strokes you gently and you have to turn away and close your eyes because there is a hand on your cock and it isn't your wife's and it is softer, smaller, and you can feel a ring on one of her fingers because it grazes the sensitive side of you. And you think this feels good, more than good, and you want to go on, but other thoughts invade your head like all your insecurities, all your woes, all the reasons you stopped having sex for over a year until this moment. She asks if this is okay. And you nod. She asks if this is how you like it. And you nod. She says you aren't getting hard. She asks if it's her, does she not turn you on? It isn't her. You can't turn on. You haven't been turned on for a long time. You look at her, but she's staring at the headboard of the bed, and from this angle she appears defeated, tired, and you can tell she is doubting you, doubting the whole situation, because it turns out you can't deliver. You are not the adventure she was hoping for. You can't fix the fractures in her life because you can't fix yours. You can't do anything, naked, in a motel room, a strange woman on top of you, the bow of her bra like pupilless eyes. And sadness spills forth, a flood, not for yourself—that sadness is and will remain in you for the months to come, even during the other encounters, in other motels and cars and dark bedrooms—but a sadness for this woman, who you, at this moment, this quiet moment save her breath and the slight electrical buzz of the alarm clock, have fallen in love with. Not a deep love. Not a love like the one you share with your wife—because you still love her, though love is not enough—but a love nonetheless. A love that is contained in this room, in between the flowery print of the walls, only at this moment. You lift her up off the bed and turn her over. The swiftness of the movement catches her off guard and she takes a quick inhale of breath, and now it is your lips tasting her neck and shoulders, it is your lips kissing her nipples through her bra, and it is your fingers traveling down the plush of her stomach, under her jeans, under her underwear, and you whisper whether this is okay, and she nods and sighs, nods and arches her back, nods when you enter the heat between her legs, nods, nods, nods.

I

I Am Sad

It's six in the morning, and the doves are cooing the world awake, the parakeets in my uncle's birdcage squeak and squawk in chaotic melody, a fountain trickles over stone, a fan points at my legs, keeping mosquitoes away. For the past ten years, I have found myself here, at my mother's home in Chiang Mai, Thailand, at my favorite spot, at my favorite table, in my favorite plastic chair, during my favorite time of day. Since my mother and Aunty Sue moved back to Thailand in 2004, having retired as nurses in Chicago after thirty-six years, I've come to make sure they are safe and taken care of, to spend a few weeks with them before returning to the States.

I'm not a stranger here, in this panhandle country where my blood runs like rivers of the earth. I first came as a boy of three, annoying the house dogs into barking frenzies. As an ornery teenager, modeling American fashions for my young cousins. As a young adult, obsessed with fast computers and faster women. I've come for weddings and funerals, cried over stray dogs and cats, feeling helpless in their homelessness. Thirteen years ago, I was married in the shadow of a looming Buddha, leaning against my midwestern bride, Katie, a white string lacing through our hands, believing, despite the heat and humidity that dampened our backs, that this would be forever.

Now, I return divorced, and the year between visits seems a deep hole I'm emerging out of.

Above me, the sun peeks through the emerald leaves of a champac tree. Green clings to everything, a wild green that climbs and laces through bamboo fences and around telephone poles. Wherever there is a crack—in the earth, in cement, in tar—green finds a way to sprout. My father used to say the green in Thailand was the jewel of the world, that everywhere you turned you were able to find unimaginable riches. He'd point to rubber trees and terraced rice fields and say this was mine, every bit of it. It didn't matter that I was a boy born in Chicago, a place grayer than green. "Home," he would insist, "is here."

I've come to see Thailand the way my father sees it. Each time I return, however, it's like someone has changed the locations of all the light switches. It takes time to adjust. To figure things out. Language trickles out of my mouth. I will stumble with my Thai for the next few days, and when I return to America in four weeks, I will stumble with my English. Still, there is a comfort here I have not experienced in any other place. A comfort that is both chaotic and enigmatic.

Everything in Thailand is chaotic and enigmatic.

At the moment, the country is without a government and under military rule, divided by colors like Chicago gangs of days past—the reds and yellows. For months Bangkok was rocked with demonstrations, violence escalating and escalating until the military took control. Now the country is quiet, the green time before a storm. Life continues. With soldiers carrying semiautomatics while patrolling public areas. With stern stares at any citizen wearing red or yellow. With whispers in small corners of markets. James Baldwin spoke of this pent-up silence in his essay "Notes of a Native Son" during the 1943 race riot in Harlem: "All of Harlem, indeed, seemed to be infected by waiting. I had never known it to be so violently still."

My mother brings me a cup of instant coffee and two hard-boiled eggs. She sits next to me. I know she wants to ask about my year away, about my life after the divorce. She wants to know whether I'm happy. She wants to hear my story because she worries. I know this, know she has stayed up late at night wondering where I am when I don't answer her calls, and when I do, why I'm quick to say everything is fine. She wonders, I'm sure, about how heartbroken I have been, and what it was like to be apart from the woman I married thirteen years ago, what it was like to start another phase of my life the way she had when my father left. She wonders, I am sure, about Katie, a woman she has learned to love, a woman she has given her son to with the expectation that she would care for him as she had. My mother knows I feel too much. She tells me all the time. "Yah kliat mak." *Don't stress.* But she knows that is impossible. Worry clings to me like cockleburs in a dog's coat, digging deep into the skin.

Beside me, an orange hibiscus blooms like a new sun. We sit and watch it. It nods slightly in the whispering breeze. Geckos scamper along cement walls. Sparrows grab day-old bread crumbs in the driveway. The day begins with the small sounds of the living.

*

In the early evening, on the television, Iran faces off against Argentina in the 2014 World Cup. Aunty Sue cooks outside, egg-drop soup with sliced scallions and cucumbers. She's stir-fried squash with large cloves of garlic, perfuming the house. If there is a heaven, this is what I wish it to smell like—my aunt's cooking, a reminder of my childhood in Illinois, a taste of Thailand in the urban sprawl of Chicago. My aunt is a culinary wizard, a woman who is not related by blood but one I consider my second mother. She met my mother in 1968 as they were starting new jobs in an inner-city hospital, eight thousand miles from home. They have been inseparable ever since.

My mother goes about the kitchen, arranging and rearranging mugs and plates. She scrubs the sink, and it makes a sound like a baying hound.

The kitchen in her Chiang Mai home resembles the kitchen of our Chicago home before she moved. My mother shipped over the cream-colored refrigerator, though it is at least twenty years old; the dining room table with my eighth-grade scrawl underneath, *Ira was here*; the black leather couches that occupy the adjacent living room, purchased before 1976, the cushions held together with electric tape. On the refrigerator are the same magnets. A cardinal, her favorite bird. Dopey, one of Snow White's seven dwarfs. And the various states my mother and aunt have traveled to—Maine, Alaska, Ohio, New York, and more. There are pictures of me all over it, in various phases of my life. I ask my mother why she brought all of these with her, why she insisted on keeping the old silverware and cutting board and blunted kitchen knives. There are refrigerators and couches in Thailand, I say; it is more expensive to ship these things than to buy new ones. She shrugs. "Memory," she says. "I keep them for good memories."

My mother dries her hands on a washcloth. "Tell me the truth," she says in Thai, "do you still love her?"

"Katie's my best friend."

"Americans," she says. "Friends after a breakup. So strange."

It is not Americans who are strange. It is my relationship with Katie that is.

"In Thailand, sometimes women cut off the man's pee-pee after a breakup." My mother makes a snipping gesture with her fingers and laughs. "You know what a pee-pee is, right?"

I roll my eyes.

"Just making sure your Thai is still sharp."

Earlier in the afternoon I gave my mother and Aunty Sue a letter from Katie. I never read it. Whatever was communicated would be between them and them alone. When my mother finished reading, she first commented on Katie's use of font. "Big letters. She knows she's writing to old women." Then she said, "Such a good girl. Like Thai." Then she said, "I am sad."

Sadness exists in all breakups. Not just for the couple. It was like this for our friends in the States, too. One of them, this wonderful specimen of a boy Katie and I nicknamed Baby Beluga, said he felt like his parents were breaking up. Another kept apologizing, and I reassured her it was okay. One said, "Well, shit, you two have really fucked it up for the rest of us." Despite this, Katie and I agreed to remain amicable, to be in each other's lives, no matter what paths we found ourselves on.

What my mother knows of breakups is heartache and betrayal and infidelity. What she knows is long days and nights with a sense of loss so deep it has never healed, a scab constantly picked at. Even now, over twenty years after the split, when I speak of my father, she tightens, her back hunches as if she's a cat about to attack.

Aunty Sue brings in the soup. Sweat bleeds through her thin T-shirt and drips down the flat of her nose. The three of us sit around the table for an early dinner. Jet lag tugs at my eyes. I yawn and eat. The soup slides down my throat, warms my belly.

"Things begin and end," Aunty Sue says. She says things like this, little fortunes. She said this when she read the letter, too.

"It's still sad," says my mother. "How many years?"

"Twelve of marriage," I say. "Fifteen since we first met."

"So sad." My mother stares at a picture of Katie and me on the refrigerator, when we were young and living in southern Illinois, our golden retrievers giving us wet kisses.

"I'm okay," I say. "Katie's okay."

"And you have a new friend." My mother pats her forehead with a handkerchief. The thermometer on the wall reads thirty-five degrees Celsius. She says my new love's name, Deedra, but mispronounces it. I tell her she needs to add an r.

"American names," she says. "So hard."

"Thai names," I say. "So long."

"Is she a nice girl?"

"The nicest."

"Does she cook for you?" Aunty Sue says. "You were going to die from all of Katie's grilled cheeses."

"Deedra is a good cook," I tell her.

"Do you think she is the one?" my mother asks.

I don't know how to answer this. I've heard "the one" endlessly in the past year. *You can now find the one. Maybe there's one out there looking for you. Do you think she's the one?* I've fallen for Deedra, despite my fears. She was the constant reminder that I didn't have to go this world alone. Part of me believes she is the one—whatever that means—but the other part knows that it has been a year since Katie, and though that year was long and arduous, how smart is it to fall so hard and so soon?

Aunty Sue spoons stir-fry onto my plate. "You've inherited your mother's curse," she says.

"All our curses," my mother says. She speaks of her sisters' marriages, all failed save for one, all disillusioned by men and love.

I spent most of the year in a state of disillusionment. This disillusionment led to sleepless nights and poor choices. I did not want to wake up.

And when I did, everything seemed too bright, so much so that I took to wearing sunglasses everywhere I went, even indoors. I found myself at bars and drank until I was dizzy. Sometimes, I could not make it into the house. Sometimes I found myself in someone else's bed next to the alien warmth of a foreign body.

I don't tell my mother and aunt any of this. I give them the family friendly version. I say I'm in a good place. Katie is in a good place. We have found the things we needed apart from each other, at least for the time being.

Garlic spreads in my mouth, and the subtle taste of palm sugar and soy lingers on the tongue.

On the TV, Argentina scores a goal.

My mother misses it; she misses most things. "What happened?"

"Goal," I say.

Aunty Sue squints at the TV. Shrugs. "Everything these days moves too fast."

In 1997

In 1997, Princess Diana died. Mother Teresa died. Members of Heaven's Gate committed mass suicide in a suburb outside of San Diego, and a Thai boy in small-town Illinois decided to lose weight and become desirable.

It was a decision made on the spot, like most big decisions are. One day he stood naked in front of mirror and realized how much he hated himself. It wasn't the sagging arms, the triple chin, the stomach that hid his penis, his penis between flabby inner thighs. His reflection shrieked the words of everyone who called him fat—bullies from grade school, strangers, friends, family. The loudest voice: his own. He shouldered an invisible boulder. In the mirror, he noticed fat beyond the body. Fat of the brain. What stared back was his ineptitude, disgust, self-loathing. "You are ugly," he said. "No one likes you," he said. "Fuckin' slob," he said. He wanted to extinguish the reflection. If it were gone, a new and better version of him would appear. He didn't let his gaze fall from the mirror. He stared like a staring contest, stared until he saw the person he wanted to be. Fat melted off, gathering at his feet and ankles that were now regular feet and regular ankles. Now he had defined a jawline. Now thick, juicy veins popped up along his forearms and the backs of his hands. Now the stretch marks that vined up his stomach vanished; the pear of his stomach vanished. He believed this was a better him. His self-worth was located in the opinions of others—how they looked at and thought of him. It had nothing to do with his other accomplishments. The straight As he received that semester or making the President's List again. It was in how large or small his belly was. "I'm through with this," he said.

He turned away from the mirror to embark on the journey of shedding pounds, one of many he would undertake in the course of his life.

The reflection, however, remained, remains, will always remain.

*

In 1997, the British returned Hong Kong to China. Mike Tyson bit off Evander Holyfield's ear, Tiger Woods became the youngest golfer to win the Masters, and Thai Boy fell in love with a white woman.

To friends, she was known as Teacher, a poet who was nine years older and taught at the university where Thai Boy was a student. He idolized her. Saw her as a guide in life. Someone who would lead him on the right path. Like Buddha, Buddha with long, wavy brown hair and green eyes. Buddha, who was born on a horse farm in central Illinois and waxed elegant about the beauty of flat land. Buddha, who taught him how to read poetry, love poetry, and how one line in verse can vibrate the inner core, like a prayer, like a blessing.

One day, Teacher invited him to a poetry reading in a small coffee shop at the edge of town. She was the featured reader. It was late fall. He wore the new leather jacket he had bought at a regular department store and not the Big & Tall one town over. He was working out. Losing five to eight pounds a week. His body was a new body. Not a specialty store body. His body was a capable body, allowing for long hikes with Teacher, whom he was spending most of his days with.

He took a seat in the back of the coffeehouse, which was noisy the way coffeehouses are—the whirl of the cappuccino machine, the grind of beans, the hot whip of hot milk. College students sat at a few tables, doing college things. Some of Teacher's students came for the reading, and Teacher flitted between tables to talk to them. He watched the easy way Teacher lived her life, the comfort she felt in whatever setting.

A redheaded kid hosted the reading. He had a strange name like Po-ee or Poem-Tree or something equally artsy. He wore the garb of a tortured poet—the cigarette-burned jeans, the Birkenstock sandals, the grungy flannel over the obscure punk rock T-shirt. Poem-Tree stood in a corner of the coffee shop, on a raised stage. He read something by someone deep, and people made the audible satisfactory groan that happens at all poetry readings. Then Poem-Tree introduced Teacher. She took the stage, a dim light hitting her hair and face.

One of Thai Boy's literature professors once said a book begins before the first word. The act of cracking open the cover is the literal start to the story. He always thought the professor was a little hokey, but here, he understood. The poem began when the poet stood in the light. Out of her mouth came song, and the song was about blackberry brambles, the sound of whip-poor-wills, the secret wild areas, the loss of a farm, a childhood. Words never sounded so light. Words like clouds. Words like delicate bubbles.

Thai Boy didn't fall for her poetry.

He fell for the poet.

"How was it?" she said after the reading.

"Nice."

"Just nice?"

He could have said what he was feeling, the swoon that saturated him in a blushing warmth, but he remained quiet. He shrugged. The fall breeze chilled the air. He took his leather jacket off and draped it over her shoulders. It hung loose on her body, arms dangling, a devouring shadow.

Touch

Touch has a memory.
—John Keats, "Lines to Fanny"

Five in the morning. My birthday. I have been up for hours, adjusting to the eleven-hour time difference. My lower back and hip ache, a dull thrumming that radiates down my right leg. The bed is board stiff, like most beds in Thailand, and the wooden frame creaks and cracks with my every toss and turn. Outside, the neighborhood rooster stirs the world awake, and downstairs, I hear my mother humming "Happy Birthday to You" while preparing coffee for the spirit home that protects the house.

I do not want to start my day. The older I get the more I am aware of time. I want to feel this new age of thirty-eight. To see if thirty-eight has made me, somehow, more enlightened. On days like this, my body feels the effects of time heavy on my joints and muscles, on my eyes that take longer to focus, on a brain that fogs. So, I stay in bed. I half-watch a movie starring Tom Cruise as a Nazi soldier, dubbed in Thai, his voice full of bass and tremor, the vein on his forehead about to burst. I want to flick it until it pops.

On my last night before this trip, Deedra massaged my back and then collapsed onto me, her body warm, her breath tickling my ear. I think of her touch, her voice, her everything. I think of her beside me now, her leg draped over me, her breath on my neck. The early morning, the back pain, the jet lag makes it easy to imagine her warmth.

"Is this all I'm good for to you?" she said that night. "Your personal massage therapist."

"Yes."

"Really?"

"Yes."

Her head rested on my chest, her fingers tracing the hair on it. "Are you going to miss me?"

"Yes."

"I like feeling you."

What I would give for her now—the slants of sunlight peeking through the slit of the curtains, the air conditioner buzzing above. Her hands. Her fingers. Kneading. Pressing. Her body moving in tune with mine. I was relearning the body. My body. Her body. She was teaching me touch. I was teaching her to receive. "We are broken," she would say. We were. The two of us had forgotten what it was like to touch with a sense of love and reciprocation. To share. To trust. To give in and let go.

*

For a long time, I felt undesirable. This feeling went beyond my size. This feeling has followed me for most of my life, since those grade school days when I crushed on every girl in class. I crushed easily then, but most of my crushes were never requited. I presumed it was my Thai blood, my "yellow" skin that was like lady kryptonite. I believed what my mother constantly preached: "You are not like them"; *them* were other boys, other men; *them* were white. Being an Asian man in America meant you were emasculated. Meant you fit the mold of "inscrutable" and "effeminate." Meant what Frank Chin and Jeffery Paul Chan theorized about Asian masculinity was somewhat true: "Our nobility is that of an efficient housewife." It did not help that I was raised by two women most of my life, though they were the greatest parents a boy could ask for, and what they ultimately instilled in me was a sense of being that went far beyond gender. But growing up in south Chicago, where men clung to fragile notions of masculinity, being Thai seemed a hinderance to my youthful desire for sexual satisfaction. So instead, I tried to be white. White was the only accepted version of maleness. White gave you freedom to move and do anything without the self-conscious cloud that always followed. White was the color of my friends and my friends' fathers. My father suffered from being stripped of his masculinity in America. Here, he was seen as a short, pastel-wearing golfer. Here, he was half the size of other fathers, who possessed booming voices and booming bodies. My father only possessed a booming sneeze.

While I was married, I never got over the weight of my ethnicity. I blamed my easy-to-please Asian demeanor. If I were more manly . . . If Katie saw me work in the garage, change the oil, build a fence with my own two hands . . . If I could kick off dust from a trail ride or wrangle a steer . . .

If I could . . . If I could . . .

After Katie moved out, I sought to eradicate that notion of Asian man sexlessness. Sought to obliterate the Asian man. That slanty-eyed gook. That wing-wong, ching-chong Chink. That boy who inhabited every Asian ethnic slur he had been called, every stereotype, everything that declared he was without a sex drive. I sought to obliterate that Thai boy.

Online dating made it possible to do so. I presented myself as the person I wished I was. One who possessed confidence. One who craved adventure. One who might be able to fuck the socks off of you. I chose my profile photo carefully, trying to deemphasize my Asian-ness, which, of course, was ridiculous. In the photo I wore a leather jacket and did not smile because smiling connoted niceness and what I wanted to portray was dark and brooding and hot as fuck. The computer screen provided cover. Provided anonymity. Meeting and chatting with women took over my nights, the light of the computer in the dark rooms of the house that Katie used to occupy, my fingers rapidly tapping.

At first, it was innocent correspondence, which sometimes progressed into sex on the page. I was good at sex . . . on the page. I knew how to string words together, play with syntax and pace, knew when to quicken the heart with short monosyllabic words and how to stall a moment with a sentence that took on the cadence of the sweet and slow movement of satisfying syrup. My desire to become a writer first came from my yearning to write romances, those penny novels I secretly bought with my comics at the used bookstore. I'd tear off the scintillating covers featuring buff Caucasian men who seduced voluptuous, corseted women. I did not want my parents to know my secret, did not want them to know I was learning the language to woo. With words you can reshape your existence. I was reshaping who I was and who I wanted to be. Lewis

Carroll wrote, "I'm beginning to think the proper definition of 'Man' is 'an animal that writes letters.'" Sometimes I was an animal. Sometimes I ripped opened blouses and sucked and bit into flesh. Sometimes my metaphorical hand glided over curtains of skin down to the wet spaces of the body. Sometimes my metaphorical tongue tasted the sweetest of nectars. Yes, the writing was cheesy. Often, I let it get the best of me, swept away with waves of language and how I made some women feel. "You made me come over and over again." "God, your words got me so wet." "We need to meet. Now."

It wasn't long before I took it to the next step. I started scheduling meetings at coffeehouses or bookstores. Many of these meetups were for friendly conversation and concluded with broken promises to meet again. Some were for the body and its urges. A hotel room. A bedroom. A basement. A car. I allowed the body to take over, to experience all the things it had never experienced because of its fidelity to one person. But now that evaporated, so the body gave in. The body acted on the things it had wanted to do for years.

To fuck and fuck and fuck.

I was a body. A selfish body. A greedy body in movement. In exertion. Touching and being touched. Touch was this chaotic echo of sound and meaning and meaninglessness. Touch was not caresses and kisses. Touch was rough and sometimes painful. Squeezes and twists. Pulling and pushing. Biting and sucking.

Touch.

Old French *tochier*, to hit.

Latin, *toccare*, to strike.

I was struck.

I struck.

Giver.

Receiver.

Touch.

Touch without reciprocation. Without appreciation. The type of touch my mother warned me about. "Be careful of a white girl's touch," she'd say. I was not careful. White women touched me. Women of different shades touched me. I touched them. Touch that led to excessiveness, to the sin Buddha warned against: "Don't give way to heedlessness or to intimacy with sensual delight. . . ." Touch in the erotic, neurotic, sadistic, never platonic sense. For a time this touch quenched my desire that wasn't desire but emptiness. I existed in the seventh terrace of Dante's *Purgatorio*, this desolate land where static lives dwelled. "There, on all sides, I can see every shade move quickly to embrace another shade, content—they did not pause—with their brief greeting, as ants, in their dark company, will touch their muzzles, each to each. . . ."

*

My mother sits on the cool tiled floor, reading a newspaper, glasses perched on the tip of her nose. She wears pajamas that she's sewn from scraps of leftover fabric; they hang off of her like rags. The morning light tumbles through the curtains, and she mumbles something about the red shirts and shakes her head. When she sees me ambling down the stairs, wincing with each step, she smiles and says, "Birthday boy, you're walking like an ostrich."

"A crippled ostrich," I say and grimace.

"Back hurting?"

I nod.

"It's from the plane," she says.

"Probably."

"Come here," she says.

I do. Step by delicate step.

"Lie down," she says. "On your front."

I do. Groaning on descent.

She sits on my back and crosses her legs, the newspaper resting on the top of my head. She reads me the news of the day. Tells me Thailand is stupid. Tells me there is too much corruption in the country. Tells me stuff like this never happens in America.

"I think this country needs a hug," she says.

It's a phrase my mother has clung to since her days as a nurse, when a coworker complained of an ornery patient. "Room 503 needs a hug." I love the phrase in its simplicity. That yes, touch can melt our inner core. That it can steal the jadedness we possess about the world, momentarily, and give us the joy of being in a body. A hug. A hug has the capability of stilling a child in a tantrum. A hug steals the rigidness in the body, and we surrender into it. The movements of a hug: the open arms, the gathering of another human being inward. I imagine mortal enemies hugging. Arabs and Jews. North and South Koreans. Red shirts and yellow shirts. Human beings have a natural inclination to cling. From the moment we emerge into the world, our first cry is not just an inhalation of our taste of air; it is a cry that demands touch, demands to be held tightly to a chest. *Hold me*, we scream. *Hug me*. We will continue to want this. Our arms are made to hold. Our bodies are made to be cradled. Humans are puzzle pieces looking for other puzzle pieces.

I need to believe this.

I hide my head in the dark of my arms. My mother's voice is muffled. She rocks back and forth, the weight of her bottom shifting to various parts of my back. Occasionally she touches the back of my head, soothes her small hand in the cushion of my hair. Occasionally, she says I'm still her baby, though much, much bigger. "Your fingers used to be this small, like peppers, and now look at them. Thick sausages." Heat radiates from my back to my skull. The weight of her—only about 120 pounds—loosens tight muscles. But not enough.

"You carry too much tension, like this country," she says. "Let it go."

*

Deedra's touch is accompanied with voice, with stirrings in the stomach, with a level of intimacy that delves beyond the physical. All I want to do is return her the favor. To trail my finger along her back, connect one freckle to the next, feel her thudding heart when I lay my palm on the middle of her chest. Her pleasure is mine. Her sighs are mine.

This touch, our touch, was a possession. We wanted to possess each other, with voracious greed, the way wild vines devour houses in the South. And it was a devouring. The way we kissed, the taste of need, like a succulent peach ripe on the lips; the way we clung hard to each other and how we kept pulling each other in, as if we were trying to meld into one; the way our legs twisted and twined. We would say this need, this desire, was unhealthy. We would say we were being selfish. We would say we couldn't help it. Our lovemaking was fixing the fissures in us—we believed—these long wounds we'd carried for years. With every sigh and moan, with every orgasmic release, something healed.

"I want you to use me," I said, my arms wrapped around the soft of her, our skin slick with sweat.

"I am," she said. "Do I want too much?"

I shook my head.

"I worry you will tire of this."

"No," I said, but the truth was I could not assure her of a future. I could not dwell in the days and months and years that had yet to present themselves. I was, for the moment, in my body. I was feeling what Buddha preached, this acceptance of the current state of things, this ability to stay rooted in the now.

Touch, her touch, delivered this recognition.

It seemed too perfect. Too coincidental to meet someone who would heal me, someone who needed me to heal her. I would tell my writing students that if this were a piece of fiction, they would have to convince me to believe in the unbelievable. The haze after the divorce *was* unbelievable. Because here was this woman who had suffered an exhausting fifteen-year marriage, and here was this man who had lost the sense of himself. Among the things we needed from each other, despite the fear of losing ourselves again, despite the fear of giving ourselves over, was touch, meaningful touch.

This was absent in the last three years of the marriage. It was not Katie's fault, or mine. Fault is not why good marriages fail. Not exclusive fault. No one person carries that weight, that burden, that regret. No one person bears sole responsibility. There was a time when all Katie and I did was touch. Intimately. Romantically. Lovingly. There was a time when we were ravenous for each other. But something happened. Or a lot of things happened. Or time happened, and we found ourselves suddenly distanced, and we found ourselves wanting what the other could not offer.

Our relationship never lacked for touching, however, even in its waning months; in fact, it was excessive. A poke. A prod. A peck. A tap. A pat. A push. A nudge. A hug. A grope. Our touches spoke very little. At night we tickled and played like children, but then we turned our backs and fell asleep, a canyon forming between us. We dreamed of others touching us, and us touching others, which made Katie silently cry from guilt, which made me wall up and suck down my sorrow. And then, the next day would begin, and we would touch each other, as if we believed our wandering hands, our bodies, would wake something in us, would set fire to our relationship.

For a long while, we did not give up. How could we? We loved each other. We clung to the notion that we could be saved. We clung with the tinniest tips of our fingers. For fifteen years, we were all we had. So for ten weeks, in an office building in south Tampa, we sought the counsel of a sex therapist.

The room was small and comfy, not a room I imagined a sex therapist would have. Not that I assumed there would be charts of sexual positions or a clinical explanation of the orgasm. Not that I assumed sex toys would be hung on the walls or that there would be a sex swing dangling from the ceiling. No, the office was nondescript in its wood-paneled walls, and I found myself staring at a small framed quote across the room: "Reality is something you rise above," which irked my writer's sensibilities because I hated the word "reality," which put me in an irritable mood from the very get-go, which I think I needed, that disposition for me to complain, to air out, to share, to be angry, an emotion I rarely let out.

Katie and I would sit on opposite ends of a couch, the therapist taking notes, prodding us with questions and observations.

"I notice the distance between the two of you," she said during our first session.

"I'm a big guy," I said flippantly. "I like my space."

In those sessions, Katie and I were free to say things that hurt.

"You're selfish," I said.

"You sound like an asshole," she said.

"You're spoiled."

"You're stubborn."

"I want more."

"I want less."

There was safety in that room. There was safety with that one witness to the things that bubbled inside of us. To the rest of the world, Katie and I wore the facade of the perfect couple. We held hands. We kissed. We kidded. It was easy for us to pretend because we weren't pretending. Not really. We projected publicly what we wanted to have privately. I believe we loved each other more during the waning years of our marriage, during those hour-long sessions with the therapist, and it was this love that kept us together longer than we should have been. It was this love that we did not want to lose because it was rare and it was special.

After every session, the therapist, this kind and patient woman, sent us home with assignments. She wanted us to experience "sensate focusing," a term derived from Masters and Johnson. Orgasm should not be the end goal of sex. One has to be in the present to enjoy the sensorial experience of touch.

"Touch each other for ten minutes, lightly, gently, but do not engage in intercourse," the therapist said. "I want you to explore each other's bodies for yourselves."

Katie and I were eager students. We scheduled our assignments in our planners. "We can't forget to do our homework," we said and giggled. Each week the therapist added something new to the assignment, like kissing, like tasting. Each week we were allowed more intimacy. The therapist wanted us to carry sensate focusing into every facet of our lives. When we showered, we should take the time to feel the water, how it glides down the back. The sting of the heat. The slick and froth of soap. Breathe the subtle scents of clean. When we ate, we should do so with deliberate slowness. Enjoy food. Taste every ingredient. Let the tongue learn new textures, new flavors. The therapist believed we had disconnected from touch. Especially each other's touch. We had to become that child again, experiencing the world anew.

We did. We did with vigor.

But what happened after those ten weeks? What happened when therapy ended?

Nothing.

Nothing is the death toll of any relationship.

*

My family surprises me with an orange sponge cake and songs in Thai and English. They have set up a party outside, on the old, long canoe turned table. My mother tells me they used to paddle the canoe to school, and the family could not bear to part with it. Now it is beautifully lacquered with a glass top; under the glass, in the hull of the boat, are mementos from their past, like Grandfather's pipe, old farming equipment, and stuffed animals. Birthdays for my family are important, and because I'm two years closer to forty, they joke about my bad back and the abundance of gray in my hair and beard. "Like Santa Claus," Aunty Sue says.

Earlier in the day, Katie called and wished me a happy thirty-eighth. We talked for a bit, my mother on my shoulder telling me to tell her she misses her, Aunty Sue echoing the sentiment from across the room. They love Katie because Katie loved me. Until my mom and aunt meet Deedra, until she stands before them so they can squeeze her hand and pull her into their embrace, she is only a name, a passing thought, a ghost.

This is the power of touch. It tells us we are here. We exist.

After cake and song, I visit Wat Phra Singh to pray for a healthy new year of my life. The temple is near the center of the city, closest to the tourist culture of Chiang Mai; it is the temple I was a monk at ten years ago to accrue karma and fulfill a familial obligation, a rite of passage for many Thai men, which, for me, lasted six weeks. Because of this, Wat Phra Singh remains close to my heart, a place where I always feel at peace, despite the chaos of taxis and tuk-tuks clogging the circular entrance to the temple, despite the cheap souvenir tables selling dragons made of rope or Buddhas made of resin, despite the backpackers and tourists who go in and out. In this urban setting, nature finds a way to invade. It is this I love, the combination of the natural and unnatural world. "Beauty exists in conjunction of everything," Buddha said. "With the things that belong and the things that do not."

Monks sit in orange robes on a raised platform along the left wall. My family organized prayers for me. For the first time today, I feel thirty-eight. It is like a rebirth of sorts, a new emergence into the world.

Outside the temple is hustle and bustle and car horns and loud voices and an ever-moving life. Inside the temple is a hushed silence and the crisp click of cameras, is a sense of peace and unity, like the white string that laces around the perimeters of the structure, a delicate barrier between harmony and chaos. Tourists aim their cameras at the big Buddha looming in the front, a Buddha with an abnormally large head; at the ornate European chandeliers hanging high above; at the money trees of donations from parishioners.

When the ceremony starts, I give offerings of food to the statues of Buddha. The prayers begin, voices humming. The swallows in the rafters stir in sound and song, almost deafening. A hairless cat meanders out from a cluster of Buddha statues at the front of the temple, licks its paws, and stares at me. A white dog scratches a tick at one of the side entrances and shakes its coat like wet laundry.

I bow my head, letting the prayer reverberate into my heart.

A monk prepares holy water in a copper bowl, a lit candle perched at the lip, dripping yellow wax. He is young, but his face contains the wisdom of sages. When done, he whisks the water onto me and my family. I close my eyes. My hands press tightly together. The water wets my hair and back, seeps through my shirt, like the cool of a summer rain. And though I do not believe in such things, when I rise from the temple floor, the pain in my back is gone, and in that spot is a strange warmth, as if from a hand.

A Brief History of Sex

after Brenda Miller

"How many have come before me, my love?"

I loathe the question.

It spurs a playback of partners, a flash of all the coitus encounters of my life. It is a question that tempts a lie, like the one I used to tell in high school, adding two to my none, so I would not look bad in front of the guys, these South Side toughies, who I'm sure were lying, too. The question can make me doubt my self-worth by implicitly asking other questions—what is too few, what is too many, where do I rank in order of competence? It does not need to be voiced to be real, this question, because it lurks in the shadows of the bedroom.

I loathe the question because I hate talking about sex. Talking about sex is akin to watching sex on TV with your parents. My insides become worms. My eyes wander. I fidget. I pick at my cuticles until they bleed. All I want to do is flee. A friend of mine likes to chide me about how I stare at the ceiling at the mention of sex. It is an uncontrollable impulse. I stare fixedly above me as if what is up there will save me from whatever discomfort I feel down here. This discomfort makes me ponder whether in the area of intimacy I have failed, am failing, will continue to fail, will die a failure.

Brenda Miller does a hell of a job taking the question on in her essay "A Brief History of Sex." She weaves three cultural sex tales (the Japanese courtesan, Adam and Eve, Krishna) with her own sexual history. What stands out, what I cannot shake, is the true or false question Miller poses near the middle of the piece. "TRUE OR FALSE: A lover is someone who loves." The simplicity of this statement illuminates the complexity of sexual life. Sex is more than physical. It is words, and words are made malleable. Like bodies.

True or false: Many marriages fail because of sex.

*

"How many have come before me, my love?"

When I was eighteen or nineteen, my mother relayed to me the story of her nursing school friend's son. She liked to pit me against other Thai sons as a way of motivation. Or sometimes a warning.

Once there was a Thai boy who fell in love with a white woman. This white woman was the whitest of white, but her hair was the color of silky sand. The Thai boy—so frail, so delicate—was enamored with the white woman. It was as if her whiteness cast a spell on him. He groveled for her affections. He became her supplicant.

The poor, poor Thai boy.

Every day, he said, "I love you with the entirety of my heart, and I will always love you with the entirety of my heart." And for a great many years—two—he lived blissfully with the fact that this was enough. This would hold them together.

The poor, poor Thai boy.

One day, a fog came to rest over the household, and the Thai boy—so innocent, so kind—detected something amiss. He sensed in the white woman he loved with the entirety of his heart that something bothered her. So one day he scrounged up his courage and asked her what was the matter.

"My lovely white woman, what's wrong? Have I done something to displease you?"

The white woman, whose hair was no longer the color of sand but of serpents, said, "You no sex good."

The Thai boy said, "But my lovely white woman, our love transcends physical intimacy. Our love is of a higher nature."

One of the serpents in the white woman's hair hissed. It sounded like an old man's wheezing laughter. "Want sex. Need sex. You no good sex."

"Darling white woman," the Thai boy said, "is my heart not good enough for you?"

"Sex!"

"Darling white woman," the Thai boy said, "are you not happy with the life I have given you?"

"Sex!"

"Darling white woman—"

"Need sex. Want sex."

What is the Thai boy to do? Who is he to prevent this white woman from having happiness?

So he let her go and moved back in with his mother, who said, "I told you so, stupid."

What happened to the white woman? She sexed every man in the kingdom.

"The end," my mother said. Then quickly afterward, "That's what *they* care about. That's what *they* want. Don't be like him."

Out of all her stories, this one keeps popping up in my head. I tell myself there is no sole reason for the failure of the marriage. But I cannot help but return to the cold bed Katie and I shared—or did not share—those last two years.

True or false: My marriage failed because of sex.

*

"How many have come before me, my love?"

This morning, I watch my mother and think about her happiness, about what finds her at this moment, sitting outside on the porch, waiting for my T-shirts hanging on a clothesline to dry. A car passes outside the gates, then another and another, and she counts the sound of them, sing-songing numbers. She is not a woman pending eighty, but a child amused by sound and the sun that sweats her skin. I believe I am witnessing my mother's true nature, before becoming a mother, before the divorce that hardened her. Perhaps she was a happy-go-lucky girl, one who skipped and danced and was amused by everything in the world, like now, when a dove streaks out of a tree and startles her into giggles. Perhaps, before everything that came in her life, she was a woman harnessing desire, a woman with many partners, many boyfriends.

I want to ask but don't. I want to know but don't.

The Chihuahuas across the street yap for their owner's attention. A woman pedals a food cart of homemade coconut ice cream, her bicycle bell trilling for customers. My mother hums. It is in vast contrast to the sounds on this street, her soft song in a world of harsh noise.

True or false: I think my mother is happy.

True or false: I need her to be happy.

True or false: In her, I see the future of my happiness.

*

"How many have come before me, my love?"

I never had the conversation with Katie, but I imagined a line of faceless men, serpenting an endless staircase. When we met, I was twenty-one. She was nine years older, more experienced in every facet of life. I felt like the character of Bruce in Tony Hoagland's poem "Self-Improvement," determined to improve his skills at the art of oral sex:

> Use nothing but his tonguetip
> to flick the light switch in his room
> on and off a hundred times a day
> until he grew fluent at the nuances
> of force and latitude.

I didn't practice on a light switch, but I did buy cherries to tie knots in their stems only using the dexterity of my tongue.

I had not been with enough women to know whether I was good or bad. I thought in polarity, like a teacher who only gave As or Fs. I had to be good—more than good—in whatever I did. "You must be the best," my mother said. "You must win everything," my father said. Being good enough, just okay, average, was never an option. "You will be erased," my mother said. "You will be forgotten," my father said. I didn't want to be forgotten. I didn't want to be erased. In grade school, I suffered moments of invisibility. Invisibility was worse than being bullied. Despite my size, despite the color of my skin, I had been vanished by the world. To make myself visible, I put my all in everything.

"Perhaps," the sex therapist said during one of our evening sessions, "you are thinking too much about whether she's having a good time. But are you having a good time?"

I wasn't. What occupied my thoughts was my body and its limits, was what Katie saw and felt and whether it was enough. I would lie there tortured, thinking myself a failure. The thought made me soft. Perhaps I was bad at sex. Perhaps my mother was right when she told me the story about the Thai boy and the white woman. Sex can eviscerate you.

During that last year of the marriage, I couldn't turn off my thoughts that screamed my inadequacies, perceived or otherwise. This would be my very own type of sexual suffering. This mental hell I had created. It was a cold and lonely place. There was no one to talk to except myself, and fuck, I hated myself.

So instead, I closed in. I didn't engage. I created a shadow. The shadow of incompetence and doubt.

Do I please?

Am I good enough?

True or false: I made myself invisible.

*

"How many have come before me, my love?"

The women after Katie left—I knew I would never see them again. They would disappear into the folds of my life; I would forget their names. Because of this, I let go. I went into the entanglement of limbs with the selfish thought of personal pleasure.

I angry fucked.

I sad fucked.

I fucked.

Sometimes we never exchanged names. Sometimes we barely exchanged a word. I drove to different states, to Georgia and Tennessee, or distant Florida cities, like Melbourne and Naples. I went over to their homes when babysitters took care of the kids or when it was the ex's weekend or when the husband was not home.

One enjoyed being choked. One kept asking if she was beautiful. One cried at the end. One insisted a horror movie—*The Mist*—play in the background. One had her black Lab in the room, ever staring. One liked her hands bound. One blindfolded me. One passed out. One called me Jim. One kept apologizing.

Some came. Some couldn't. Some would call afterward, and when I didn't answer, left nasty messages. Some emailed me love letters. Some thought I would be their listening vessel and would relay the heartbreaks of their lives before kicking me out of their beds. Some held on too tightly.

This was a form of mourning. This was a form of healing.

I wasn't mourning the marriage. I wasn't healing from the wound it left. It was something much deeper. Something that surfaced because of it. Something that had been there for a long while, perhaps before Katie and I were married. The word *something* is all I have to describe the machinations of my psyche. What I suffered from didn't have a name or a shape. It resisted logic or sense, elusive, like a ghost.

I was grieving. This grief made me lose myself. This grief made me play a dangerous game. I hated thinking of it as a game. Games have rules and strategies. Games have endings. Here, there was no clear path. No ending. Who would be victorious and what would be the prize? A clearer understanding of the self?

True or false: I didn't give a fuck about the self.

Stupid Men

I wait for my cousin Oil at a coffeehouse off Nimman Road in Chiang Mai, watching a couple flirt. When they enter, they track in lots of sound and laughter, disrupting the quiet ambiance of the shop. The other patrons lift their eyes from their computers. Some of them have that glazed look of leaving the virtual world and reentering the real one. The couple seem to be in a world of their own, also, speaking in a way that draws attention to them. They don't care. The woman is Thai and petite. She wears an elegant black summer dress that travels along the curves of her body. A tan fedora floats on top of her head. Her partner, whom she hangs on, is a Caucasian man wearing a backward baseball cap and camouflage cargo shorts. He towers over her. He's English or Australian, judging by his accent, and spends much of his time in the gym.

"Do you love me?" the woman says.

"No," he says.

"Do you love me?"

"No."

"Do you love me?"

"No."

She keeps asking. He keeps responding the same way. Until, finally, her tone turns severe. She hits him in the belly with the back of her hand. He fakes hurt.

"Do you love me?"

"I'm hungry," he says and pulls her out of the coffeehouse, not purchasing a thing. The girl's dress trails behind her, her hand on top of the fedora.

An American woman with an eagle tattoo across her shoulders stops typing and rolls her eyes. "What a dick," she says.

An hour later, Oil arrives in a black Benz. She drove from Bangkok to spend a day with me before heading back south for work the following morning. A belated birthday outing. The past few years it has become increasingly hard to find time to get together. Oil manages the finances of a medical organization that sends her on business trips all over Asia. If she's not working, she tends to the needs of her older brothers, who are always at her for money.

Oil is the closest thing I have to a big sister. Most childhood memories of Thailand come back to her. My love for her is like what my father describes when he speaks of past lives. He says we carry parts of our former selves into this life. We find the people we love, like family, like friends, like lovers, again. And this feeling is instantaneous, as if you are picking up where you left off.

Oil's been driving for about eight hours, but you wouldn't know it if you looked at her. Her hair is kept in place, tied up into a ponytail. She dons large Gucci sunglasses and a navy-blue sleeveless dress with a gold-buckled belt. She looks like a Thai Audrey Hepburn, the one who appeared in *Breakfast at Tiffany's*. Oil is thin, though she complains she is fat. I could wrap my fingers around her wrist and then travel up her arm without disconnecting. Her weight is the first thing she addresses when I enter the car.

"I'm so fat," she says and makes a bloated sound.

I buckle in. "What do you weigh now?"

"A whole forty-five kilos." About a hundred pounds.

"Yood," I say. *Stop*.

Oil mock slaps my head, something that's stuck since we were kids, this fake play of hitting. "Let's go," she says, pulling into the stream of Chiang Mai traffic.

When I was in high school, Oil came to do her master's in finance in Saint Louis. On breaks she would spend time with us in Chicago. She knew my father's departure made me spin out of control, knew how angry I was, especially at my mother for reasons I didn't understand at the time. Her presence, however, was a respite from this anger. She made the mood lighter with her kindness, with her smile that never waned. Later, when her boyfriend Bob came to get his degree, too, she stayed with him in a small apartment. I saw less and less of her, which made me hate Bob, who was already easy to hate.

"How's your mom?" Oil says.

"Old."

"How's Aunty Sue?"

"Old."

"You're old, too, birthday boy," she says.

"You're older."

"But I'm *soi*." Beautiful. She takes one hand off the wheel and puts it under her chin, batting her eyes. A motorcycle swipes by, inches from her side mirror.

I tell her Aunty Sue doesn't walk well anymore, and my mother spends her days sitting on the floor reading a newspaper.

"You need to make them move."

"I'm only here for a few weeks each summer. What happens after I leave?"

She nods. "I'll be on them."

Oil needs a sweet fix, and the restaurant she drives us to is famous for a hundred different types of roti, a crispy flatbread made on a well-buttered griddle.

We opt to sit outside and people watch. Tourists walk by, their heavy backpacks slowing their steps. The restaurant is located in busy part of the city. Across the street is a megamall, built like a futuristic spaceship, many waves of metal. Oil checks her emails and complains about the incompetency of her coworkers. "I leave for one day," she says, "and they ruin everything." The sun scorches, but we are under the shade of an umbrella. Oil asks for a fan to be aimed at our faces.

I tell Oil about the couple at the coffee shop.

She shakes her head. "Stupid men."

I nod. "Men are pointless."

"They are the worst."

"Completely."

"Don't be a man like other men," Oil says.

"I'm a man already, though."

"But don't be like them. Don't be stupid."

"Too late."

"You're one marriage down," she said. "Like me."

"Bob, another stupid man."

"Stupid men are everywhere." She laughs, and I notice her straight and white teeth. Last year she was in braces. Braces at forty. I chided her endlessly. Calling her metal mouth. But now, her teeth are pristine. Gone is the slight overbite. Gone are the moments when she would cover up her smile.

"Does Mr. Bob still call?"

"Occasionally."

"Is he with his mistress?"

"They're married and have a kid." She shrugs. "Sometimes he leaves a message asking if I can pick him up a chicken for dinner. He wants me to deliver it to his new home. To him, I'm still first wife."

"Are you?"

Oil throws her arms in the air. She possesses the movements of a stage actor—big and overly dramatic. "Bah." *Crazy.*

"He's such an asshole," I say in English, which gets my cousin to giggle. Any English cuss makes her giggle.

"He's in the shadows now," she says.

Shadows follow, I want to tell her. They grow. They shrink. They disappear. Oil knows this. She has had six years to deal with heartbreak, to deal with Bob. She—like the other women in my family—has hardened herself, has made her spirit unbreakable.

The waiter comes to take our orders, tablet and stylus in hand. I order a traditional roti smothered in sweetened condensed milk and sugar. Oil picks the roti topped with candied squash, chocolate sauce, and mounds of whipped cream. While we wait for our desserts, we catch up on small talk—work, friends, food. Oil complains about how she does not have any time for herself, how they run her ragged at work, how she wants to retire and disappear. I nod. She reaches over and tugs at the point of my beard. "Get rid of this," she says. "And your tattoos."

"I'm getting a new one."

"Are you kidding me?"

"Nope."

"So ugly," she says. She raises her hand to mock hit me again. "I swear."

I tell her our cousin Thong is taking me to get a tattoo in a week, one I've been planning since the divorce.

"He's another troublemaker," she says and rolls her eyes. "The two of you."

When the roti arrive, Oil's plate is massive, double the size of mine, whipped cream like mountaintops. The candied squash are fine threads of gold, chocolate sauce like meandering dark brown rivers. I instantly have order envy. It doesn't matter; Oil takes one bite and places three on my plate.

"How's your dad?" she says.

I shrug. "Okay, I think."

"Is he healthy?"

"I think so."

"You think?"

I shrug again. "I'll see him when we go to Bangkok."

She takes a bite and chocolate clings to her lips, but she quickly wipes it away. "Get over it," she says. "He's still your dad."

I smile. Oil cuts through bullshit and calls me on my stupidity. On the issue of my father, I'm stupid. I know when I get home later in the afternoon I will call my father and ask him how he is, ask him about his health, confirm our plans to meet and how long I'll stay with him. Oil has that effect on people. She makes them do better.

"How's your dad?" I ask.

"He had a stroke a week ago." Oil says it like she says anything else. As if she is pointing out the dog that is across the street, barking.

"He was with the other family when it happened." She shakes her head. "They are not that bright over there. They found him disoriented and unable to speak and called me instead of the hospital."

I tell her I'm sorry, but she swats my apology away, as if all of this doesn't have an effect on her beside inconvenience.

"I'm paying for everything because none of his family has any money." She places more roti on my plate. "Here. Eat."

Oil's father is like many fathers in Thailand. Like mine. He married Aunt Jeeb, the second-oldest sister in the family, the sister my mother is closest to, the two of them sharing heartbreak. After producing four kids, Aunt Jeeb discovered her husband lived a double life. Another family existed on the other side of Bangkok. He saw them on weekends. When she discovered his deceit, she expelled him out of the house, but because her children loved their father, Oil most of all, she allowed him to visit the kids in the mornings on weekends. During that time, Aunt Jeeb made herself a ghost, vanishing upstairs, coming down when his car pulled out of the gate.

When I was younger, I didn't think anything was peculiar about this arrangement. I didn't know the complexities of the family. To me, Oil's father was a jolly man who liked to pick me up over his head and spin me until I was drunk with dizziness; he was the man who brought me my favorite foods, like chicken and rice and fried Chinese doughnuts. I called him Uncle Raisin, because of his dark, dark skin and the deep folds around his eyes and mouth. He resembled the California raisins on the cartoon commercials in the States, the ones playing instruments and ever smiling.

This story is all too familiar—Thai men having multiple spouses. In Thailand's polygamous days, a man of elite status could take three wives—*mia muang* (first wife), *mia noi* (minor wife), *mia tassee* (slave wife). Polygamy has since been outlawed, but the practice still lingers. Ask Aunt Jeeb. Ask my mother. Ask Oil. They will tell you stories of stupid men.

"Do your brothers help out?"

She hits the table and hisses. "Stupid men," she says. "They keep asking for money."

"For what?"

"A down payment on a house. A loan to get through the month. Start-up money for a business that will never happen. Whatever they dream about. They always have the same line: 'Sister, I'm building myself up. Please help.'"

"What do they do all day?"

"Play the stock market."

Oil updates me on her older brother, a traveling salesman who drives to beauty salons in Chiang Mai and the surrounding northern towns.

"That cosmetic business of his costs more than it makes," she says.

"Do you use his whitening cream?"

"It gave me a rash. Don't buy any of it."

"Why don't your brothers get real jobs?" I ask.

She shrugs. "I don't know. Why don't they?"

"Stupid men?" I say.

She nods. "Stupid men."

The roti is good. Every bite coats the mouth with sugary decadence. I close my eyes a few times and chew slowly, trying to make the moment last. When I open my eyes, my plate is clean and so is Oil's. I order hot tea to help me digest. We sit with two steaming cups between our hands.

An American couple walks by. They are in casual tourist garb; the man in cargo shorts and a loose-fitting Hawaiian shirt that V's open at the neck, exposing chest hairs. The woman wears a bright red tank top and white Thai pants bought at one of the many shops along this street that cater to Westerners, I am sure. The pants look like puffy pajama bottoms. I've never seen someone Thai wear these pants, only tourists. I catch snippets of the couple's conversation, about checking in with Mom, about noodles later. When they pass us, they smile and nod. We smile and nod.

"I remember when I was in America," Oil says, "how different couples were." She points to the backs of the Americans, walking in sync, their flip-flops slapping their heels. "Look at them. They are equals. They are in it together. I remember always walking behind Bob or making sure he was happy. He insisted I get only what he wanted because what he wanted was the best. I was more 'thing' to him than person."

I tell her I don't think it's an American thing. I tell her there are plenty of stupid men in America, probably more.

"But it seemed like women mattered in a different way there."

I lean in closer, as if imparting a secret. "The things you don't see behind closed doors. Like . . ."

And I am off. I tell her the story of the white American couple who just passed us. The man looks like a Ralph, and not because of the Ralph

Lauren cargo shorts, but because the Ralphs I have met possess a calm and calculative nature. This Ralph is no different. This Ralph is the definition of cool, suave, charming. He doesn't walk; he saunters. He doesn't watch a movie; he watches a film. And the woman, her name is Tiffany, like the Tiffanys I knew in Chicago, rosy cheeked and ready to appease. Tiffany smiles with her whole being. She is quick with praise. If you are sick, Tiffany is at the door with chicken soup. But once you get to know her, you find out Tiffany tugs on every nerve. Tiffany has a way of talking that is like nails on a chalkboard, this high-frequency screech that makes your face pucker. It is her voice that chips away at calm and collected Ralph, who behind closed doors, is not calm and collected at all. Ralph is a bull in a china shop. He is red-faced anger. In the privacy of their hotel room, Ralph and Tiffany bring out their true selves, as if shedding their outer coating only to uncover gelatinous beings. These beings are not the happy tourist couple we see. They are not going to check in with Mom because gelatinous Tiffany hates Mom and gelatinous Ralph hates gelatinous Tiffany for hating Mom. The gelatinous couple isn't going out for noodles later because in the hotel room they will fight. Fight so loud management knocks on the door to ask if everything is okay. What they find are two white gelatinous tourist bodies, entangled in struggle, dead.

"The end," I say.

Oil shakes her head and then pours me more tea. "This is why you write."

"Here's another one," I say. "But you may know this one already."

Ralph and Tiffany *are* the perfect couple. In public, among friends, they hold hands and sneak pecks on the cheek and say cute pet names to each other, like Attila the Honey or Butthead. Their friends tell them they are perfect. Their friends say they want to aspire to be a couple like them. Ralph and Tiffany smile and blush. They say love will get you through anything. But when they go home, silence follows. Silence squeezes their vocal cords, a slow choke. At home, they dwell in different spaces. Sleep in different rooms. Tiffany spends her days on the computer. Ralph obsesses over how much weight he has lost in the past month. The two of them move about as if they shoulder boulders. They spend evenings in front of the TV, their dogs in between them, and say nothing of value. "That show is funny." "Yeah." "I really like that actor." "What's his name?" "Manny something." "Patinkin." "The dude from *Princess Bride*." "Yeah." "Yeah." "Cool." "Cool." This is the extent of their talk—TV and the happiness of their dogs. Ralph and Tiffany do not say what is never far from their thoughts. They do not voice their worry. The marriage is not working. Love won't get them through this. They've become lonely strangers, despite the years they've been together. It is not because they don't love each other. They do. But love alone can't bridge the distance that widens by the second, until the two of them stand on two separate islands with too much water between them.

Oil doesn't say anything. She sets her eyes on the moving world in front of us. The midafternoon light bounces off the hoods of cars and blinds me. I block my eyes with my hands. Oil puts on her sunglasses.

"You and Katie were good," Oil says.

"We were."

"Good doesn't always last," she says.

I nod.

"But it was no one's fault."

"Maybe," I say.

"You should've taken the garbage out more," Oil says and sticks her tongue out.

I raise my hand to mock hit her. She raises her chin like a South Side toughie.

"Everyone hated Bob," I say.

"I know."

"I hate Bob."

"The heart says one thing," she says. "The brain says the other."

"So true."

"You know why he left?" Oil says.

I shake my head.

"Because I lost the baby."

Eight years ago, Katie and I visited my uncles in the central plains of Thailand. Oil was four months pregnant and was on sick leave. Her pregnancy had been difficult. She was having all-day sickness and not gaining enough weight. She complained that her stomach was in perpetual ache. She put on a good face and didn't let on to her discomfort. The ride to my uncle's house was bumpy. They were repaving the road, stripping the old layer away, leaving holes and gravel. We were in a continuous state of jostle. When we arrived, we ate lunch at a seafood restaurant, and while my mother and uncles talked, Oil drove Katie and me to Wat Pho Bang Khla, a temple known for its bats. It was an eerie sight, bats on every tree limb, weighing branches down like taut fishing poles. Some bats clustered together in the rafters of the main hall, pulsating like a black heart. I remember Katie saying that bats were about rebirth. At dusk, every night, they darted into the world, again and again. Oil spent a long time praying in front of a statue of Buddha at that temple. She liked holding her stomach. She did so the entire day.

A week later, after I returned to the States, my mother called to tell me Oil lost the baby. When I talked to Oil, she said Bob blamed it on the trip, the bumpy roads, that bad omen of bats.

"That's why he left?"

Oil shakes her head. "That's what he says. But I believe he left me because he left me. It's what Thai men do."

"That's stupid. He's stupid." I could feel myself reddening. I could feel heat flushing my face. If Bob were in front of me, I would punch him right in his rhinoplasty nose. I would take that chicken he wanted and shove it up his ass.

"God," I say, "why are Thai men like this?"

I am angry at Bob, yes. But I am also angry at the unknown, the uncertainty of the days to come. I don't want to be a Thai man. I hate what bad Thai men stand for. Hate how they hurt without remorse. But the fear of becoming one is always there. In my year alone, I didn't give a fuck. Not giving a fuck was easy and selfish. But I was good at it. It was a shrug of responsibility. Nothing mattered but my libido.

"Stupid men," I say.

Oil nods. "You have to think beyond your wiener."

This Bed That Was Not My Bed

There were times I did not know whether I was awake or dreaming. It felt like looking at the world through a wall of water. This happened often after Katie left. I would wake up next to a stranger, whose name I could not remember. The night was deep, and sometimes the residue of alcohol weighed heavily in my head. At first, I thought I was in my bedroom. I thought I could hear the sounds of the wave machine that lulled me to sleep. But there was no machine, only the whirl of a creaky ceiling fan. I turned and put my hand on a hip, believing it to be Katie's. When you are with someone for fifteen years, when you spend nights studying the body, you know when something is not right. The curve in my hand was not familiar, not at the right angle, not the deep slope I was accustomed to. The texture of this hip was smoother, cooler. And then I registered breath, the sound of it, the soft whistle through the nose. It was not the breathing of a wife I knew. My wife snored the dead awake. It was a stranger's breath, a stranger naked beside me. A stranger naked and asleep. I could smell the scent of us in the room, sloppy and sweaty. I closed my eyes. I was stuck in a dream, and at any moment I would awake to the familiarities of my world. There would be the stuffed white tiger we bought at a Colorado zoo at the foot of the bed, the old cherry dresser on which sat the box of my watches, and above that, the Japanese painting of cranes swooping in tight circles. The more I willed myself to wake, the more I realized I was. The more awake I felt, the more shame crawled into me. I rolled out of the bed that was not my bed, slowly, careful not to stir the stranger beside me. I kicked the bedside table that was not my bedside table. It was larger and round. A glass of water perspired on it. A digital alarm clock read a late hour. I searched for my clothes, but my body was heavy and unfamiliar; it felt as if I wore a looser and clumsier suit of myself. I fumbled in the dark. Once I'd found everything, I searched for the door, but the door had moved because it was not my door. It was at the opposite end of the wall from where my door was supposed to be. I turned to look at the stranger in the bed that was not my bed, but this full-size spring mattress. She remained still, her dark hair over her eyes. Her mouth was slightly parted. If she was awake, she did not indicate so. If she was awake, I wondered if she felt the same as me. I wondered if she thought if she closed her eyes hard enough, if she remained as still as possible, I would disappear.

I wanted to disappear. From this room. From this life.

And so I left.

I drove to a home that was not my home anymore. Streetlights were violent assaults to the eyes. Passing cars roared in my ears. I found my bed. I lay awake until the sun clawed high in the sky.

Mount Crested Butte

It might have been the fourth or fifth date after we decided to be a couple when we talked about marriage. That night Katie took me to a Mediterranean restaurant, and I tasted for the first time dolmades, rice and ground lamb wrapped in grape leaves; it was like biting into clouds of heaven. Afterward, we ended up at her rented farmhouse, on the back porch, sitting on the concrete steps.

As the night wore on, the conversation delved into deeper terrain; most deep conversations seem to happen after midnight. The lightning bugs constellated over the prairie of her backyard. The shadow of a tire swing swayed under the dark limbs of an oak. The air carried with it the faint sweet scent of newly bloomed hyacinths. Katie lived so far into the country it seemed we were the only people on earth. Her dogs—Mick and Bonnie, who would become my dogs in a few years, too—snoozed by my side, their warmth like a blanket.

Katie was passionate when she spoke, passionate and a little drunk, especially when we happened on the topic of marriage. "Marriage is an institutionalized way of controlling something uncontrollable. You know? You don't have to be married to be in love. It's just a paper, a fuckin' paper. And then what happens? Domestication. You fall into roles you never wanted to be in. The role of husband. The role of wife. And don't get me started on kids. . . ."

I nodded. I kept nodding.

I said: Amen.

I said: Marriage sucks. Kids suck.

I said: Who wants any of that?

"Not me, not ever," Katie said to the air. "I don't think I will change my mind."

And then she looked at me with an intensity that made me aim my eyes at the dark fields beyond. That was the power she had, one where I could not hold her stare. In that look was an invitation to speak up. To add to this late-night, drunken conversation. That look was her way of saying Please tell me what you think because I've been up front with what I want and don't want. We could end this now if you don't agree. It would be easier. Not years later, not even months later, when we'll fall even deeper for each other. So tell me, What are you thinking?

I was twenty-one and already in love with this woman who knew so much about the world, who had fully formed ideas and opinions, who, unbeknownst to her, was shaping my future, my wants and desires. She wasn't a Greek god who molded mortals into versions of herself. Not manipulative. Not malicious. I was reshaping her, also. That was the power and beauty of our relationship. Whatever firm ground we stood on could be tested, could waver and crumble, and suddenly, the thought of marriage wasn't so bad, was possible, even for someone who decried it one drunken night.

For a few summers Katie and I vacationed in Colorado, a strenuous exercise of being with Katie's family and eating mostly white food. After a couple of days, I would yearn for rice and anything Asian, even from the Asian-ish restaurant in town with the overly sweetened sauces. Despite my culture and family shock, Colorado remains one of the most beautiful places I've ever been, a place I've often thought of living the rest of my days. In my darker moments after the divorce, I fantasized about disappearing into the Colorado woods and living in solitude with an unruly beard and a black bear as my only company.

One of Katie's and my favorite things to do was ride the ski lift at Crested Butte. It gave the sensation of flight. In the rare moments we were without her family, I decided that was when I would do it. In my right pocket was the ring. I kept fingering it the whole day. For months, I planned something mega-romantic, some grandiose gesture, full of melodrama and sentimentalism. I would begin with, "My love, my dear . . ." and end with, "I'm happy to have found you." In the middle of my profession of adoration, angels would hover over us strumming harps. But on that ski lift, the ragged top of Mount Crested Butte to the right of us, all of this built-up romance slipped away.

Halfway up, I said, "Hey."

Katie said, "Yeah."

"I like you."

"Yeah."

"I was wondering. . . ." I pulled the ring out. Because we were fifty feet above the ground, because the green meadows of the mountain lay underneath, because I knew if I were to drop the ring at this moment I would never find it again, I shoved it into Katie's hand.

"What?" Katie said. She opened and closed her fist. Blinked at the ring nestled in her palm. Then she slipped it onto her index finger.

"You wanna?"

Katie said nothing.

Katie said nothing for a great moment of time. Up the mountain we went. Then down again. Up. Down. We made three revolutions on the sky lift, each revolution about ten minutes long. In the distance, thunderclouds hung over some far mountain. Wrens and sparrows swooped in and out of the wildflowers below. The world happened all around, but not a word passed between us.

"Well?" I said.

"Okay."

"Cool."

Later that day, I stopped at the local library for a particular short story by George Saunders about an obese man who foolishly falls for the wrong woman. That entire year I had been researching stories with fat characters. My body was growing again, and I obsessed about fat, especially my fat. When I returned to the station wagon, I caught Katie staring at the ring. The sun glinted off the diamond and made prisms on the roof of the car, on her face. I hid behind a concrete column. I watched her. I watched her and thought, This woman loves me. Loves the ring. Wants to be my wife.

Now, I crawl into this memory. I stand beside the boy behind the column who watches that girl watching the ring. I know what that boy thinks. In this quiet moment, the boy believes he is observing the happiest instant of his life. Perhaps of hers. I ghost past him, toward the car. The girl's face is windburned, cheeks and forehead red. She wears a baseball hat that sits awkwardly in the tangles of her hair. Her face wears no expression. Not a smile. Not a frown.

The boy doesn't see the nothingness on her face. How can he? He is too far away.

July 10

On this day thirteen years ago was a wedding. A Thai boy was marrying a white woman from the plains of Illinois during the monsoon season. The night before had brought a storm that knocked the power out. The air conditioner was still, and the absent buzz of electricity made the night disconcertingly quiet. The couple tossed the blankets to the side. They sweated. They sighed. They said things like, *I'm so, so hot.* Or, *It's so freakin' hot in here.* Or, *What the fuck?* No air-conditioning in Thailand was a death sentence for two people accustomed to midwestern winters that chilled the core.

The Thai boy was bored. To occupy his time, he inched closer to the white woman. He thought about the next day. It made him fidget, made him want to annoy the person next to him.

"Hey, you," he said.

"Don't," she said.

"What?"

"Don't touch me," she said. "It's too freaking hot."

"Our love is hot." He grabbed her hand.

"Let go." Her voice grew shrill. She was annoyed and dramatic and amused, all at once. This was one of the things he loved about their relationship. These moments of levity. These moments of fun in spite of the physical discomfort they were currently feeling.

He held her hand tighter. "Cuddle time," he said like a child.

"I'm going to kill you."

"Kill your husband?"

"Not husband yet."

"Let's hold hands." He then put his leg over hers and snuggled into the clavicle of her neck.

"I swear to God," she said. She tried to squirm away, but he clamped his leg on her tighter. She tried shaking his hand away, but he would not loosen his grip.

"Bucking hand," he said, a play on "bucking horse." "Bucking hand."

"I'm going to wreck you."

"Please do."

She whined and laughed, and then he laughed because the world was too stinking hot not to.

Not long after, the power came on. The air conditioner kicked in. He never let go of her. She never let go either, and the next morning, on July 10, they leaned against each other in a cavernous prayer hall of a seven-century-old temple, a golden Buddha looming over them, nine monks praying for a blessed future. Outside, two temple dogs rolled in the dirt under a rubber tree, oblivious.

II

After the Hysterectomy

When you meet someone at twenty-one, someone nine years older and wiser, you learn the world through her eyes. You are a blank slate, a boy who hasn't lost enough. You adopt what she wants and her views on life. Her interests—nature, birds, the infinite flat of Illinois—become your interests. And suddenly, you, the urban misfit, find yourself donning a pair of binoculars and aiming them in a tangle of branches, leaning your ear to every tweet and twitter, any rapid flap of wings. And suddenly, you want to retire in an old farmhouse in central Illinois, near her family, and grow corn and strawberries, raising horses you will never ride. And suddenly, you begin to write poetry, love poetry, want to be a poet, like she is—deep, dark, and mysterious, with a gift for composing perfect iambic lines. Because of her you don't want children, complain of their noise and ruckus on planes, the way they can't control the yarn of drool dripping from their toothless mouths. But then a sadness sets in, a sadness that feels like a hand to the throat, because after all these years, you don't know what you want. You, with the graying beard. You, with a belly distending over the waistline of your jeans. This dawns on you, as you sit in the waiting room of a hospital because your wife is having a hysterectomy. You think this is what you want, too, because you can't bear the pain she suffers every month she menstruates, her headaches that fetal her in the center of the bed. You want this, but you don't understand why your right knee bounces with a ferocity that shakes the bench you share with other people, people waiting for loved ones, people who stare at the crazy Asian man with an unstillable knee. You want this, but the finality of this decision has taken away a path in your life, and the Buddhist you are wonders whether that path would've led you to Nirvana. In that waiting room, you imagine a child, one you've created, one without a face, a child, your child, yours. And you hear that child's laughter. And you feel that child's breath. And you understand why your mother clings to you, why she squeezes your arms and legs, even now, as if she thinks you are not real, a dream she does not want to lose. In that waiting room, for perhaps the first time, you find yourself wanting. It fills you like the fragrant flood of a pond of lotuses. Beautiful gaping blooms hungry with want. But you keep quiet. You do not voice this. What good would it do now? What good would it do, when you are allowed to see your wife, dazed from surgery, slipping in and out of the conscious and unconscious world with her new body? What good would it do when you hold her hand, her voice weighted down with weariness, asking how the dogs are, asking whether you put the garbage out and gathered the mail?

A couple of years later, you will remember that hospital room. You will remember the overcast light entering the curtained window, and the gray that permeated that space. You will remember how your wife's long hair fanned the pillow, how even in post-surgical sleep she was beautiful. You will remember the slight murmurs in her sleep, some mysterious conversation had in a dream. This would be the end, though you did not know it then.

The end.

The end.

And you will remember this, in that gray hospital room: your fingers feeding ice chips to her cracked lips, one cold chunk at a time, this last intimacy, this last act of love.

The Gastropub

A week before my annual visit to Thailand, a few weeks after Katie's hysterectomy, I was a couple hours early for a doctor's appointment in the fancy part of Tampa, and instead of going home to let the dogs out or sit on the couch with Katie watching her favorite show at the time, *Dead Like Me*, I parked the car and went into the new glitzy restaurant next door, which wasn't labeled a restaurant but a "gastropub."

The gastropub was hip in the way I wasn't. It was soft lighting and high ceilings and rich dark wood floors. It was European electronic mood music. It was Florida men with pec-exposing shirts that V-ed so deep revealing squiggles of chest hair and Florida women with short skirts and high heels and blouses that barely contained bosoms. Every table had a tablet where patrons ordered food and drinks. Though it was still early in the evening, the restaurant was a loud beehive of conversation, a mixed cocktail of hormones.

I wanted to leave and sit in the car, blasting Chicago's Greatest Hits. This brand of music was what I had been listening to in the past three months, sappy ballad bands of the seventies and eighties that immediately brought back my teen years. Every song covered adolescent heartbreaks—which were many—and the teenager I was locked myself up in my room and listened to "Open Arms" or "Can't Stop Loving You" recorded over and over on a cassette tape, while writing in my journal how love sucked.

Love did suck. Love sucked now.

The distance between me and Katie had grown too wide and too deep. There was a time we shared every facet of each other's life, when there were no secrets. There was a time I would have called and told her about how ridiculous the restaurant—no, gastropub—was, and we would have laughed at the absurdity of people. I missed my wife, though I saw her every day.

Why then was I here?

Why then did I take a seat at the bar?

Why did I slip my wedding ring off my finger and put it in my pocket where it rested heavy against my thigh?

I ordered a beer and a basket of fancy fries and watched. I watched how people interacted, and whether it was possible for me to interact like them. I noticed the lean of young lust, the way the woman at the table nearest me laughed at something the gentleman with her said, laughed and leaned into his chest. Or how some men, like the one farthest from the bar, kept talking and talking, nonstop, minutes straight—I couldn't hear what he said but it seemed important and exciting only to him— and the woman he was with obliged him with nods. Or the couple that seemed to know each other, perhaps married, sat and talked with the intimacy of close friends, and when she rose to go to the restroom, she gave him a soft peck on the cheek.

A woman in a business suit took a seat next to me. I scooted over to give her more room, but it seemed like I moved because I thought she smelled.

"Hi," I said.

She smiled. I liked her smile. I liked the sea-glass pendant around her neck.

I remembered terrible pickup lines I used pre-marriage. Like, "Your hair smells so good. I was wondering what shampoo you used?" Or, "Your smile is like a Cheshire cat." Or, "I think you've been missing me." I didn't know why these lines came to me now. The same reason I didn't know why I took off my wedding ring. I didn't know. But I knew.

The bartender planted a Bloody Mary in front her with a tall stalk of celery.

"I need this," she said to herself.

"Hard day?" I said.

"Been better."

I nodded. "I hear that."

I sounded like a fuckin' idiot.

The woman drank her Bloody Mary. She sighed with pleasure, with exhaustion. I sighed because this was not where I was supposed to be. But it was where I was. It would be where I would end up months from now—at bars like this, at gastropubs like this—only I wouldn't be shy to talk to strangers. Sometimes strangers talked back. And my wedding ring would be elsewhere, stored in a cigar box of pens and Buddha pendants, taken off permanently, my tan line on my finger disappearing.

I finished the beer. I finished the fries. I moved to leave.

"Have a better day," I said to the woman, but she didn't hear me.

Sex Education

Bangkok is overly crowded and polluted, the air a dizzying mix of car exhaust and garlic. The city moves at a pace antithetical to my own. Even for a Chicago boy like me, Bangkok sets me on edge. I believe a mugger will jump out at me at any moment. I believe my ears will explode from all the sound. This is what Buddha meant when he spoke of chaos: "It is inherent in all compounded things. Strive on with diligence."

After the hour flight from Chiang Mai to Bangkok, we spend the afternoon at Tui's recycling center. Tui is one of Aunty Sue's nephews. I refer to him as the Godfather because his workers step lightly around him. Because when he speaks his voice reverberates and people listen. Because he gets whatever he wants, whenever he wants it. Recycling is one of his businesses. Construction is the other.

At the recycling center, thousands of plastic bottles gather in mounds. Old newspaper and discarded tires find resting places along a blue plastic fence. The inside of Tui's office is filled with old toys and sporting equipment—golf clubs and tennis rackets, teddy bears and gum ball machines. I find books on bonsai-ing, Thai cooking, and novels by Peter Straub and Danielle Steel. This office is like Bangkok, too—overwhelming, claustrophobic, a hoarder's heaven.

I make myself as comfortable as I can on a leather love seat, my mother next to me. She tugs at my hair to keep from falling asleep. We have hours to kill before Tui and his wife Bee close shop, and because we're staying with them for the next week or so, we wait.

Aunty Sue sits behind the main desk, a queen, spinning on an old office chair that squeaks. I am on the phone with Deedra, asking her why she's up when it's one in the morning, asking her if she misses me. She tells me she has gotten used to sleeping with me, my warm presence in the bed. "It's too cold without you." I talk openly even with my two parents in the room. I assume they aren't listening, assume their English has deteriorated past the point of understanding. Deedra and I say I love you a bunch of times and bye a bunch of times more and I miss you even more. Our talk is sickly sweet, the way new love talk is. When I hang up, I'm smiling.

Aunty Sue stops her spin. "You never spoke like that with Katie," she says.

"Like what?"

"Love you, love you. Joop, joop." She puckers up and exaggerates kisses.

My mother laughs, playing with a Matchbox car on Tui's desk, a red Corvette.

"I don't know what you're talking about," I say, but I do and my insides flush.

"I want to ask you something," Aunty Sue says. "Don't be embarrassed."

"Oh boy," I say.

"I want to ask you about sex."

"Oh boy," says my mother.

"When you and Katie had sex, did she . . . ," Aunty Sue hesitates, searching for the right word, "climax?"

"Oh boy," I say.

"Oh boy," says my mother.

"I want to know," Aunty Sue says. "Maybe that's why she couldn't get pregnant and maybe that's why she got a hysterectomy and maybe that's why you've broken up."

"It might be hard to believe," I say, "but Katie never wanted children."

"Impossible," says Aunty Sue. "She's a woman."

I shake my head.

"This is what women are made for," Aunty Sue says.

I do not want to get into an argument about feminism and body empowerment with my aunt, though she and my mother are two of the biggest feminists I know. These two feminists have spent their lives raising a respectful and open-minded man.

I do not want to point out that she is childless because I know what she will say. How can I have a child without a man? Aunty Sue, who speaks freely about anything, like she does now, seldom spoke of a past boyfriend or partner. In all the time I've known her, it has been my mother, my mother who now hums "Jingle Bells" to herself.

"I think my boys are a little dumb," I say. I speak in English, hoping Aunty Sue won't understand and forget all about it.

"Boys?" Aunty Sue says.

"Swimmers," I say.

"Swimmers?"

"Sperm."

"Oh boys," says my mother.

"How do you know?" Aunty Sue peers over her glasses. "Are you a doctor?"

"A feeling," I say.

"A non-doctor making a doctor's diagnosis on a feeling." She laughs and then gathers herself, leaning on the desk. "I'm asking, did she climax?"

Heat creeps into my face. I aim my eyes at an old robot toy, black with gold knobs. It's identical to the one I had when I was small, the one my father bought for me from the Alsip Flea Market. Outside the main office, Tui talks on a cell phone, pointing and wagging his fingers. Bee is busy with empty bottles, stacking them in a cardboard box. They are childless, too. I wonder if Aunty Sue has had this same conversation with them.

"We can speak frankly," Aunty Sue says. "I want to know."

How do I tell my aunt that sex was a complicating factor in the marriage? That we went over a year without having it. That we consulted a therapist. That I often slept in the guest room or my office. That I hated my body.

"I don't know," I say.

"Listen . . ." and Aunty Sue is off. She lectures on and on about the idiosyncrasies of the human body during copulation. The opening and closing of parts. She speaks terms I have never heard of before, terms never covered in sex ed when Mrs. W. directed a pointer at a diagram of a penis, and the class howled when she slapped the testicles with it. Even then, in seventh grade, sex made me squirm and shudder. I was not like the other boys in the 'hood who spoke of sex unabashed, who bragged about banging so and so and getting BJs behind the bleachers at school. Even when I had sex for the first time, I kept it to myself because verbalizing it was too embarrassing.

Aunty Sue is not embarrassed. She is a fountain of facts. When she speaks medically, her English is crisp, the language of nurses. Twenty minutes later, I feel like I can deliver a baby.

"Oh boy," my mother says.

"Thank you for that," I say.

"If you had a child," Aunty Sue says, "it would be beautiful, and you will know a love like no other." She begins spinning again in her chair. Round and round, counterclockwise. "Give your mother a grandchild. You'll complete her life."

"Oh boy," my mother says.

The Abyss

On one of the nights I couldn't sleep, I spiraled into the abyss of the internet. Katie had been gone for a month, the house unfamiliar without her. But with her absence came new possibilities. For hours, I read articles, visited websites, watched online videos. All on the topic of adoption. My mind was filled with the idea of having a child. Caring for a child. Raising a child. Adoption became a possibility. Being a father, a possibility. I wasn't planning on meeting a future partner. I wanted a child but not a wife.

The next day, I had lunch with a friend, who has a name like a birdsong but the mouth of a shit-talking sailor. I liked this contrast about her. It was a marvel to see someone so slight contain the bluster of giants.

When I told her I was thinking about raising a kid, my friend said, "Fuck you," which meant, Really? And then, "Are you motherfuckin' kidding me?" And then, "Holy fuckin' Christ on a stick."

"Yup," I said.

My friend drew the scowls of two older women at the next table. I mouthed, *sorry*, but my friend didn't stop. "Are you sure this isn't a fuckin' rebound thing? Because this sounds like a rebound."

"Isn't a rebound the first person you date after a long-term relationship?"

"Dude," my friend said, "having a kid is the relationship of all motherfuckin' relationships. The longest of long-term. Fuckin' forever. You understand this, right?"

I shrugged.

"What—you gonna knock someone up?"

"Maybe I've already have," I said. "Maybe there's a little Ira running around somewhere in the world."

"You're a fuckin' idiot."

I laughed. "Adoption."

"They let single dudes adopt?"

I sighed. Out of all the things I read the night before, not many articles offered hope for single men looking to adopt. They, by law, could, yet it was a rarity. From one of the sites: "As men were (and sometimes still are) seen as the less nurturing sex, the idea of a single man wanting to adopt a child was perceived as out of the ordinary." Other websites reiterated this. A gay couple could adopt. But a single male, no way.

"I mean, yeah," my friend said. "Fuckin' creepers out there. What would you think if a single guy went to an adoption agency?"

"Nothing good."

"Fuckin' A right," my friend said. "How about a black market baby?"

"I looked that up, too," I said. "It's not cheap. It's not like I can just go to an underground mall and say I want a baby and they'll have one in stock."

"Fuckin' duh."

"I read crazy things," I said. "Child trafficking. Sick pedophiliacs. Babies sold for medical testing. Messed up stuff."

"Because the world is a fuckin' mess. Fuck me. Fuck you. Fuck all of us. Fuck."

The women the table over paid their bill and left, shaking their heads on the way out. My friend took no notice.

"You're fuckin' serious about this?"

I shrugged. "I don't know. Right now, I'm not serious about anything."

"Because this is no fuckin' joke."

"I know."

"How about meeting the fuckin' one and doing it that way?"

"Fuck the one," I said. "I don't believe in it."

"Right now you don't. Time."

"Maybe," I said. "Maybe not."

"I know one thing—and don't get a big head—but you'd be a good fuckin' father. And there aren't many of them out there, believe you fuckin' me."

The Impossible Dream

Outside rain taps on the roof of the house. The wind whistles through the screened windows and tree branches tickle the white cement walls. Bee and Tui promise a large dinner when they get back from the recycling center. They know we have been cooped up, the weather denying us fun. I don't mind. The sound of the rain soothes me. It gives a temporary respite from the heat.

On days like this, I roam their expansive house, climbing up and down stairs, taking one slow meditative step at a time. Bee and Tui live on the outskirts of Bangkok, close to an outdoor market. Their home stands out, a fortress above derelict other houses a quarter of its size with rusted roofs and gates. One of the neighbors raises fighting cocks, and they announce the morning with alarming viciousness. Tui likes his privacy, so the cinderblock wall is high, the banana trees are high, blocking any ray of sun. Roaming their home is like roaming a luxurious catacomb, with dark parquet floors, gold-patterned wallpaper, and portraits of the king and queen in the long living room, who in the shadowed dark look like vampire royalty.

I spend the day writing postcards. I take postcard writing seriously. I do not fill them with details of how great the trip is. I do not wish my friends were here with me. Most of the time I tell them of my dreams. Most of the time they are nonsensical, little poetic riddles. Last year, a friend said, "I don't get your postcards. They seem kinda sad."

Last year, I was sad.

The rain lingers, steady. It brings with it a breeze that billows the curtains of the house. My mother screams something at my aunt who screams something back, the two of them losing their hearing, their talk loud and speckled with impatience. Outside, the neighbor dog barks to be let in from the rain.

After I write friends, I find a shadowed corner. I look around to see if anyone is watching. It feels like I'm twelve again, sneaking off to write love letters to Brenna Murphy, the girl who won my heart by chasing me around the block with a butcher's knife. I have another stack of postcards, most of them for Deedra and her daughters. I buy them wherever I go—pictures of temples, water buffaloes, rice fields and the shadowed mountains of the north, monks walking for morning alms, children playing under a waterfall, statues of Buddha with his dreamy expression.

When I write to Deedra, I want no one around. It feels wrong, like I shouldn't be happy, like I hadn't suffered enough. And now, I'm writing postcards to this woman that contains the same giddiness of those letters to Brenna, the language of first love. I hesitate to write the word "love," however, because to write it is to make it real. Right now, I need the unreal-ness of it. I need to feel as if I am dreaming, as if this woman belongs to another world, that she at any moment can evaporate, leaving only lingering images that begin to fade until there is nothing left. These postcards are windows to another life, and I imagine taking this dream woman there, imagine showing her temples, waterfalls, the mountains of the north. I want to take her to the secret places in this country, the places only my family knows of, containing stories only they would tell. This is the other half of my life, and I want this dream woman to be part of it; not many have privy to this. I keep it guarded.

Thailand is my heart. I don't show my heart to just anyone.

*

At the end of our marriage, Katie had vivid dreams. They came to her like TV shows. Some dreams brought about sadness, childhood ghosts lingering among the fireflies of her past. Some dreams she savored like chocolate ice cream, especially the ones that co-starred Colin Firth; in these dreams he always reprised his role of Darcy in the BBC's version of *Pride and Prejudice*. Some dreams—the really bad ones—circled around

Katie's sense of helplessness, the inability to save a dog or to raise her voice against opposition.

Katie obsessed about her dreams, keeping a dream dictionary close by, looking up meanings, as if they would tell her something that would change the course of her life. Her own writing began to change, her poems exploring this dreamscape, her language taking graceful leaps between the real and surreal, the speaker of her poems possessing this voice—this true voice—that seemed absent in her life. Though I was enchanted by this new change in her poetry—I thought they were some of the best she'd ever written—I was also wary of it. "I only write about relationships when they are about to end," Katie said before we started dating. She never wrote explicitly about the state of us, but in her poems, I was there. In the move and curl of her lines. Peeking behind the lone oak in the prairie. In every scattered flight of sparrows. I was there. Her dreams, her poems, were about a life absent of me, about a speaker trying to find her footing on this planet, longing for something I could not name, wanting something I could not give. Her poems, her dreams, were messages I did not heed, or perhaps I did but did not believe it was possible.

I was dreaming, too, dreaming that nothing was wrong, dreaming that this was a rough patch we would get through, dreaming that I had the strength to save us.

*

In the early evening, I wake from a nap, pen still in hand, postcards on my stomach. I am disoriented. I turn on my side thinking my face will be in a nest of dark hair, expecting the warmth of another body, the greediness of limbs, the sound of soft breathing. Sometimes I forget I am in Thailand. Sometimes I think I am in the States, body pressed against Deedra. Sometimes—this time—I wake with fragments of a dream. What I find is cold, blowing air from the air conditioner above me. What I find are my two parents watching the news, talking back and forth about the state of the country.

The rain has not ceased. My mother says the sky has a lot to cry about today. On the TV, the newscaster looks serious, her face overly powdered, her lips an astounding red. Aunty Sue shakes her head. She says this is not what the prior kings wanted for the country, this infighting, this coup, this corruption.

"Kie kee nah," my mother says. *Embarrassing.*

But kings are dreamers, too, perhaps the biggest of dreamers. And the kings of Thailand bigger still. It is the reason Thailand has come so far, has defied odds, has risen against opposition and retained its independence for centuries from countries who have tried to take it over.

More news: another politician was found to be corrupt, a wild elephant sat on a car, and Chile is the Cinderella surprise of the World Cup.

"Look," Aunty Sue says, "the princess is awake."

I am the princess. I yawn and sit up.

"Days like this are for sleep," my mother says.

I nod.

"Did you dream?" Aunty Sue says.

I did, but the story has left me.

"If you dream," Aunty Sue says, "tell us and we will buy lottery tickets."

"So we can be rich," says my mother.

"Then we can go anywhere in the world," my aunt says. "See everything."

My mother shakes her head and looks at her arms and legs. "Too late," my mother says. "I'm dreaming now for the next life." She wears a sleeveless shirt and orange tie-dyed shorts. Her arms are pale, her underarms sagging. As a joke she likes to jiggle them, which usually drive her younger sisters into fits of laughter. Her legs are plump, ankles thick, and I have noticed on this trip how she needs help getting up, how her grunts are more pronounced.

Despite what my mother says, despite her insistence that her dreams are for the next life, there comes a certain age where your dreams are movies of the past, when you relive youth and the capabilities of the body. There was a time my mother and aunt were more capable than they are now, when they lived and played golf without aches and pains, and energy propelled them to take extra hours at the hospital, to take care of their son, to mow and garden and shovel snow. They dream the mundaneness of youth. They dream about what slips from them with each passing second.

This might be the reason Buddha does not dream, something I was taught many years ago in a class at the Thai temple in Chicago. I remember the monk-teacher, whose shaved head reminded me of an alien's, said, "Dreams, as pleasant as they are, present us with unreality, the unattainable. We dream and then we want what we can't have."

We do. I do.

To dream is to also hurt. To dream is to hold onto what is lost. Like what Buddha left behind: his son, his wife, his family, a kingdom, his sins; or the suffering that drove him to seek a monastic life. Or perhaps, enlightenment is another dream, a burst of color in the mind, a kaleidoscopic achievement of peace and understanding.

I am standing at the juncture of past and present where part of me is looking into the future, still dreaming and hoping and wanting; and the other part is beginning to think of what I have lost and what I will continue to lose.

The other thing about dreams: sometimes they break your heart.

The Red Balloon

My mother keeps balloons everywhere. Her doctor says for her to exercise her lungs once a week by blowing balloons. On some mornings, I would come down to both my mother and Aunty Sue huffing and puffing into balloons, and when they notice me, they let them go and laugh at how they flatulate around the house. When I first arrived, at the height of the stairs in my mother's house in Chiang Mai were an assorted array of balloons in different colors, hung around a sign written in perfect print, *Welcome Home.* As the weeks go by, the balloons will sag, depleted of air, appearing like shriveled multi-colored squash. The balloons are a reminder of how much time I have before I have to return to the States.

Even in her purse, my mother has balloons. When she sees a child, like the bouncing boy at a small temple in the middle of Bangkok, she quickly pulls one out and blows into it. The boy is bored because his mother is talking to a monk, her hands pressed in front her in deference. The boy goes from one puddle to the next. The temple dogs watch him intently from a careful distance. I watch him from a careful distance, noting his socks pulled to his knees and speckled in dirty water.

It takes my mother a few minutes before the balloon fills and another minute for her to tie it adequately. It is red. The sun makes it glow. She goes to the boy in the middle of a puddle, who stops and watches her.

"Come here," she says, beckoning him with her hand. The boy looks at his mother. She stops her conversation and smiles. The boy looks back at the balloon.

His mother tells him it's okay. She is young, in her twenties, wearing a red dress to her ankles. She looks the age I was when I got married. "Go ahead," she says. "What a pretty balloon."

The boy hesitates. He is computing my mother with a tilt of his head. Who is this old lady who wants to give me a red balloon? Why is she so old?

"Every boy should have a balloon," my mother says. She extends the balloon to him.

This boy is all dimples, his hair in the typical boy mess. He takes a step forward. Grabs the balloon and then rushes back to the puddle. He stands there hiding behind the balloon, his face shaded red.

His mother says, "Tell Grandma thank you."

The boy puts his hands together sloppily and bows his head.

My mother says he is polite. "How old are you?"

He puts up five fingers with his left hand, while the right one clings to the balloon.

His mother laughs. "He's not quite four."

The boy goes off running, balloon bouncing in his hand. His mother chases after him, saying luke, luke, *son, son.* Be careful.

Monks watch and smile. The temple dogs bark and scamper away.

This could be the sequel to *The Red Balloon*, a movie I watched years ago in grade school. In the original, a red balloon follows a little French boy everywhere he goes. They form a friendship, until bullies pop the balloon. But then the miraculous happens! Balloons from all over France fly to the boy and carry him away.

In the imagined sequel to this movie, set among jeweled temples in the scorch of central Thailand, there is one balloon. It is red. And there are no bullies on the temple grounds, just temple dogs and monks and parishioners come to pray. And this balloon is without helium to fly the boy anywhere. In fact, it is not the balloon leading the boy; it is the boy leading the balloon. It is the boy putting the balloon in his mouth. It is the boy making the balloon slick with saliva. It is the boy being a boy with a balloon. And in this movie there is a man who watches the boy's mother, who watches the boy. The mother smiles and it is a smile that says he is mine and there is nothing in this world I love more than this boy and his balloon. And the man wonders what it might be like to have a boy to blow a balloon for. He wonders about the simplicity of a balloon and the awe it inspires in boys. The balloon is the container of air. It moves as if not from this world—hovers and floats and bounces. The balloon is a wonder. The boy is a wonder. At the end of this sequel, the balloon will pop, and there will be no other balloons come to save this boy. Only a mother who lifts him up and whispers everything will be okay. There will be other balloons in the future. I will give you all the balloons in the world.

"What are you smiling at?" my mother says.

"The boy," I say.

Giggles

Twice in my life my dreams felt so real I remembered them without the fade that usually follows. They were so real I questioned whether they were even dreams. Even now, they unspool with clarity. Both instances contained elements of the supernatural, like scenes from a Guillermo del Toro film—haunting and surreal and ordinary, all at the same time.

The first happened near the end of the marriage. I had purchased an oversize beanbag and put it in my office. My office was a small green box, and the beanbag took up more than half the space. I bought it so I could rest and read in between work. But the purchase of the beanbag was also the marker of when I stopped sleeping in the bedroom, when in the middle of the night, I'd leave and find my way into the embrace of the beanbag.

One day, I heard someone in my office. The dogs often came in to greet me with licks and wiggles, to tell me it was morning and that I had to get up and feed and love them. I murmured something in my half-awake stupor, probably, *okay, okay, I'm up, I'm up, chill, chill*. But no dogs came, no licks, no morning exuberance ritual. Only the sound of footsteps. Heavy. I knew it was morning. I could sense the sun behind my closed eyes. When the sun rose, it'd come up with blinding vengeance through the one window of the office. I sensed the sun. I sensed the sun and someone over me. I thought it was Katie and said something like, "Come cuddle," but she did not cuddle. Instead there was a silence that buzzed my ear, that prompted me to open my eyes and look up. What I found was the silhouette of a man looking down at me. The sun behind him creating a glow around his body, which was thick. He looked as if he wore a flannel and baggy jeans. My reaction was calm indifference, which was the first indication this was a dream. I would have screamed otherwise, cussed something fierce, jumped up and kung fu–ed the hell out this intruder. The dream version of me, however, looked, saw, yawned, and then blinked. It was the blinking that brought me awake. It was the blinking that vanished the man. And for minutes later, I sat in the beanbag and thought, Well, that was weird.

The second time: I was in bed in Deedra's house. It would be the first time I stayed the night, and we were figuring out this new configuration of our bodies, which were naked and pressed against each other. I loved the warmth of her skin, her need to press harder into me, as if she wanted to meld into one. The two of us were terrible sleepers, but for the first time in a long time, sleep came easy. In this dream, I slept on my side, my fingers dangling over the bed. Then it happened. Someone was playing with my hand. I felt other fingers, tiny fingers, tapping and tickling. And then the rapid sound of a child running away. And a child's giggle. It happened again. Someone playing with my fingers and running away. And more giggles. This went on for a while. I never took my hand away. I let it dangle there. My eyes were open. Whoever was playing with my fingers was smaller than the height of the bed. I could not see anything, but the shadowed top of a head. I remember in this dream how pleasant it all was. How there wasn't anything out of the ordinary. A naked woman pressed against me. A child giggling and playing with my fingers. Me enjoying the sensation of a child playing with my fingers, enjoying the sounds of the giggle. No thought entered my brain that said this was unusual. That Deedra did not have a small child but two grown ones who were sleeping in their own rooms. In this dream, however, this was my life. This was ordinary. I woke and sat up. Deedra was not in the room. She probably was drinking coffee or getting the girls up for school. But I still felt the phantom touch at the tip of my fingers, the lingering sensations of when skin meets skin. I looked at my right hand. I closed and opened my fingers. I searched the room that was lightening from the beginning of the day. I thought, incredulously, that I would find the child the giggle belonged to. The dream felt so real I believed a child existed, a child who loved to play with a father's fingers. The dream felt so real I thought I was a father.

Deedra found me in a daze. My eyes aimed at my hand. "I had the strangest dream," I said.

"Tell me," she said.

July 10

On this day thirteen years ago was a wedding reception at a fancy hotel with a fancy buffet and a fancy triple-tiered cake and a fancy karaoke machine, where Aunty Sue serenaded the married couple with "Chang Chang Chang," the Thai elephant song.

Before the reception, however, after the morning ceremony at the temple, Thai Boy's mother and aunts took White Woman to get her hair and makeup done. That left Thai Boy with an empty hotel suite, complete with minibar. With a few hours to himself, he called for an in-room massage and busted open an overpriced Coke and a small bottle of rum.

The massage therapist rolled out a cushioned mat on the floor.

"Sir is married today," she said in Thai.

"Yes."

"To a *farang*," she said.

"Yes."

"She is American or European?"

"American."

"Americans are nice. Is she very nice?"

"Yes."

"Does she not want a massage, too?"

"She is getting her hair and makeup done."

"Of course," the massage therapist said.

The hour went by slowly. The massage therapist walked on top of Thai Boy, her small heels digging into the meat of his lower back. She pulled his arms back, bending him into a C. She twisted his torso, and his body released in a series of pops. A Thai massage was half massage, half assisted yoga. In a Thai massage, the body is not static, but is moved and stretched and elongated.

Thai Boy was in a haze when there was a knock at the door.

"Sir," the massage therapist said.

"Okay." His head blurred beautifully.

"Sir," the massage therapist said again.

"Okay." He concentrated on the silent rush inside his body, and it was like waves on some euphoric shore.

"Sir, I'll get it for you," the massage therapist said.

Thai Boy heard the hotel door open. Thai Boy heard, "Is Ira here?" Thai Boy heard, "Madam is so pretty."

He rose up and put his glasses on.

"Madam is back," the massage therapist said. "Beautiful bride."

Thai Boy tilted his head. He stared at the woman in front of him who was not his wife. She was a clown impersonating his wife. Thick eyeliner crusted her eyes. Her cheeks were overly bruised with blush. Her lips glowed toxic red on her ghostly white face.

"I didn't think you can get whiter," Thai Boy said.

"Fuckin' fuck," said White Woman. She did not blink.

"What the hell happened?"

"Fuckin' fuck."

The massage therapist took her leave.

"I look like a hooker," White Woman said.

"You're beautiful."

"Shut the fuck up."

White Woman went into the bathroom to rub off the foundation. "Massage?"

Thai Boy nodded.

She rolled her over-mascaraed eyes that made her look like a cartoon cat. "You know where I was?"

"With my mom?"

"Roaming around this hotel trying to find you."

"She didn't tell you the room number?"

"She told me the wrong one." White Woman scrubbed a washcloth hard on her face, but the makeup was on thick. "The front desk didn't have a clue. I told them your last name. I told them my last name. Your mom's last name. Aunty Sue's. They didn't know anything."

"You're beautiful," Thai Boy said.

"You know what name the room was under?"

He shrugged.

"Ira and Kethi. K. E. T. H. I."

"You're beautiful."

"Who books a room under first names?"

"You're beautiful."

"And *my* name is spelled wrong."

"You're beautiful."

"Say it one more time," White Woman said. "I dare you."

After forty minutes, after White Woman cooled down and managed to look more like herself, after she ran after Thai Boy with her shoes, they went down to a small banquet room filled with family and friends. Night would arrive soon. Already it had been a long day, and Thai Boy felt the effects of it weighing on his body. White Woman was tired, too. He could tell by her reddened cheeks, her slight slouch, her silent sighs. There was nothing she wanted more than a nap. Unfortunately, they had a few more things to do, like the Water Pouring Ceremony, Rod Nam Sang, a tradition that used to authenticate Thai marriages.

White Woman sat to the left of Thai Boy, and in front of them were two golden tables. A white string—*mong kol*—twined around their heads, joining them. They put their hands together and placed them over the edge of the tables. Each guest then came forward, starting with the eldest, to pour holy water over the couple's hands, wishing them the best in their future together.

When it was Thai Boy's mother's turn, she looked at him. It was the same look that stilled him when he was an overly rambunctious boy. Her mouth was a tight line. Her eyes narrowed. When she finally spoke she said the clearest Thai word Thai Boy has ever heard her utter: "Grandchild," followed with, "now" in English.

Everyone laughed, Aunty Sue convulsing beside Thai Boy's mother. Cousins snickered into cupped hands. White Woman asked what happened.

"I'll tell you later," he said.

At the end of the ceremony, White Woman whispered, "This is nice."

"It is," Thai Boy said. "You're beautiful."

What I Want

Rayong is a fishing city three hours outside of Bangkok, along the Gulf of Thailand. After the fall of Ayutthaya in 1767 to the Konbaung Dynasty of Burma, King Taksin fled to this coastal town. During his time in the city he built a navy and gathered forces to reclaim what Burma had taken. This was one of the last wars against Siam's enemies of the north, wars that had been carried on for centuries over land and greed and pride. In the center of the city is a shrine in honor of the king. A statue of him sits on a gold throne, his hands on his sword that rests on his lap, his head held high, chin tilted to the right, as if expecting more danger to come, as if expecting the rise of another enemy.

I wonder if King Taksin expected us, in a hired van heading for the coast. Us, hungry for seafood, hungry for the salt air, hungry to be away from the pollution of Bangkok. Us, this silly brigade of mother, son, aunt, on a weekend trip, in a vehicle stocked with so much food and water it would survive a zombie apocalypse for years.

My mother and Aunty Sue converse with the driver, Supon, a close friend of the family. When there are long trips, Aunty Sue uses his services. "He drives the way old ladies like," she says, which means slow and attentive to bathroom breaks every thirty minutes. Supon's kindness is in his smile, his eagerness to converse. He is a good man, a full-time soldier, and because the country is under military rule, he only drives on weekends, like this Saturday, dedicating the rest of the week to the needs of the state.

The three of them talk about the intricate politics of the country. I barely understand how America works, having failed the mandatory high school Constitution test twice before finally passing. I remain quiet and listen, my gaze out the window and into the lush green of the land.

"America is threatening to cut its support," says Supon. "They want democracy now."

"Democracy, democracy," Aunty Sue says. "It is only a word."

"They don't know what's it like here," says my mother.

"Democracy is not an answer to everything," Aunty Sue says.

Supon speaks of the civil war that nearly broke out between the reds and yellows, the violence that took over the capital, the assassination attempts on political leaders. A week ago a poet-activist was murdered at a busy intersection of Bangkok. Supon shakes his head; his hand tightens around the wheel. "I love my country," he says. "I want the best for it."

Each evening, before soap operas, the TV broadcasts the amendments of martial law and updates of the country: which politicians have been removed, who has been arrested, who is corrupt, what is the timeline for the new elections. For the time being the military has restored peace. In the States, my friends would ask what was happening in Thailand, and when I tell them it is under martial law, they scoff. "Stupid military. Brutes." I understand their antipathy. I share it, too. I remember Tiananmen Square, the image of the tank and the protester. But Thailand's politics are different. Thailand's culture is different. It wants to be seen as modern, but retains its cultural identity. It is a mix of hundred-year-old temples and modern high rises. It is Pali prayer and modern pop music. It is a country that lacks an identity, having its feet in both worlds.

"What does each side want?" I ask.

My mother pins her eyes to the blurring landscape. Supon maneuvers the van around a stray dog sunning in the road. Ahead, the ocean laps the Rayong shoreline.

"For the other side not to win," Aunty Sue says.

*

"What is it you want?"

I posit this question to my college students. I often put them on the spot.

Some will say, "I want a burger."

I ask, "Why do you want a burger?"

Some will say, "Because I'm hungry."

I ask, "But out of all the foods in the world, why a burger and not a doughnut?"

Some will keep answering my questions, which I am endless with. Some will shrug. Some will become frustrated and tell me to let it go. Some, when posed with the question of want, will not know what to say. They will stutter. They will shrug. Once, a student cried. Want has that kind of power.

When I was younger, there was a simplicity to my wants. I wanted every toy in existence. I wanted every candy bar. I wanted to press every button on an elevator. Wanting, for children, is a way of experiencing life, understanding the things rotating the earth. I drove my parents mad with my wanting. My mother cursed the day I learned the word "want." My father shook his head at it. Often, I hid among the stuffed animals at toy stores until my parents gave in to my wants and bought me that teddy bear I would tire of an hour later.

But the older I became, my wants became less about material things, and more about the intangible—an emotion, a sense of well-being. My wants morphed into an existential crisis that most of the time related to mortality. I want to go to Europe before I die. I want to be skinny just once in my life. I want to experience true happiness. I want to be a father. Suddenly, we have a checklist of how we want to part with this world, and perhaps, how we want to be remembered.

For the longest time, I prayed to Buddha, as if a genie, and asked for the same three things: peace for all dogs and cats; for my mother and aunt to live long healthy lives; for my marriage with Katie to last forever.

The last of these wishes began on July 10, 2002, the moment Katie and I were married at Wat Suan Dauk in Chiang Mai.

The morning had been hectic, the wedding service long. I could see fatigue in Katie's eyes, the heat ruddying-up her cheeks, perspiration glistening her forehead. I felt it, too, this tiredness that weighed me down more than my sweat drenched shirt. So I ducked out. I sat in the main *vihan*, alone in that cavernous hall, the walls covered in murals of Buddha's life—from prince to enlightened one. A looming gold Buddha towered over me, his face serene. The Buddha at Wat Suan Dauk was different from the others in the country. He was alert, black pupils standing out from the whites of his eyes, instead of his usual dreamlike repose. It was as if this Buddha was challenging any onlooker to a staring contest. "Look at me," he proclaimed. "I dare you." I stared at him because he was beautiful; because he was the silent observer in this special day of my life; because I believed holding his gaze would somehow give me the strength for the days and years to follow. I sat on my knees, though my legs were sore, and then bowed my head three times. The sun, which had remained hidden for most of the morning, began to peek through the layers of gray.

It was there—my hands pressed together—that I made my wish. There, below this alert Buddha, I said in a whisper I wanted Katie and I to last forever. I said it in Thai and English. I said it because, though I didn't know it then, I was scared. I was scared I would end up like my parents, divorced and unhappy. I feared failure. This fear eluded me for months and years, even hours before the wedding, but it was there then and it felt like a constriction over my chest. It made me take short breaths, made me sweat even more. This fear lasted a few short seconds before my mother called for me, and I rushed out to be with my family and new wife.

It seems silly to wish a marriage forever. A long-lasting marriage is nothing to wish for; it is something to work for. Still, the notion of wish represents an absence. A child wishes for a new bike because she does not have a new bike. A man wishes for a promotion because he lacks the sense of monetary or social success, and he believes a promotion will give him that. During the years my mother and father fought, I wished they would stop and be happy because happiness had evaporated from our suburban home. I wished and wished and wished. I wished the impossible. I wished for certainty when the world provided enigmatic answers. My wishes were filled with loaded words like *all* and *forever*, words that illustrated how badly I wanted.

The Buddhist nun Pema Chodron calls unrealistic wishes "the path and the flower." You want the flower, but you do not seek the path to the flower. You want to be with your wife forever, but what path have you taken to ensure that this happens? Is a path toward forever even possible?

I understand this. I understand, logically, that we need to look at the steps we take to achieve our dreams and desires, instead of dwelling on the dream itself. I understand this. I understand this is what Buddha teaches, to think through our actions, to interrogate the self. I understand. I do.

But still.

Still.

I cling to wishes. I keep wishing. Because wishes are hope, and a life without hope is a sad one, even when disappointment sometimes follows.

After the divorce, I no longer knew what I wanted. Not in the larger sense. What happened in the year between visits was I stopped believing in the impossible. I stopped believing.

*

"You're so good with kids," Katie said one day. I was. Always have been. I found myself in tune with them. I enjoyed being around them. Katie's nieces and nephews thought I was their personal jungle gym. I was fine with that. I babysat them, while the adults played cards upstairs or went out for a fancy dinner. I knew the language of kids and had the patience to entertain their endless questions. I made them laugh with my goofiness.

Early on in the marriage, Katie expressed her concern. Perhaps we were in Wisconsin, visiting her oldest brother's family, and I had just spent the day with the nieces and nephews. Perhaps it was in Illinois with another brother, whose wife had just given birth to a baby boy, and I carried and coddled that boy for days. Wherever we were, Katie wanted to talk, and I knew in the concern in her face, the way her brows furrowed together, the way she nibbled on the corner of her lip, that the conversation would be hard.

"I don't want to take away an opportunity from you," she said.

"You're not."

"You understand them," she said.

"But I don't want them."

"Kids aren't something I understand."

"They smell," I said.

"And drool." She laughed and then looked at her feet. "But seeing you with them makes me think this is what you want."

"I don't." I reached for her hands. Held them.

"Are you sure?"

"I am."

My love for her made me sure. I reconfigured who I was. Pushed aside all the things I had planned and dreamed and wanted.

Before Katie, having children was a given. This was what Thai people did. We married and had kids, lots of kids. My mom was one of nine. Aunty Sue was one of seven. When I went to Thailand, there were lots of cousins, and each year, I seemed to meet another one.

My want for a child was more than cultural and familial expectations. It was born from a memory, one that had stuck for years, one that replayed over and over after Katie left, feeding my want into a frenzy, making me lose myself in research on adoption. When asked why I wanted a child it is this cloudy memory that hovers, this faded image that sticks, this warm and comfortable feeling—like the unwavering certainty of first love. It is a simple memory. I am four, holding the first baby of my life—a baby holding a baby. I don't remember where I was. I remember sitting in a chair and holding this baby. I don't remember whom the baby belonged to. I remember the baby was small in my small arms. I remember the baby smell, fresh talcum powder, clean detergent. I remember someone—maybe my father, a man for sure—instructing me to not touch the baby's head, that the skull hadn't hardened yet. I remember thinking what an odd notion—a soft skull. I remember how irresistible the baby's head was. And I remember someone—maybe Aunty Sue, but maybe not—complimenting me on my gentleness, and someone asking whether I wanted a baby some-day, and I said yes, and whether I'd be a good father, and I said yes. And the stillness of that baby in my arms. And the stillness I felt in my body.

I wanted a baby. I want a baby. I wanted to be a father. I want to be a father.

"Am I taking something away from you?" Katie said.

"You can't take away something I don't want," I said.

*

A week after Katie and I were married, Aunty Sue wanted to show us the Rayong beaches, one of the first tourist destinations before the development of the southern islands. We stopped first at a local market to buy dried seafood. Katie couldn't stomach the smell. She gagged and fanned her nose with a fantasy book she had been reading on the trip. "Oh my God, oh my God, oh my God," she said. I took her hand and pulled her into the nearest 7-Eleven to buy potato chips and Thai iced tea. "That was unbearable," Katie said. "I almost puked." I laughed and called her the whitest woman in America, a nickname that stuck for the duration of our relationship.

Katie is not wrong about the smell. It is everywhere in Rayong. It lingers in the salted air of the ocean, in the aisles of markets, in the temples we visit. Rayong is famous for dried seafood and fish sauce, *nam pla*, its number one export. The smell of fish sauce fills the entire cavity of the nose for hours. It is as if you've walked into a room full of dead and rotting fish.

I love the smell of fish sauce.

Younger, I used to bring a bottle of fish sauce to my nose and breathe in deeply, as if it were a bouquet of roses. When Katie and I moved to Florida, I shipped our bottles of fish sauce through the mail. I don't know what went through my mind to think this would be a good idea. I only knew I couldn't part with the fish sauce, the way Katie couldn't part with her Earl Grey tea and honey, which came in another box. When our mail lady—the poor, poor soul—delivered the box to Katie, her face green, our package with Hazmat stickers all over it, she simply said, "Something broke," and rushed away.

"The mail person hates us," Katie said.

"Probably," I said.

But the smell of fish sauce, even the overpowering stench of it from that box, made our new home in Florida feel like a home, despite the fact we had to throw the box directly into the garbage.

Fish sauce signifies Thailand. The smell of it instantly transports me there. Or not Thailand exactly, but the Thai kitchen in our suburban home in Chicago, Aunty Sue cooking our meals, our family whole.

Fish sauce has become metaphor the way Katie has become the Illinois fields, the way Deedra is whatever flower I see. When you fall in love, you see more than the person in front of you. You see all she represents. You see yourself in that landscape. You don't want to let go.

We are in the safety of the van, behind tinted windows, waiting for Aunty Sue, who is purchasing dried squid. I can tell tourists from natives. Tourists are the ones with handkerchiefs over their noses, with sour faces. Tourists are the ones my mother and I make fun of.

"Oh, he's definitely not from around here," my mother says, pointing at a man taking a breath from the crook of his arm.

I point to a group of women pinching their noses and grimacing. One of them holds a handkerchief to her face. "Look at them," I say. "They can't take the smell either. *Farang*."

"Like Katie," my mother says and laughs. "She was so funny."

It was funny, though Katie didn't think so at the time. My mother loved Katie despite her aversion to fish sauce. She became part of the family because now she had her own story; now my mother would talk about her daughter-in-law who couldn't stand the smell of the thing that made Thailand, Thailand.

The mention of Katie quiets us. I'm not sure what my mother thinks. I know she worries, but she doesn't push. No one pushes. They say they are happy for me as long as I am happy. Things begin and end.

"Does your new girlfriend like fish sauce?" my mother says.

"She likes Thai food."

"We'll take her here whenever she comes and see what happens."

*

I wanted nothing more than to kiss her. I had been wanting to do so for the last eight months. Did I say eight months? I meant eight years. I meant the very moment I met her. The instant I saw Deedra, I thought, I'm in trouble. I thought, She's going to be my undoing. Even when I was happily married to Katie; even when I would never be unfaithful. Deedra, instantly, took my breath away.

I told her that.

On her couch.

Her kids were away—at sleepovers—and her ex-husband had moved out, the end of fifteen years of unhappiness. It was the first time I had been over to her home, and we spent most of the night watching TV, saying very little, her head resting on my shoulder. The wound of her marriage was fresh, like mine. For months we had been talking on the phone, late into the evening. We texted each other incessantly. We went on long walks. Kept everything platonic.

Why was she different? Why was she not like the others who came and went that year?

She knew about me. Knew my marriage. I stripped away the persona of someone who was handling everything well, who was moving on with his life. I knew she would understand. I needed one person to know how much I was hurting. It couldn't be any of my closest friends. It couldn't be any of my family. It had to be her, this woman whom I had been crushing on for years. This woman who never thought twice about me because she was raising two girls and was married to man who couldn't keep a job, whose anger was volcanic. This woman who was sharp-tongued and strong-willed and unafraid to tell the truth even if the truth hurt. "You're being stupid. Stop being stupid."

What does want feel like in the body?

The mind races and rushes the heart and makes it so you chew the inside of your cheek. And then your knee starts bouncing. Bouncing rapidly, without pause. And your hand is locked in a fist, your fingernails embedded in the palm. And your breath is shallow and slow; it is as if you've forgotten how to breathe until you remember, and then, to take in more air, you yawn, big and long, stretching the limits of your jaw, gulping in the air you hadn't been breathing.

It was three in the morning.

"You're tired," Deedra said. "Your yawn."

"I'm going to kiss you now," I said, and before she could react—yes, no, I don't know—I moved in.

What does want feel like on the lips?

Soft and clumsy and scared. Scared is a form of hesitancy, is the question of whether to commit, because to commit is to relinquish a part of you, and you don't know if you can do that, give yourself over like that, and you don't know what she is thinking with your lips on hers and whether she wants this, any of this, and you think this is her first kiss that isn't with her husband, and you remember your first kiss after your wife, in a motel room with a woman you never saw again, and you were filled with regret but at the same time craved more, wanted more.

I kissed Deedra. I wanted to. I wanted it badly.

*

Supon stops at a market so my mother can jump out and buy fruit. Throughout the car ride, she's been moaning about how her stomach wants fruit, and fruit is nowhere to be found, only seafood, seafood, and more seafood. "There is too much fish here," she says. Aunty Sue tells her that fish live in water and we are near water. "Fish, fish, fish," my mother says. The way my mother complains is the way I complain—whiny, a spoiled child. We want what we want.

Supon maneuvers the van under a series of overpasses. Underneath, vendors sell a variety of goods—from fresh mackerel to beef tripe to Hello Kitty pencils to baskets and baskets of fruit.

There's a rhythm to outdoor markets in Thailand, ordered chaos. My mother peruses fruit while I wander aisles, dodging patrons. I take in all the food—grilled chicken livers and hearts, coconut custard cups topped with scallions, and fried fish cakes. I stop to check out the silver tubs of curry—green, red, yellow, like swirls of oily paint—and bottles of fish sauce like dark rum.

At the Publix in Florida, you grab a number at the lunchmeat counter and wait. If someone accidentally bumps you, she says excuse me. There is no waiting here. No excuse me's. Someone will bump you. Those long years my mother lived in Chicago, she was timid, always depending on Aunty Sue to do most things, but here, now, she assumes a more aggressive posture, pointing at large baskets of mangosteen and rambutan. Because she is old, my mother commands respect from the vendors.

"Is it sweet?" my mother asks, in a tone that suggests a command not a question. She holds a rambutan in her hand. It looks like a fiery red ball, an alien fruit with spikes.

"Yes, ma'am," the vendor says. She's aged by the sun. It's a distinguishing characteristic among the social classes, skin color. My mother's skin is pale and powdered and middle class. She wears a large-brimmed hat to keep the sun at bay.

"Are you sure it is sweet?" she says.

"Yes, ma'am. It's from my garden, ma'am. It's the sweetest, I assure you."

"When were they collected?"

"This morning, ma'am. I climbed the trees myself."

"You are not selling me old fruit, right?"

"No, ma'am. The freshest."

"I want to taste this." My mother thrusts the rambutan at the vendor.

The vendor cuts the fruit in half. Inside is an opalescent pearl. My mother observes it as if the viscosity of a fine wine before popping it into her mouth. She is deliberate when she chews. Slow. Purposeful. Then she spits out the woody seed.

"I'll take five kilos."

"Yes, ma'am."

"You will give me a good price, yes?"

"Yes, ma'am."

"I'm only buying from you."

"Thank you, ma'am."

"I'll come back tomorrow if your price is right."

"Yes, ma'am."

They go back and forth with numbers, settling on one that appeases both parties. "This is acceptable," my mother says. "I want you to remember my face, okay? I will come back and you will remember to give this old woman a good price, okay?"

This is how things are negotiated. A directness I am unaccustomed to. A command I never knew my mother possessed. To choose fruit is easy. To want fruit is to want pleasure. An appeasement of the taste buds. My mother wanted fruit. She got fruit.

In the van, she eats happily, staring at fishing boats rocking in the gulf. I think she has wanted all her life. A faithful husband, a Thai daughter-in-law, a grandchild. And those big wants have slipped through her fingers. Those big wants have eluded her. And now she wants fruit—sweet, delicious fruit. "Miracle fruit changes the tongue. One bite, and for hours all you eat is sweet," writes the poet Aimee Nezhukumatathil. Sweet is what my mother wanted, but it is also how the sweet is received, at what price, at what time of day, with full command and presence.

This sweet is not a gift. It is a taking.

Bed, Bath, and Beyond

The house Katie and I had bought together when we moved to Florida was still on the market. No one was buying—Florida suffering when the housing bubble popped. Getting another place would be heavy on my wallet, but after the divorce, I couldn't stand staying in the house any longer. Sometimes I slept in my car, especially after late nights out. Some nights, I stayed at friends' homes. They were kind enough to offer their spare room or couch, and for a while I felt like I was a boy again, at a sleepover. I was not a boy, though. I was thirty-seven. I was thirty-seven and didn't want to go home because home was no longer home.

After a few weeks, I began to think that I couldn't be without the company of people; that being alone frightened me, that being alone made me helpless. To prove myself wrong, some time in October, I found a nice condo to rent close to work, and each month I paid a mortgage and rent.

When I moved all my belongings to the new place, I went about the business of unpacking like a madman, working late into the night, hammering nails into the wall to hang my art without worry of my slumbering neighbors. I sometimes went without food because I needed to organize my office in just the perfect way, making sure I had a view of the expanse of green grass and the small community pool. The walk-in closet in the bedroom could've housed a king-size bed. I shoved two dressers into it. I didn't want my bedroom to have anything but a bed and one reading chair. Unlike the other rooms in the condo, I kept the walls bare. The bedroom looked sparse with its beige walls and carpet. The vacuous space was my space and mine alone. Nothing disrupted it.

Books were the hardest to unpack. I spent days arranging and rearranging them, finally settling on shelves for white writers and shelves for writers of color. White writers occupied one bookcase, while my WOC brethren took up another. The books weren't separated by genre or alphabetized by last name. They were arranged by my state of mind. Marilynne Robinson's novel *Housekeeping* occupied the first position on the white shelf. "Because, once alone," Robinson wrote, "it is impossible to believe that one could ever have been otherwise. Loneliness is an absolute discovery."

Maxine Hong Kingston's *The Woman Warrior*, the ultimate memoir about being other in this country, headed the WOC shelf. "The work of preservation," Kingston writes, "demands that the feelings playing about in one's guts not be turned into action. Just watch their passing like cherry blossoms."

With each book I picked from a box, I'd open it to a random page and begin reading. Hours would pass with me on the carpeted floor, books scattered around me like leaves.

Though I unpacked boxes of books—boxes my poor friends helped me haul up to my second-floor condo—there were considerably less than what I had when Katie and I lived together. My bookcases were emptied of poetry. The poetry books had been Katie's, and they were the only things she made sure to pack and ship to Illinois. I found myself missing her poets—James Wright and Rudyard Kipling, Sara Teasdale and W. H. Auden. In Anne Fadiman's book *Ex Libris*, she writes of the books one accrues over time: "Books wrote our life story, and as they accumulated on our shelves (and on our windowsills, and underneath our sofa, and on top of our refrigerator), they became chapters in it themselves." The arranging of my books was the reliving of much of the marriage. Each book, a memory. Each book, an unwritten story. Much of the life we had together was founded on books—those moments when we read to each other, those moments when we needed to share a poem, those moments when we silently read in bed before drifting off, those moments in bookstores buying more books.

*

While packing the house, I gave a lot away. Or I would simply get rid of things in the trash. If I were going to start over, I would start over like a fire that rebirths a forest.

The first night in my new place I realized I had none of the essentials—no silverware, plates, glasses, mugs, coffee maker, towels, soap, shampoo, laundry detergent, curtains. I thought I could live simply, like monks who needed only their alms bowls and umbrellas. The rest, the world would provide. The monks I encountered in Thailand, however, amassed stuff like anyone else—monks with cell phones, monks with personal TVs, monks with buzzing air conditioners in their *kuti*, living quarters. I pondered a life without a coffee maker and immediately called my friend Aaron.

"Three words, dude," he said, "Bed, Bath, Beyond."

Aaron and I had been friends for a few years, both sons of immigrants, both interested in the same things like video games and comics. Katie and I had often gone on couple dates with him and his wife. When we decided to separate, Katie broke the news to them first, and it was Aaron who relentlessly called me to come out of my hole when I didn't want to see anyone. That year, Aaron was going through his own breakup. It came a few months after mine, something no one expected. "You just wake up and think you're not sure you want to be with the person beside you anymore," he said. "You think this relationship has run its course. You still love her, but not enough."

I helped Aaron move his belongings into storage, and for a small bit of time, he stayed in my spare room until he got his own place. We were inseparable, "the brown boys," as we called ourselves. We got haircuts at Fantastic Sam's. We went to the gym and exerted our heartbreak on the racquetball court. We cooked each other food, and his mother, who lived not too far away, would deliver wonderful Trinidadian cuisine. It was good to have someone to talk to.

The most important role Aaron took on: my Bed, Bath, and Beyond buddy. Daily, we made trips to the store that contained every household need. We parked in the same spot, this strange slot that was not paved in with tar like the rest of the parking lot but with small sand-colored pebbles and stones. No matter what time of day the parking spot was unoccupied, as if waiting for our arrival.

In this store I went about purchasing a new life.

"Here's the goal," I told Aaron. "I don't want to get anything that Katie would like." It wasn't because I didn't like Katie's decorating aesthetics; it was because I didn't know my own.

"Don't get anything green," Aaron said.

"Or leafy," I said.

"Or things with birds and nature stuff," he said.

"Stay away from anything with a dog on it."

We went about the store filling the cart. Before committing to an item, I asked, "Is this Katie?"

Aaron would say, "Totally." Or, "Nah, but it's super ugly."

We went through every inch of Bed, Bath, Beyond, interrogated every item, all the while cracking jokes or bouncing on the display beds, like six-year-olds. Aaron was witty, his sarcasm sharp. When he stayed over the first night, he went through my bookcases. "Of course *Woman Warrior* is first," he said. "You are so predictable."

I needed his snark. I needed someone to make me laugh. I needed someone to make fun of me to get me out of my sullen moods. He needed that, too.

*

Since I was sixteen, the year my father left, I've gone on nightly drives on Christmas Eve. On these drives I try to get lost on purpose, taking turns onto unknown roads, visiting unknown towns off the interstate. I want to be lost because I need to know that I can always find my way back. On another level, in the mind of that younger self, perhaps my father was lost, too, and if I could find my way, surely he would. He never did, but I still continued my Christmas Eve tradition. That year, I asked Aaron to come with me. Up until then, I went alone, alone on the road, alone with my thoughts. This year I welcomed the company.

I took small Florida roads into dark Florida woods, the radio playing some indie band Aaron liked, bands that always sounded good in his company.

"You know," Aaron said, "if the car dies out here, we are dead. Two brown boys murdered in backwoods Florida."

"They wouldn't even try to find our bodies," I said.

"Fed to gators."

The road was dark, and the outline of trees rushed by, the sky clouded in gray haze. For most of the drive we bullshitted about the last books we'd read or the new video game that was coming out or Japanese horror films we were addicted to.

"I think I've finally grown up," Aaron said. I turned to look at him; his profile in the dark of the car was only a head with a baseball cap.

"Divorce and you grow up?"

He laughed. "When I get married again, I can say 'in my first marriage. . . .'"

"You want to remarry?"

"If she's the right one."

"You believe in that?"

"I believe that if love comes why not go head on."

"Marriage shouldn't indicate someone's love."

"You know who you sound like?"

"Who?"

"Katie."

"Fuck me."

We laughed. Barely anyone was on the road. Occasionally, a pair of headlights breezed by.

"I think if you go into every relationship with the thought of 'I'm not going to do blank,' then you don't fully commit to the relationship. And if you don't commit, you don't allow yourself to fall."

"That's some deep shit," I said.

"Merry Christmas."

I drove for a couple hours more. We were in a town east of Tampa, almost to Orlando.

"You know what isn't Katie?" Aaron said. "A fifty-five-inch flat screen TV."

Two days later we went to another B-store, Best Buy, to purchase the very un-Katie TV.

*

Five months later, when Deedra and I first got together, we went to Bed, Bath, and Beyond and sent a picture to Aaron, who had since moved to California. Our faces loomed somewhere in bedding. Our smiles big and toothy. He wrote back immediately: "You cheating bastard."

The Sleep of the Restless

At night, I hear whispering in the hotel room outside of Rayong. I think at first it comes from a lingering dream, one where I was whispering into Deedra's ear. But when I realize I am not in her bed, in her room, in her arms, I look up. To my left, Aunty Sue lies on her front, a blanket wrapped tightly around her, the air-conditioning frigid. Her snores come in slight whistles. Next to her is my mother. She sits in bed, her body blanketed in darkness. Her hands are in prayer, her mouth moving. I keep still, holding my breath. The bedside clock reads 12:32. I watch her until my eyes grow heavy, and I drift off.

*

My mother seldom sleeps. Her late-night shifts when she worked as a nurse messed up her REM cycle. She is a sleep sprinter, taking small naps an hour or two at a time throughout the day. When I lived in Chicago, during summer breaks from college, I used to hear her footsteps through the house at late hours. The creaking floors gave away her restlessness; it was as if a ghost wandered the upstairs.

After my father left, my mother was a ghost. She smiled. She laughed. She put on a mask that said everything was okay, but there were times I would watch her at the sewing machine and notice the dark bags under her eyes, the weight of her life heavy on her shoulders. I would watch her and think all of her sadness was located in those sleepless eyes. If only she could blink them away. If only she could gather that sadness like an eyelash and blow it out into the world.

My sleep is no better. On average I get four or five hours a night. I am a light sleeper, but need white noise—a fan, a sound machine, sometimes the TV. My insomnia is a symptom of my state of mind. The more tumultuous my life, the more I cannot still my brain. I lie in bed, tense, my shoulders to my ears. Thoughts run into one another like pinballs, a messy swirl of them. My imagination revs up, and I envision worst-case scenarios and tragedies. At the darkest moments, I fantasize about my death. I pull the trigger. I swallow pills. I slit wrists. All of which makes me shudder in bed. Then I imagine a world without me. And the world would be fine. I would be one less person. I would be forgotten. No one would mourn. These thoughts are not rational, but sleeplessness does that. Makes us believe in our fears. Makes us see them as real.

I wake again at two.

The toads outside croak something fierce. Aunty Sue has not moved. When she sleeps, she is dead to the world. My mother has fallen back to sleep, her mouth slightly parted and misshaped because her dentures are out. My eyes are clear, awake, my mind alert. I know I won't be able to get back to sleep for a couple of hours. I know if I try to sleep I will roll around and around, frustration mounting and mounting.

So I sneak out.

I sneak out the way I did when I was a boy, tiptoeing to the door, making sure to turn the knob without anyone taking notice. When I was younger, I pretended to be a ninja and stealthily hid along the walls until I was in the backyard, sitting on the ledge of the chimney. Eventually, a parent would notice my absence and find me. During my puberty years, I escaped to the high school bleachers behind the house and looked at the stars. I did this most nights after my mother and aunt went to the hospital to begin their shifts. I had a couple of hours before my father returned from work. Sometimes he never came back, spending his nights with another family. I sat at those bleachers and did not think about my mother and father. I convinced myself that I was past the point of caring, though I wasn't. I cared deeply, so deeply that when I thought of my father, I shook and cursed. When I thought of my mother, the same. So I didn't think about them. Instead, my mind went to all my crushes. I had many. Kristen, Claudia, April. Rosalie, Delphine, Jean. I thought about them in so many ways. I was a boy, and sex bounced around my brain like lottery balls. But I was also a romantic. I believed in flowers and candies. I believed if you loved someone it would last, like the romantic comedies I devoured, the ones starring Meg Ryan and Tom Hanks. Even though my parents hated each other, even though my friends' parents were divorcing left and right, I somehow thought I would be immune to it. I thought that there was someone out there who would solely be mine. The one. I imagined her on those bleachers with me. I imagined her until my eyes got heavy, and I returned home for sleep.

There are no bleachers to go to in Rayong, but the stars are bright under a pink haze. Rayong is hypnotic at night. I lose myself to the sound of waves, the occasional rumble of a passing car. The heat lifts, especially by the shore. The humidity, however, is still thick enough to fog my glasses. In the distance, docked boats rock in the water, a single light left on. Stars in the sea.

I sit on top of a picnic table, about to call Deedra, wondering what she is doing, when I notice Supon leaning against the van. He is smoking; I didn't know he did. I walk toward him, and when he sees me, he puts out the cigarette, as if I've caught him doing something illicit.

"You can't sleep?" he says in Thai.

I smile. "I'm still not used to the time change."

"How much is it?"

"Eleven hours."

He whistles. "Our night, your day."

I nod.

"I've never been out of Thailand," he says. "I wish to go to America."

"Someday," I say.

He shakes his head. "In the next life perhaps."

"You sound like my mother."

He laughs. "I'm a realist."

We stand under a light. June bugs buzz and bump the bulb.

"I don't smoke much," Supon says.

"I used to smoke when I was a kid."

"Aunty wouldn't like it if she knew I did."

"She probably does already," I say. "She knows everything."

Supon laughs. "She is the sharpest person I've ever met."

I tell him how Aunty Sue has the ability to tell the future, how she seems to know everything before it happens, how she has covert ways of finding secrets out, like pretending to give my cheek a kiss, but secretly sniffing my skin for the scent of tobacco.

"She has this ability to know a person will call," I say, "and within seconds the phone will ring."

Supon smiles. "Maybe she is a witch."

"Maybe."

He asks if it is okay to light up another.

I tell him of course. I ask why he is still up.

"When I'm away from my wife, she worries. She wants me to call."

I ask him what she worries about.

"She thinks I might get in an accident. She thinks the worst kind of things."

I understand this. When Katie and I were together and one of us had to go on a trip alone, I worried I would somehow lose her, that she would come to the realization that I wasn't the one she was looking for at all. I worry about this now, away from Deedra, who I imagine is crocheting on the couch with her small dog cuddled against her.

"My wife is more worried now that the country is crazy," Supon says.

"Aren't you worried?"

"I'm more worried for the country."

Supon wears his brown military uniform. It is the only thing I have ever seen him in. The uniform fits him tight around the chest and stomach, accentuating how fit he is. He is about fifty, but possesses the athleticism of someone much younger. It is what my mother and aunt always comment on—how good he looks in uniform. I laugh and make fun of their old lady crushes. Now, cigarette smoking in his hand, Supon's first three buttons are undone, exposing a white T-shirt underneath.

I ask him how long he's been married.

"Twenty-seven years."

"That's a long time."

"Doesn't feel like it," he says. "Even when our kids are about to graduate high school."

"Time goes fast."

"She is a good woman," Supon says and smiles.

The van door is slightly open. There is a pillow in the reclined front seat. Tonight Supon will sleep in the car, though we offered to get him a hotel room. He said he felt more comfortable in the van, said he would not know how to sleep in a bed with all that space. This is what drivers do on long trips; the van becomes their home.

"There was a party a few hours ago." Supon points toward the other building across the way, part of the hotel. Earlier, I noticed a large group of women on a tour bus, wearing pink polos. My mother said it was probably a class reunion. They came to the hotel with a storm of chatter.

"People were karaoke-ing," Supon says. "It sounded like tortured chickens."

"I'm not good at karaoke," I say.

"When I got married, I had to sing at the reception. My military friends made me." He shakes his head at the memory and exhales a cloud of smoke.

"My students made me karaoke this year," I say. "I sang 'Sexual Healing' by Marvin Gaye, but I didn't know the words. Do you know it?"

He shakes his head.

"It's very embarrassing."

"What is it about?"

"Sex is the answer to everything."

"Americans," he says. "You are not shy."

"I guess not."

"I sometimes drive for American tourists, and the young ones are very excited for each other. I don't know what they are saying, but I know the word 'sex,' which comes out of their mouths often."

"My mom always said to fear white women."

"Speaking of," Supon says, "how is your wife?"

I don't know what to say. Supon has met Katie on numerous occasions, driven us around for the last ten years. They rarely talk but share smiles and nods. I play the translator between them. Sometimes, Katie says "bathroom" in Thai, and Supon finds one quickly for her.

"She's good," I say. "Looking after the dogs."

"Please tell her I say hello and hurry back."

"I will."

He looks at his watch. "I should probably sleep. You should, too."

I tell him okay. I tell him I might go to the pool. He nods and heads into the van. When he shuts the door, the car light goes out.

*

I have tried counting sheep and counting backward. Sometimes, I would pretend I was snorkeling in the Andaman Sea—my favorite activity—allowing the underwater world to hypnotize me. That sensation of floating in the ocean was as close to sleeping while awake, and I wanted to have that sensation. I needed that sensation, the way water rocked you, the weightlessness, feeling as if you were not anchored to the earth. But in the end I was a boy with a lot of weight, both physical and emotional, and my thoughts would jolt me out of my reverie and then I became all too aware of my body in bed, unable to succumb to slumber.

Katie, on the other hand, did not have a problem sleeping. She was a sleeper. She was a professional sleeper. She was a professional sleeper, who possessed a snore that rocked the floors. This snore came from the back of the throat—no—deeper still, in the depths of the gut. How a sound like that came out her I didn't know. Her snore seemed demonic, a call to the devil to rise and set fire to the world in apocalyptic sorrow. There were times I would stare at her sleeping, wondering if horns would sprout from the lush of her hair. I wondered if she would grow fangs, and then and there, her eyes would pop open and that would be the end of me. In one glorious thunderous snore.

Dramatic, I know.

But her snores were dramatic.

I kidded with friends that it was her snores that drove me to the guest room. Or the demise of our marriage was because of the sounds shaking the walls, this snore of snores. Of course, that was not the case.

When we were struggling, she slept more. I slept less.

I've been in other relationships where sleep was an issue. My first college roommate thought he was a vampire. He slept with his arms crossed in front of him and rose at sundown the way Nosferatu did from his coffin. The rest of the night he rollerbladed the southern Illinois woods in a trench coat.

My father before the divorce would come home after his shift at the tile factory and stay up until two or three watching late-night TV. Sometimes I joined him, falling asleep in his lap. Later, he would be on the phone with other women, flirting and laughing, his voice keeping me up.

My insomnia after Katie left was like my mother's after my father left. I was prone to wandering. When I couldn't sleep, I took to moving through the empty house. Most of the furniture was packed up, the house for sale. Sometimes I packed boxes. Sometimes I watched TV. Sometimes I chatted with women online. Most of the time, I listened to the sounds of the world: the eerie screech of owls, the slinky scamper of armadillos, the raccoons traversing from trashcan to trashcan.

*

The hotel pool is empty and dark. Statues of fish and mermaids sit on the edges like menacing sentries. At night they are featureless, foreboding shapes. The sign at the gate of the pool reads: Closed at 9:00 p.m.

I go in anyway in my pajama shorts. I feel like that boy again sneaking off to the bleachers.

How do I describe this night swim? How the water instantly cools my body. How I dive under and hold my breath for as long as I can. How when I break the surface my intake of air echoes. How wonderful it feels to be weightless, to let the water slick off of me like pearls on my skin. How this silence is an embrace.

The quiet is different. It is not frightening. Not like those long stretches of nothing in that lonely house. Not like the silence after sex with strangers; that silence filled me with loathing and guilt and embarrassment. Not like the silence of absence; the fact that for fifteen years I had come accustomed to familiar sounds, like the jingle of dog collars, like the rattle of vitamins or the burst from Katie's nose spray, or even her monstrous snores.

I tilt my head back and float. Above me are stars and the silvery streaks of clouds, and below me nothing.

It's Raining

Bee drives. She drives and swerves. She drives and swerves and calls the Godfather, Tui, from the phone in her right hand, her face puffed from frustration. We are meeting him for dinner at a Chinese restaurant in the middle of Bangkok, a day after our trip to the coast, and he has organized a feast of Peking duck, stewed pig leg and radishes, Hong Kong stir-fry noodles, and deep-fried crab sausages. Tui has been at the restaurant for forty-five minutes now, impatient and hungry, while Bee traverses the congested Bangkok traffic. My mother and Aunty Sue sit in the back, quiet, trying not to interrupt Bee on the phone.

"I'm lost," she says. The car drifts. A Toyota blares its horn and blazes past. Scooters buzz by, missing the side mirror by centimeters. A bus filled with uniformed students spouts dark fumes into the evening sky.

"I just made a U-turn," she says. "There are lots of places for U-turns."

Through the phone's receiver I hear the Godfather's exasperated voice. I don't need to know what he says to know the sound of complaining.

"You don't have to talk to me like that," Bee says. "I'll call in a minute." She hangs up. The car swerves. A motorcycle swifts pass. The sky is patches of gray clouds and gray overpasses.

"He's always like this," Bee says. "He always comes at me."

"He should tell you where to go instead of yelling," Aunty Sue says.

"I wonder if it's going to rain today," my mother says, voice distant.

"U-turn, U-turn," Bee says. "He tells me I'm not listening to him."

"There's been so many places for a U-turn," says my aunt. "Which one?"

"Forecast says rain," says my mother.

"He talks to me like I'm dumb," Bee says.

The phone rings, an electric guitar solo.

"There are so many places for U-turns," Bee says. "Which one?"

The car glides into the other lane. A pickup filled with fifteen field workers steers away. The workers stare, faces dark and dirt-caked.

"You always talk to me like that," Bee says. "You're not listening to me. There are a lot of places to make a U-turn."

She hangs up.

"He gets so angry," Bee says. "I've never been to this restaurant before."

"He should tell you what U-turn," says Aunty Sue.

"The clouds are dark," says my mother.

Phone. Electric guitar solo.

"I'm trying, Tui," Bee says. "Which U-turn? What street? Why do you talk to me like that? Stop talking to me like that."

She hangs up and starts crying. She's driving and crying. Students in backpacks and briefcases wait at a bus stop. Under a bridge, stray dogs settle in curled circles.

"I don't understand why he gets so angry," Bee says. "He keeps telling me I'm not listening. But I listen to everything. He gets so mad at me."

"There are so many U-turns," says Aunty Sue.

Bee sucks in her breath. She grabs my leg. "Don't think bad of me for crying."

"I don't," I say.

Bee hits her cheeks. She dries her eyes.

"I bet it'll rain," my mother says.

*

When my father and mother fought, when I was thirteen and watched from behind the laundry basket upstairs, my mother's anger vicious and red, like her face, like the heat emanating off of her, I cringed at my father's defenselessness, at how he picked a spot on the wall and stared at it, at his posture, that of a deflated balloon. My mother's voice cracked and trembled. Her spit hit his face. Her whole being shook, such a contrast to her husband, a man who sank into himself, sank into the silence of his creation.

Even when she struck him.

Over and over.

On his face.

On his chest.

He showed not a flicker of emotion, not a flinch at her balled up hands. Anger rose in me instead, like the dark churn underneath this earth. Anger at him, anger at my mother, anger at myself, though I did not know why. And sometimes, I screamed out. And sometimes, I ran off. And sometimes, I sneaked back into my bedroom and raged on my pillows.

Why does the child carry the weight of two arguing parents? Why does he internalize blame though he is blameless? Why—goddamn it— was his father soft?

My father created the illusion of an impenetrable bubble. It was only an illusion, however, because eventually, his passiveness led him away from us. Eventually, he could not shoulder his wife's anger, but worst of all, his son's, who seethed in silence. I don't know what I wanted from my father on those stormy days when my mother screeched herself hoarse. I don't know what reaction, if any, would have appeased me. I only know I wanted something from him, some fight, some assertion that this marriage, this family, mattered.

Now, I recognize him in me, despite how hard I fought to be his foil. I saw him in my blank stare. I saw him in the way I tried to please everyone. I saw him.

The truth was I contained in me a ferocity that could cloud the sky. I was angry. At Katie. At her need for something I could not provide. At her wandering eyes at other men and her naturally flirtatious nature in public. I feared I would be inconsolable in my rage, become not the Incredible Hulk but the Incredible Ira, turning a deeper shade of yellow instead of green, Ira smashing the shit out of walls and furniture, dogs and cats, and those I loved the most. In the end, there would be nothing incredible about any of it. Just sadness. Sadness in the recognition that this anger was my mother's anger, one fueled by deep betrayal and jealousy and, worst of all, helplessness. My mother was helpless. She didn't know how to save her family. She didn't understand why her life had steered her this way. My father's infidelity was something she could never forgive, so the only way she could hurt him was to unleash this fury, this rage of fists and voice.

Anger and passivity.

I am both my mother and my father.

*

One of my good friends' sole purpose in life is to argue. He loves it. He pushes people. He tests their intellect. He is relentless. He controls conversation with his loud voice and erratic hand gestures. I believe the term "pulpit" was made specifically with him in mind, because if I close my eyes and listen to the cadence of his talk, I can see the Sunday morning televangelists who speak powerfully about God and salvation and always enthralled me when I was younger. Sometimes he plays devil's advocate just for the sake of argument. Sometimes he pushes too far and gets slugged. Sometimes out blossoms this beautiful discussion about art, politics, the meaning of life, and there is a shared respect and understanding of each other's viewpoints, even if at one point, we existed on opposite ends of the spectrum.

I envy my friend's fearlessness in the face of conflict, envy his mouth and intellect and his quick wit. I wonder if my lack of wanting to engage is a sign of fear. I feel my body respond the same way it did in my youth, when my parents fought   this recoil, this urge to flee. I feel this way in tense meetings at work or when watching overly dramatic TV dramas. When I am confronted, I am quick to apologize even if I am in the right. I find myself apologizing a lot.

Before arriving to Thailand, at the connecting flight in Seoul, an older man looked me up and down in security and said, "I hope I don't sit next to you." His hair was thin and white and cycloned the top of his head. He limped along with a cane and wore trousers well above his navel, leaving his very white socks exposed. I knew, by the tone of his voice, this gentleman meant what he said as a joke, even if the joke was insensitive, even if the joke was at my expense. My thoughts were first filled with violence—red and wild violence upon his white, impervious face—and then, instantly, remorse.

"I'm sorry," I said. "Where are you going? Maybe we aren't. I'm sorry. We can get that changed."

In Pam Houston's essay "Out of Habit, I Start Apologizing," she recounts her impulse to always apologize for her weight and the freedom she feels out in nature where the critical eye of our judgmental culture does not roam. She speaks of herself, but she speaks for all women who suffer day in and day out over body image. I have inherited this same habit. Not just about the body. This act of apologizing. I say I'm sorry. I try my damnedest to avoid any altercation. But sometimes an altercation is what is needed. Sometimes someone needs to be confronted. Sometimes someone needs a verbal slap. Sometimes someone needs to be slapped. Or punched. Or kicked.

It is not Buddhist of me, I know.

I remember one afternoon at a beach near Tampa when Katie said she was worried. The wind was loud, and so were the gulls swooping and crying around the two of us. Waves crested and foamed.

"I love you," she said, "but I'm scared."

By then I was already gone. I retreated far. I heard her voice, but it was as if it was syphoned through one of the shells on the shore. I heard her, but somewhere between ear and brain, I had changed the meaning of her words. I heard how worthless I was, how unattractive, how unintelligent. I began nodding because I believed this. I believed so wholeheartedly what was reverberating in my head, a hive buzzing violently with so much disdain.

Voiceless, as if someone welded shut my mouth, as if someone snipped my vocal cords. I pinned my eyes on the cloudless sky, at the pelicans plummeting into the water. I could feel the intensity of Katie's stare. Could sense that she was crying. I could not say anything to right the situation, to comfort her, to comfort us.

My silence, however, didn't present a lack of thinking. The contrary. In fact, on that beach, I was flooded with words and phrases, as if my brain presented a long list of multiple-choice options, an infinite list of them, so many that I froze and picked "none of the above."

Also, on a subconscious level, this silence was my way of establishing control in an otherwise uncontrollable situation. Once at the sex therapist's office, I walled up. I felt that wall, the brick and mortar of it, building in my throat. My lips thinned. I could feel it. My eyes settled on the various knickknacks in the office. My breath shallowed out. I do not remember what brought about this silence. I do not remember what was said, but I imagine it to be something harsh, some secret Katie had disclosed. And I was gone.

"Do you feel this?" the therapist said.

I didn't respond. One of the bulbs in the lamp beside her had blown out.

"This silence is powerful," she said.

I heard the sound of Katie's body shifting on the leather couch. I could not look at her. I could not look at anyone. Looking at someone meant I had to address the situation. I remember thinking how the situation was stupid. How everything was stupid. How being here was stupid. How the therapist was stupid. Katie was stupid. I was stupid. Stupid. Stupid. Stupid.

"When you do this," the therapist said, "you control the conversation. You know that?"

I gave her nothing. Not a nod. Not a sound.

"Wow," the therapist said. "This is very adolescent of you."

I wanted to make a W with my fingers. *Whatever*. I wanted to stick out my tongue. I wanted to say it was them who needed fixing, not me. I was perfectly fine. I was amazing. Greatest. Husband. Ever.

But I kept silent—in that therapy session, on that beach. Silence choked the marriage. Silence slithered into our lives and settled there until it was too late.

*

Six years ago, Bee took me out for late-night dim sum. She knew I was bored, having been cooped up at the house all day, watching badly Thai-dubbed American movies. My mother and Aunty Sue were suffering from heat exhaustion from a day of temple hopping all over Bangkok and taking Katie to the airport for her flight home; she always left two weeks before me so she could return to work and the dogs and give my mother sole time with her son. So when Bee came back from work she asked if I wanted a late-night meal.

Bee has been close to my heart from the moment I met her. She loved Katie like a sister, taking her by the hand the way women do in Thailand, trying her best to make Katie feel comfortable in a foreign country. During the wedding, she stuck close to Katie so she wouldn't be disoriented by the slew of Thai family. What I love most is how expressive she is. She touches—a hand on a shoulder, taps on the back, squeezes on the leg. She listens, as if whatever you're saying is the most important thing on earth. She constantly asks what certain words mean in English, and each year I come back, her vocabulary grows. But it is her laugh I cherish. Bee laughs with her body. She then becomes self-conscious and covers her mouth, still shivering from the aftereffects.

The restaurant was poorly lit, making everything sickly looking, the walls suffering from jaundice. Bee served me pork dumplings, *kanom jeeb*, but I didn't want to be served, like she served her husband. I told her I wanted to eat like friends.

I put a dumpling on her plate, and she smiled.

"Do you miss Katie?" Bee said.

I shook my head.

"Really?" Her eyes widened.

"We are confident in our love."

I sounded like a fool, young and brash.

"Do you guys fight?" Bee said.

"Never," I said.

Bee made an incredulous sound, a sharp suction of air, an exaggerated exhale. "Tui and I fight all the time. We fight almost every day."

I nodded like I knew the secret to a healthy marriage. Like my relationship was far superior to Bee and Tui's.

In many ways, though, my marriage was better. Especially then. Tui was the Godfather, after all. And like all godfathers he possessed power. He came and went as he pleased. He sat at the kitchen table like a king, and Bee served him multiple dishes of food and prepared his pills and packed his clothes for long trips to construction sites. He came home every night at three or four in the morning, out with friends, out who knows where, and she'd have to wake and open the house gates for him. Their marriage reflected Thailand's patriarchal society, a reverence to gender inequality. They did not seem like husband and wife but master and servant.

And they fought. All the time.

And she cried. All the time.

"I wish I had a marriage like yours," she said. "No fighting."

"Katie and I—we're a good match," I said.

Bee sighed. The dumpling I put on her plate remained on her plate; it remained on her plate until we left.

*

When we arrive at the restaurant, Tui has already eaten two full plates of fried crab sausages, a toothpick dancing in between his lips. Next to me, he may be the biggest Thai man in the country, but his girth brings him prominence in the way of fat presidents, like Roosevelt or Truman. The Chinese restaurant, like the ones I've been to in Bangkok, is gold and red, filled with large round tables and spinning lazy Susans. Bee sulks into the restaurant, eyes wet and swollen. Her mascara smears the undersides of her eyes, and she resembles a Thai goth girl, a Thai goth girl with a floral print blouse and black slacks. Her shoes shuffle the tiled floor. Aunty Sue tries to lighten the mood by saying she wants to order everything on the seven-page menu, that she is properly hungry after the long drive; she gives her nephew a kiss on the forehead and demands the waitress's attention. My mother sits with her purse on her lap. She keeps talking about the sky outside that is darkened by night.

"You're finally here," Tui says. "I was starving."

"You didn't have to talk to me like that," Bee says. Her voice is soft. When she sits, she aims her knees away from him.

"Are you mad?" he says.

"No," she says.

He laughs. When Tui laughs, his cheeks jiggle, and he wheezes. "You *are* mad." He puts his hand on the back of her neck.

Bee shrugs him off.

Aunty Sue talks to the waitress. She says she wants hot jasmine tea. Wants scrambled eggs with shrimp. Wants stewed radishes. Wants blue crab fried rice. She ticks off one dish after another. She isn't kidding about ordering the menu. "What spicy food do you have?" she asks. "I want the spiciest."

I keep listening, keep watching.

There is a love poem happening, the move and sway of language and bodies. The return and denial of affection. The sounds of a restaurant, the whispers of other tables, the kitchen hidden from view. Amid all of this, the give and take, the push and pull, of this relationship.

Bee looks at her hands, her lips in puckered resistance.

"Why are you mad?" Tui says. He is confused. Truly.

"You don't have to talk to me like that."

Tui smiles again. Laughs again. His laughs are like end-stopped lines of a poem, a definitive stop, a commanding presence. Bee, on the other hand, displays the perfect pout, punctuated with alliterative precision.

Metaphor in movement.

Bee turns further away from him. He leans in closer.

"Don't be mad," Tui says.

"Don't be mean," Bee says.

He places his hand again on the back of her neck and squeezes. This time, Bee does not pull away. This time, her body melts into her seat, into his touch, her shoulders releasing all that tension she had built up in the car.

"I'm sorry," Tui says. "But you feel too much."

"You can treat me better."

"I do," he says. "I will."

He laughs again. And that is it.

Forgiveness in the form of a smile, a peck on the cheek.

Plates of food come to the table—a bronze duck, with thin pancake wraps, spicy papaya salad, sesame-oiled jellyfish. Tui puts food on Bee's plate. He chopsticks jellyfish and feeds her a bit.

Bee smiles. Everything about that smile shows me how much she loves her husband, how much she would continue to do anything for him, how much control he has over her heart. And though I think their relationship is not ideal—what relationship is?—and though arguments like this will happen again, will always happen, for the moment, this is love. A different form of love. A love that feeds on words, on fights, and on disappointment. It's happening here, this love. Tui, with his arms around Bee. Bee, smiling and taking food from his chopsticks.

My mother, quiet for most of the dinner, comments on the weather outside. "There it is. The rain."

July 10

On this day last year, Thai Boy and White Woman ended. And it was Ira and Katie. It was the beginning of Ira apart from Katie. It was the beginning of Ira.

IV

Ruins

I meet my father at the McDonald's at FuturePark Rangsit, a mall that spreads over many city blocks. Malls are serious business here, upwards of seven floors, crowded and loud. Advertisements plague the exterior, and inside is consumerism at its best or worst, depending on how you look at it.

My mother and Aunty Sue accompany me but do not want to see my father. They sit at Auntie Anne's pretzels. Aunty Sue nibbles on one. My mother sips a lemonade. They say they wanted to make sure I arrived without trouble. They say they've never been to this mall. They say they need new underwear.

I know why they are here. They have come to spy on the man they despise, to see what has become of him. The last time they saw him was twenty years ago.

"Don't follow me," I say.

Aunty Sue makes an incredulous sound. "Why would we follow you?"

"We are here for underwear," my mother says.

"Ask him for money." Aunty Sue takes a large bite from the pretzel.

"Don't ask him for anything," says my mother.

"Don't give him anything," Aunty Sue says.

"Make him pay for meals," my mother says.

"Make him pay for the last twenty years," Aunty Sue says.

"Be nice," I say.

"We are the nicest," my mother says. She sips her lemonade, the tartness causing her to pucker her lips.

"Find out how many wives he has," Aunty Sue says. "You may have many brothers and sisters."

My mother laughs but it is a laugh born from years of hurt—too loud, too forced, too many years holding on to the snake of resentment.

"Family reunion," Aunty Sue says.

"I'm late," I say.

"Go," my mother says.

"Have fun," Aunty Sue says.

"Call me tonight," my mother says. "Make sure he drives you home tomorrow. Call me. Don't forget to call me."

I nod, shouldering a backpack of clothes and toiletries, turn to look at my mom and aunt one last time. They sit and eat and wave.

Unlike in the States, Thai malls offer some of the country's best food, from every culture, from every part of the world. Except, I'm meeting my father at McDonald's, the most American of American establishments. I haven't seen him in three years, and when I do—sitting at a table, staring into the distance—I pause and take him in before he registers me. He has become shriveled, skin the color of a terra-cotta pot. I not only tower over him, but my shoulders are twice as wide. His breath comes out in rasps, and I can't help but smile at how utterly goofy-looking he is with oversize glasses, a pink-striped button down tucked in tight, white shorts pulled above the navel, a gold-buckled belt, and black sandals with black socks.

When he sees me, he smiles. "Fish fillet?" he says. "You like fish fillets."

I shake my head.

"How are you, my son?"

"Fine," I say.

"You look fine."

Outside the McDonald's are souvenir carts selling keychains and Japanese cartoon figurines and oil infusers. They are like the mall kiosks back in the States. The carts circle the outside edge of the food floor, in front of ramen and sushi establishments. My mother is in front of a cart of handmade dolls. When she sees me noticing her, she picks up a raggedy one and examines it like a precious diamond.

"French fries," my father says. "You like french fries."

Another shake.

Aunty Sue hides behind a cardboard cutout of a Thai celebrity, advertising whitening cream. She pokes her head from around a hand holding up a peace sign.

"You're not hungry?"

"No, sir," I say in extreme politeness. This is how I talk to my father. Formal. Like strangers.

He pats my arm. "I've missed you."

I smile. In front of him are the crumpled up remains of a Fish Fillet sandwich and an unfinished scattering of fries.

"Coke," my father says. "You like Coke."

Another shake. I haven't had soda in ten years, but I don't say anything.

Now, my mother and aunt find themselves sifting through bootleg CDs at a music cart, though they do not own a CD player. They play cassette tapes of Buddhist sermons in what I believe is the oldest tape player in the world, the same one my mother had when she lived in Chicago, when I was a boy, and during Christmas, when we were all a family—my father transforming our home into a winter wonderland, Aunty Sue cooking in the kitchen—my mother would put Sinatra and Crosby into the player and the house was filled with song. I wonder if any of them remember that or any of the good moments of the past.

"Are you ready?" My father stands.

"Let's go, please," I say.

I help him up. He's a little unsteady, but otherwise strong. I shake my head at my mother and aunt, who are pretending not to see us, pretending to be interested in a bootleg Beatles CD, pretending the man I am with never existed.

*

When Siddhartha left to become Buddha, he also left his family behind. It was a sacrifice he thought was necessary in order to find a way to alleviate suffering. For years, his father, Suddhodana, lamented the abandonment of his son. He sent ten thousand messages, asking Siddhartha to come back. Finally, when Siddhartha became Buddha, he returned to his father's kingdom and preached the Dharma to Suddhodana, who later would die as an arahant, a perfect being.

My father is not a perfect being. My father did not send ten thousand messages, but he did call. A lot. I would listen to his messages that always sounded the same. "Ira, this is your father. Are you there? Hello?" For three years, I never called him back. "All he wants is money," I would say. "I'm too busy," I would say. "I'll do it later," I would say. Later became much later, and later came with guilt like a stone in a shoe.

Guilt is what I feel most of the time when I think about my father. Even now. Beside him in the car. I will spend the next two days with him, and though he is happy to see me—always happy to see me—I calculate the most minimal amount of time to be in his presence. My father will ask if I can stay longer. He will ask often. He wants to take me to the dentist office he sometimes works at. He wants to introduce me to his friends and to the students he tutors in conversational English. "You can stay with me for as long as you want," he says. "Dad will take care of you." But I keep telling him two days. I keep saying I am busy traveling, that Mom and Aunty have my days filled with appointments, a lie. My father nods and smiles and never pushes.

And then there it is—guilt.

My feelings toward my father, I believe, will prevent me from enlightenment, will prevent me from stopping the cycle of reincarnation. I will have to come back and resolve this issue of forgiveness. I carry hurt close to my heart. His infidelity those years ago. His abandonment. His way of jumping in and out of my life. What I want is his recognition of this gap between the two of us.

This, of course, I will never say.

Instead I sit in his tiny car as he, at eighty-one, traverses the Bangkok streets like a pro. The city recedes, and the color green from the flat of rice fields blurs by oppressively, making me squint against the glare of it.

*

My father takes me to Ayutthaya, where he was born and raised, and though I have been here a few times, I never tire of the ruins of the former capital. They are everywhere, the remains of a pagoda eroding in the harsh Thai heat, the crumbling foundations of kingdom walls. In Ayutthaya ruins are beside shops, ruins are in empty fields, ruins are perfect canine sunning spots, ruins are being consumed by the lush Thai greenery. I want to imagine this place as it once was. Before the Burmese burned the city in April 1767, before the loss of golden temples and Buddha statues, before the destruction of ancient art and literature. What was this world like? What paradise might this have been?

Along the trip, my father points to this and that. "Your grandmother and I used to walk this alley," he would say, "and now it's a highway."

I listen and nod.

Once, my father told me I was a high commander in a past life, here in this city, leading an army to war against the Burmese. Perhaps he was right. There is a comfort here that calms me. The air, though stiflingly hot, feels familiar. I hear sounds not from this life, but from another— clashing swords and prayers. The stray dogs look at me as if they too recognize I am as I once was. They bow and stretch in greeting.

Outside of Wat Mongkhon Bophit, my father and I find a resting spot. The temple houses a towering Buddha, over fifty-five feet tall, constructed around 1538. Sometime in the 1700s, lightning struck the temple, and the Buddha was decapitated. He has since been repaired, and parishioners come to pray to him for luck.

Behind my father, a potted bougainvillea blooms pink and orange. He asks about Katie. I don't know what to say, so I say what I usually do. "She's fine." Then a few seconds later, "We've split up, sir."

"Huh?" he says.

"Me and Katie. We've split up."

"Huh?" he leans his bad ear closer.

"Split. Up. Me. Katie."

"Oh," he says, nodding. The news passes over him without shock or surprise.

"We're still friends," I say.

"That's good."

A family of tourists takes pictures among the temple ruins to the right of us, the father and son wearing German soccer jerseys, the mother and daughter fanning themselves with German flag fans. I wonder if they prayed to Buddha for Germany to win their next match against Belgium.

"Are you okay?" my father asks.

The question catches me off guard. I stammer. "I'm good."

"It's never easy," he says, "but you will find your way. Eventually."

"I have a new friend," I say. I sound like a boy who wants to show off for his father. "She's really nice. Pretty."

"Of course," he says. "What's her name?"

I tell him, and he repeats it. "Sounds like yours."

He sits facing away from me, his hands on his knees, like some of the statues of Thai kings I've seen. He speaks in the direction he faces. I face the same direction. The two of us look as if we are simply enjoying the day and not having a conversation.

"Can I ask what happened?" he says.

"We weren't working,"

He nods.

"We're still friends," I say again.

"You guys are not like your mother and me, huh?"

I laugh.

"She hates me." He smiles and sighs.

The sun is vicious today. It is cloudless, so there is nothing to deter its rays. Sweat beads on my father's forehead. Strays dogs find shelter under the overhanging limbs of a Bodhi tree. Moving in weather like this is like swimming. My father opens a golf umbrella. He tells me to scoot in. We share a circular shade. Mynahs squawk along the crumbling base of the temple. There exists a beauty here among the desolate, a beauty in the charred and broken remains. I do not remember the last time I was this close to my father.

"Can I ask you a question?" my father says. "Who broke it off first?"

"It was mutual."

"These things happen. You don't plan for it. But they do. And then sometimes you end up alone. Like me. It happens."

*

I see my father in me.

I have his chin, his nose, his long dangling earlobes. My hair is thick in the front, and my beard grows coarser year by year, like his. At the height of my joy, I have his laughter, high-pitched and loud. It is something I try to avoid, this laugh, but it comes unannounced, comes with genuine happiness. My sneezes are his, too, booming and rattling floors. You can hear the wind-up of it, this long inhale of breath before he lets loose. It sounds more like the *kiai* of a martial artist than a sneeze. I have inherited his way of dreaming, his constant curiosity about everything on this earth, the way he would touch poison ivy to see its effect or felt the bite of a piranha on purpose when he was a boy. I also see him in my competitiveness; he strove to appear bigger than himself, the way he puffed out his chest and boasted when talking to doctors at the Chicago temple, the blue-collar factory worker who earned a quarter of their income.

I possessed his quick wit, his ability to make a woman smile and feel wanted. His gift for speech was never an act, his language measured in time. He will love you. For a time. He will be there. For a time. He knows this. Whatever bridges he burns—there have been many—he burns to the ground, he burns them until what is left is smoldering ash. Ask my mother.

I grew up with dudes who turned up their charm and would say anything for a quick lay. My father was different. Who he is and how he presents himself is his way of being in the world. He was never out to consciously deceive, though my mother would argue otherwise. At one time, I agreed with her. I have come to realize, however, that he never lied about his infidelities or his shortcomings as a father and husband; he just didn't open his mouth, so no lie could come out.

And this last trait we share: we love women. Love them with a sense of urgency and pleasure. Not just physical love, not just sex, but love that burrows deep into the bone. We love the sensibilities of a woman, their inherent empathy, the power they can have over us, how they can dismantle us with a look, a word, a touch. In each woman my father meets, he recognizes a sort of love. When I slept in other beds, I understood this, too. There was a thrill in the meeting of someone new. The first smile. The first flirt. The first kiss. The first fuck. It was thrilling to have secrets. To not tell my friends where I really was, or who I was really with, or that I subscribed to dating sites, and at night, I wrote letters until the light of morning. It was thrilling to move from one bed, go home and wash up, and two hours later be in another bed. There was even a thrill in getting caught, though paranoia made my eyes dart around department stores or parking lots, hoping not to encounter a one-night stand or a date while on another date.

This thrill made me selfish. My father was selfish.

After the divorce, I understood him more than at any other time of my life.

I leave my father on a stone bench. He does not have the energy to walk with me through these ruins. He tells me he has seen and been everywhere. The ruins of Ayutthaya were his playground. There, he points, was the tree he climbed and hid in. There, he points, was where he threw crumbling pieces of ruin at egrets. There, he points, was where he swam with the piranhas. My father was endless with stories. "Let me tell you," he begins, and then we are off in some tale about boyhood mischief or heroics.

In Chicago, during sleepovers, my friends and I would gather in the bed, and my father would regale us with his stories. Thailand was this foreign land to them, and I imagined they envisioned a world of wild green, a world filled with monkeys and tigers and slithering snakes, a world opposite from Chicago concrete and yapping dogs behind chain-link fences. "Your dad is so cool," they would say. "Indiana Jones cool."

My father is cool. Or trying to cool off.

European and American tourists wander the temple grounds, posing for photos: one group flexes in front of a throne of Buddha; another places their heads on decapitated stumps of Buddha statues; another climbs on giant eroding Buddhas, despite the signs posted everywhere—"no climbing."

Peace still pervades, an internal one that rushes over me like a blush. I find myself in rhythm with my breath, my steps, my heart. I let history wash over me, transport me to another time and place, of kings, of dynasties, of war. There is romance in the ancient, as if the land itself were folding me into its arms, making me feel all my other lives. My father would tell me this was the allure of Ayutthaya, this sense of being a part of a continuous world, a continuous history.

I circle a crumbling temple lined with Buddhas eroding from centuries of sun and wind and time. The Buddhas have a horror movie feel to them, some faceless, some missing earlobes or eyes or noses, or fingers and hands. My imagination revs up. I envision a swarm of Buddhas rising from the ruins, and the world would not suffer a zombie apocalypse but rather a Buddha one, and these Buddhas would not devour brains, but rather they would touch our foreheads and cure us of whatever suffering we carry in us.

I look toward where my father is seated. The sun descends, the horizon bright and red. He is framed by two crumbling pillars that once anchored a beautiful golden temple. Where I am, he is a speck, a statue himself, eyes surveying the land of his youth, which is a land of loss.

*

The day's heat has taken a lot out of us. The car ride is silent save for Thai folk music playing through the car speakers, which to me, sounds like cats mewling. We order grilled chicken and sticky rice along the side of the road and eat in the car, the sun making its way down to the line of the land, then disappearing.

It is night when we arrive at my father's house in a gated community. A uniformed guard salutes us when we enter, a formality in most gated communities in Thailand.

My father's house is two floors but small. He lives in a neighborhood of identical homes with carports in front. Everything is a box—the bathrooms, the living room, the bedrooms, the outside kitchen. Small boxes.

At the bottom exterior of the house, the signs of water damage creep up halfway to the front window. There is more at the lower fringes of the front door, the wood bowing and fraying from rot. "The floods," my father says. "I lost all my furniture, but friends gave me their old stuff." He refers to the 2011 floods that decimated Thailand and were some of the world's costliest disasters, leaving 815 people dead and over $45 billion in damages. My mother and Aunty Sue were at Tui's at the time. His workers had fortified the outer edges of the property with hundreds of sand bags. They parked their cars on the overpasses of highways. The water kept coming, my mother said, kept rising and rushing through the spaces in the bags, but it never reached the house. Because most of Bangkok was without electricity, at night my mother and aunt read by candlelight, and during the day, they sat on the marble porch watching the water rise.

My father turns on the television. He wants to know what is going on in the World Cup; he is an avid soccer watcher. When he was in the Thai Air Force, he bragged about being a soccer star. I never appreciated the sport, born in the age of Chicago football and basketball legends like Walter Payton and Michael Jordan. During Sunday school at temple, my father was appointed to teach soccer after Buddhism classes were over. He and a couple of other fathers made Thai boys run drills between cones and practice passing the ball back and forth. I never understood why you could not kick with the tips of your toes. This frustrated my father into a whistle-blowing frenzy. "Like this, like this," he would say. I continued doing what I was doing because it amused me to see my father's face grow a deeper shade of brown.

"Who will win this year?" My father hands me a can of iced green tea from a fridge that contains only iced green tea and collapses on a light blue pleather couch.

"Germany, probably."

He shakes his head. "Brazil."

"The Germans are too big, too quick."

"But Brazil has history. History is important."

I shrug. "Chile tied them a couple days ago."

"Fluke," he says.

I am tired and leg weary. My head pounds from not enough water. I can't keep still. Already, I think about the morning, about when my father will drop me off. I have had a good day with him, enjoying his company. Our silences have not been awkward but comforting. Still, the need to return to my mother is strong, a magnetic pull that forever draws on my fidelity to her.

I wander my father's boxy living room. He has framed photos on every surface of the house. I notice the ones of me immediately—my senior-year high school portrait; receiving my bachelor's degree; a wedding photo of Katie and me, in traditional Thai dress—me in emerald green, Katie in burnt orange.

My father could not make it to the wedding in Chiang Mai. Back then, he flew to and from Thailand to the U.S. every six months to collect his social security checks. He lived at a friend's house in Chicago, working at a McDonald's to gather some cash before flying back to Bangkok. He made it to our second wedding, though, in Katie's hometown, Champaign, Illinois, a month later, a wedding for friends and family. My father came with his usual bluster, talking with anyone who would listen to him, talking about his only son and how accomplished he was—*did you know he is a writer and he has published in magazines?*—about the union with this prairie girl—*they are perfect because I've consulted the star charts*—about how his life had been made difficult after the factory closed down—*my heart, my heart, it's not so good*—about stories of my youth—*let me tell you about the one time Ira kicked a boy in the face. . . .*

The one thing I am sure about when it comes to my father: he is proud of me. This pride is his way of showing his love, all these photos of times he has missed in my life—my senior year, my college graduation, my wedding.

"Are you hungry?" my father asks.

I shake my head. I tell him I am heading upstairs, that I am tired, that tomorrow Mom expects me back by noon—a lie.

"No problem," he says. "I've missed you. Goodnight."

I head up to my boxy room. A framed photo of my father sits on the nightstand. In this picture he is not yet my father but a young man of about twenty in a military uniform, his face absent of his thick glasses, absent of loose skin and graying hair, absent of his prominent mole on the left side of his chin. This is the face of man who believed the world would deliver on its promises. You can see it in his smile, his eyes. You can still see it now, even on his eighty-one-year-old face.

I turn on the air conditioner, setting it at a frigid temperature. I'm hot. No matter what clothing I peel off, no matter how fast the fan spins, I can't cool off.

Fortune

When my father met my mother, it was his mole that attracted her. His mole was a prominent focal point, and when he didn't shave, it had fine fuzz that looked like a burying tick. But then, my father's mole was attractive, like super model Cindy Crawford, the thing that brought your attention to his face and eyes and hair. My father was handsome; it was easy to see how women fell for him. It was all because of that mole.

My father and mother shared a mutual friend, who was having a party at her new home in Orland Park, a suburb of Chicago. This was the first time they would meet, and my father and his mole spent the night wooing my mother.

Since she'd immigrated to America in 1968, my mother rarely had the attention of a man, except for the doctors she worked with at Englewood Hospital, who complained about her English. She spent most her time in the nurses' dorm with Sumon—Aunty Sue—whom she met when she first arrived, the two of them becoming fast friends, confiding hopes and dreams, homesickness and fears. What my mother didn't tell my aunt was she secretly yearned for a man to take her out of the crumbling inner-city dorm and into a house where she could raise children. Her younger sisters in Thailand were married and had kids. They sent photos and letters written on thin blue airmail stationary, telling my mother about their smart and obedient children. At the end of each letter, her sisters asked about the prospects in my mother's life.

Here was my father with his mole.

Here was my father with his mole and smile.

She didn't know anything about him. Not many did. She didn't know he had been married once before. She didn't know about the daughter he left in Thailand to pursue American dreams. She didn't know he was in the country illegally, working at some steel factory, fleeing immigration officers on more than one occasion. My father was a "Robin Hood," a Thai term for being in a foreign country illegally. No one knew how he arrived, where he stayed, and what he did. Surrounding him was mystery, and it was this mystery that drew people in.

"Who is that man?" my mother asked her friend.

"A friend."

"Where does he come from?"

"I don't know."

"How do you know him?"

"I don't remember," her friend said.

That evening, my mother went against her caution. She allowed herself to enjoy the company of this man with a mole, who possessed a startling high-pitched laugh that made her blush.

They sat by the fireplace, the fire warming their backs, plates of food on their knees. My mother picked at grains of jasmine rice. My father spoke about his youth in Thailand. He was endless with stories. He was a boxing champ. He owned a vw car dealership. He managed a hotel. Stories I would hear, too, when I came into being, stories I was not sure were true. It didn't matter. Love was happening. And I want to imagine it like a fairy tale, like some serendipitous moment where two people from the same country meet in a foreign one. Two people who needed each other, and that need was vital, so vital my father and his mole took out a notebook from his back pocket. "I can read fortunes," he said, and though my mother didn't believe in astrology, she believed in this man and his mole. He drew lines resembling a tic-tac-toe grid. He asked her questions: What day were you born? The time? What animal are you in the Chinese zodiac?

After she answered all his questions, after some scrawling in his notebook, he smiled. "According to this," he said, "we will be happy together for a long time."

I kept Katie a secret. For the first six months we dated, my mother and Aunty Sue did not know of her. They only knew I was not home at the regular time they called, 9:00 p.m. When I returned their call and they asked where I was, I told them I was out with friends.

One day, my father called at four in the morning from the Amtrak station in Carbondale, Illinois. I was in my last year at Southern Illinois University. My father was in town for a spontaneous weeklong visit in which I'd designate myself to the couch as he took over my bedroom. I was used to this. It was my father's way. Coming in and out. Disappearing for long stretches of time.

His visits were quiet. We went out to eat at Chinese buffets, and when I wasn't in class, I took him to state parks in the area. He'd bring a camera with him and snapped pictures incessantly. Stand under that tree, he'd say. Cross your arms, he'd say. Smile, he'd say. We would end our days in my small apartment, watching TV before going to bed. When I started dating Katie, I would leave him at the apartment at night, go out with Katie, and return well past midnight. He'd be already asleep, shaking the walls with snores.

On the last night of his visit, Katie came over to meet him. I felt a filial obligation, already guilty that I had been keeping Katie a secret from my mother, unable to determine her reaction to a girlfriend who wasn't Thai—worst—who was white. In my mind, if I introduced Katie to one of my parents, I was still following the rules of a good Thai son, alleviating the guilt I harbored over this secret relationship. Katie never asked about my parents. I had met hers, stayed in her mother's home, drank with her brother and played cards with her sister. But my family was this hole I didn't want to jump into yet. When Katie asked about them, I'd make a joke. "They're crazy Asian. They do weird things." I hesitated to introduce Katie to my mother and aunt because of their reaction, but also because they were Thai. I was beginning to reconcile this other part of me, beginning to merge Thai and American instead of keeping them separate. In my jokes, Katie sensed my hesitancy and did not prod.

But now, she was meeting my father.

In my apartment, I cooked. I was trying my hand in the kitchen for the first time, calling Aunty Sue for her garlic chicken recipe. "We can bring some down this weekend," she said, and I was quick to squash the idea. "I want to try to cook," I said. "I want to learn." Aunty Sue said I was becoming an adult.

My father was at his best—charming and talkative, telling Katie about my childhood: the time I quit martial arts because I hated violence; how I was one of the best golfers in the state; how I caught poison ivy on a Boy Scout camping trip. As the night went on, I began to see the man my mother fell in love with, the man with the attractive mole. And then I remembered them together—how he kissed my mother's cheek before leaving for work at the textile factory, remembered his nightly phone calls to her and how she answered within the first ring, and his whispers that made her giggle when they thought no one was looking. I especially remembered how I modeled myself after my father, copying his every move—his high-pitched laugh, his duck walk, his always-inviting smile. People loved him. I wanted to be loved.

"Your dad is charming," Katie said. "I know where you get it from."

Around midnight, my father brought out the astrological books.

I shook my head. "He reads fortunes," I said. It was a side job. He had a long list of clients in Chicago, who would call him for guidance.

"I am the best," he said. "Never wrong."

Katie smiled. "Why don't you read Ira's first?"

My father shook his head and waved his hands.

"He never tells my future," I said.

"Why not?"

"It's not good for a father to know what's to happen to his children," my father said.

"I understand," Katie said.

My father asked the same questions he asked my mother years ago. He drew in a notebook, wrote Thai numbers and intersecting lines. He knew Katie had been ill with chronic fatigue, but in terms of health, she would be much better in the coming years. True. He said her parents were opposites of each other, and that caused turmoil in her. True. Money was on the upswing after a few years of drought. True. Then he said in the Chinese zodiac, a monkey (Katie) and a dragon (me) were a perfect match in heaven.

"According to this," my father said, "you will be happy together for a long time."

After Katie left, my father asked if my mother met Katie yet.

I shook my head. "I'm not sure what'll she'll think."

My father frowned, the waves on his forehead deepened. He looked like he did those moments when I'd disappointed him, like when I didn't win a golf tournament or received a bad grade in math. "Be a good son. Do not keep secrets. She is your mother."

*

When I wake up, my father says he wants to read my fortune before I return to my mother in a few of hours. "Really?" I say. He nods. My father is in his eighties, and I wonder if he believes this might be the last time he is going to see me, his son who visits and calls infrequently. One year he might be gone, and this time together might be the last. Telling my fortune is his last gift, more special than the house he has promised, this two-story home filled with gaudy mother-of-pearl paintings and fake flower arrangements.

He brings out his fortune telling books and sits at the dining room table. I know the books well. They look like the ones he had for years but rebound with duct tape. Inside of them are diagrams and Thai numbers and Thai writing. My father keeps his eyes toward his books, his right hand drawing and writing on a sheet of paper. He peers under his glasses, extending his neck like a lizard about to catch a fly. "Tell me your birthday?" he says.

I tell him.

"What year?"

I tell him.

"What day were you born?"

I tell him.

"What time?"

I tell him.

These might be the things a father might remember. Perhaps age has fogged up his memory. Or, he's treating me as a client and not a son, so as to not cloud his readings with biases. There's a professionalism he wears—how deeply engaged he is with his books, how quickly he draws my fortune, pencil scratching paper rapidly. I imagine this is what I look like when I'm composing a sentence.

My father doesn't speak, but nods and occasionally makes groans of approval.

"Ira," he says, "your health is good. You need to exercise and drink hot water every day. But you are strong. Very strange, but you will be stronger the older you get."

"Good," I say.

"And you travel a lot. Am I right?"

"Yes."

"I'm right. You travel a lot. You're going to keep on traveling. It's good for you. You like it. Going from place to place. You like new places. You are fearless when you travel. Asia and Europe—that's what I see in the next couple of years. You also have big travels soon. Is this true?"

"It is," I say, thinking of the two-month road trip I am planning in the fall when I drive from Florida to Wyoming, sleeping on friends' couches or rest areas along the interstate.

"Of course it's true. But your money," he pauses, shakes his head, "your money right now is not good. You've been struggling. You hear what I'm saying?"

I have struggled. With a house that will not sell. With credit card debt accrued to stave off unhappiness.

"Things will turn around in six months. Trust me. Your fortune speaks it." He taps his pencil on his books for emphasis.

I have never thought of my father as smart or stupid. He is simply my father, a man who comes and goes, whose dreams are much bigger than his five-foot-four frame, much bigger than even me. But watching him now, this is how he gives back to the world. He reads fortunes. He gives answers. He gives hope. When I was younger I never thought too much of it. My mother never believed, and neither did Aunty Sue, who seemed to laugh at the mention of it. But here, in this moment, he possesses an authoritative persona, a confident look, his spine board straight, wearing his oversize glasses that seem to be his way of peering into the future and past.

"What about love?" I ask.

He looks over his doodles. "Tell me the birthday of your new friend."

I tell him. Time, day, date.

He gives me a thumbs up. "No wonder she's a good match." He tells me about her star and how it intersects with another star, which passes this moon and reflects this light and because it circles close to this sun, Deedra and I are destined to be.

"According to this," he says, "you will be happy together for a long time."

"I want to know more." I lean toward my father. I want him to say the things I need to hear.

My father studies the grids. Sighs. Nods. He sighs and nods for long minutes. "She's had a hard past, yes? Lots of secrets. Lots of hurt. Yes?"

An unfaithful husband. Depression. Anxiety. "Yes."

"This girl is strong, though. Very smart. Can be stubborn, but not unyielding. Such a hard worker. Does a lot in one day that many can't do in ten. Am I right?"

"Right on," I say.

"Tell me. Is she good with paperwork?"

"The best."

"That's right. I know. She's very good at paperwork. Very neat and organized, right?"

"Right."

"And she's financially secure. She keeps tight, doesn't she? She likes to check her accounts."

"She does." What my father says is right on the money. Deedra is all these things. But I want to know more. I want my father to answer a very specific question. "What if we have a child, Dad?"

"Let me check." He consults his books and jots down more notes. He nods. "Let me tell you, Ira. If you have a child, that child will love you to no end. Do you understand? You'll be a good father. The best. You will give everything to this child. Sometimes too much, but it is because you will love this child with your entire fiber. You will want a lot and you will give a lot, and this child will cling tight to you. Do you hear me?"

I do.

"I speak the truth, son. Your future, I've read it."

*

The thing about fortunes is that you believe everything that sounds good. You disregard everything else. It's why I keep fortune cookie fortunes that seem to guide me toward some revelation, some modicum of hope, like the one I have in my pocket, from a dinner with Deedra a few weeks ago. *A new path will present itself and you will take it.*

The thing about fathers is they will love you with their entirety, but sometimes they dream too much for you; sometimes you carry their disappointments on your shoulders for years; sometimes, despite your best efforts, you will see them in you—beyond the physical traits, beyond personality similarities—and you will find yourself wondering and worrying whether you will end up like them, alone and sad; sometimes they make mistakes and you hurt for it and that hurt turns to stone; and sometimes, you find your way back, and it feels good, feels like a budding flower, a new bloom, a new life.

Before I leave my father's parked car in front of Tui's house, I hand him some money, shoving crisp bills in his hand. It is not much, but enough to sustain him for a couple of months. He looks at the money and makes a sound I have not heard in years, a sound of joy, like when I won a golf tournament, like when I became a black belt at the age of nine. He makes this sound, this quick inhale of breath that is both astonishment and elation. "Thank you," he says.

"You're welcome."

"Thank you," he says again.

"You're welcome."

"You will call me, yes?"

"Yes."

"You will stay in contact, yes?"

"Yes."

"Dad will miss you."

"Okay." I put my hands together and bow my head.

"Bye," he says. "Bye."

Inside Tui's house, my mother waits, legs crossed and swinging on the dining room chair. She smiles when I enter.

"You're back."

"Yes."

"So soon."

"Yes."

"How is he?"

"Old," I say.

"Are you hungry?"

"Yes."

She tells me to sit down. She brings out a plate of steaming rice and a myriad of side dishes—stir-fried bean sprouts, salty pork chunks, chicken in green curry. She sits with me as I eat. Sits and watches, saying very little, but saying enough.

July 10

On this day last year, Katie sent an email.

I was in Chiang Mai, but I sensed something was wrong, even eight thousand miles away. Katie wasn't answering the phone. When I'd send her a text message, she'd write back in brief phrases, like *Everything is fine. The dogs say hi. Woof.*

On the day of our twelfth anniversary, this email arrived, and I already knew what it contained, knew because the email had no subject, knew because I knew.

I read it around six in the morning when the neighborhood roosters were mad with their alarm. I read it without my glasses, and the words were a blur, and I thought this was a dream and if I rubbed my eyes hard enough, if I squeezed them so tight they teared, I would wake and see the real message—an anniversary message, an everything will be okay message, a you are the greatest and smartest and most handsome husband ever message, an I am just so damn lucky to have you message, an I wish I were with you so we can be together and celebrate this glorious day because I realized how wrong I was and how right you were message, an I'm sorry message, an I love you message.

I put my glasses on.

I read it again.

This email—I hated it. I hated it because it expressed everything that was right. I hated it because it was eloquent and poetic and heart-breaking. I hated it because I envied Katie's writing, and how diligently she conveyed what was devastating her heart, which was us. I hated it because I wanted to hate Katie.

I couldn't find hate for her. Only guilt. Only sadness.

What she expressed was inevitable. Sometime in the twelve years of our marriage, we had drifted in different directions, and no matter how hard the both us tried—the counseling, the therapy—something had irrevocably shifted; the tectonic plates underneath us had ripped.

I knew this.

I knew this.

I knew before I arrived in Thailand that year. When Katie dropped me off at the airport, this trip would be different, and when I returned, everything would be different. What that difference would be I didn't know. But I felt it. It felt like the absence of a wedding ring that had been on a finger for years.

Inked

In 2004, I found myself lying on my side in a tattoo parlor in Syracuse, New York, getting a dragon that twined along the side of my right calf. The first signs of spring were emerging through the thin layer of remaining central New York snow—daffodils and crocuses, and the first sprouts of tulips, like hands in prayer shooting for the sky. My hands were in prayer shooting for the sky with every moment the needle jagged into me. Katie recorded the whole experience, taking photos and laughing at my grimaces and the bubbles of sweat on my forehead.

The reason for my tattoo: to reclaim my body.

I am and was a big man. I am and was a big Thai man. Possibly the biggest Thai man in the history of Thai men. At my largest I was over four hundred pounds. I crumbled under the gaze of gawkers, whose O-mouths reflected my very O-body.

Before the tattoo, I stopped looking forward to my trips to Thailand. They made me aware of how large I was. I believed I was failing at being Thai, worse yet, failing at being human. I imagined myself as Jabba the Hut from *Star Wars*, which many of the bullies in grade school nicknamed me with unique variations: Jabba the Stupid, Jabba the Chink, Jabba the Fatso. During my trips, I'd begun hiding into myself. Aunts and uncles were confused at my reluctance to come down from my room; they only knew the young Ira who was unafraid, who spoke to every Thai person like a native, who walked with confidence through congested streets. My family had itineraries for day trips to temples and gardens. Instead I watched endless television and plagued myself with self-destructive thoughts, like mutilating my body. Causing it harm. Like digging a spoon into my stomach and gutting fat off of me. Like cleaving the sag from my thighs and waist. Like burning my fat off, having it sizzle like bacon on a skillet.

I had created a distorted story of the body, a story of hatred. I hated my body. I believed others hated it, too. I felt their hate in their stares, their judgment, their ridicule, their thoughts of my lack of self-control. My body said everyone hated me because who could love a fat body like mine. My body was writing itself. I was a tragic character in its story.

The year I got my dragon, I read Natalie Kusz's essay "Ring Leader." In "Ring Leader," Kusz speaks of her life as an overweight and disfigured woman. She speaks of the stares and this overwhelming sense of helplessness. So what does she do? She gets a nose ring. She gets one to reclaim herself. "Somehow now, the glances of strangers seem less invasive, nothing to incite me to nunhood; a long look is just that—a look—and what of it? I've invited it, I've made room for it, it is no longer inflicted upon me against my will."

My will. My terms.

I didn't suck.

My body didn't suck. It was big, yes, but it was mine.

My mother's, too.

In Thailand, tattoos were absent in upper-middle-class families like ours. Only the lower class had them, the poor. "You are not them," my mother said. I understand my mother's possessiveness of my body. She, who birthed me. She, who made sure I was kept safe. She, who bandaged every cut, salved every bruise. I understand her reticence, her perked eyebrows, her frown, when I arrived to Thailand in 2005 with an enormous dragon on my leg.

Then a Buddha on my chest the following year.

Then a Thai Buddhist wheel.

Then a turtle with Thai art on its shell.

Then a Bodhi tree on the other calf the year after that.

Then . . .

*

My cousin Thong and I had planned it for a couple of years. He would take me to the beaches of Hua Hin for a seafood lunch, and on the way back, we would stop at a friend's tattoo parlor for quick art on my right shoulder blade.

Thong is the free bird in the family, the son of one of my twin aunts, Jeem, the youngest of my mother's sisters. He is a dreamer like me. His goals are simple. Be rich and live a wealthy life. Thus far he has been successful. At one time he was the face of a cellphone provider in Chiang Mai. I'd see him on billboards and mall advertisements, his white complexion and rhinoplasty-ed Anglo nose, his wide toothy smile, giving the peace sign. Now he helps his wife's family with their multimillion-dollar company that sells herbal balms, while writing erotic novels in English.

When we were younger, he'd conjure up some weed, and we'd take quick puffs in his room, while he regaled me with tales of his youth. "Once, me and some buddies went to the woods to smoke and I found a lizard, *kingka*. You know what a *kingka* is? They have the sharpest claws, like razor sharp. Because I was drunk and high, I grabbed it and threw it against my friend's back. The lizard dug in, and my friend screamed and bled. I assure you, Cousin, it was hilarious."

The main reason I like Thong: he is a storyteller.

Thong is at the wheel of his fancy SUV with a dash that looks like something from a sci-fi movie, speeding through Thailand green. "Are you sure you want to do this?" he says.

"Absolutely."

"What will Auntie do?"

"My mom? Probably kill me."

"Will she kill me?"

"Probably."

He makes an exasperated sound, stolen I am sure from the Korean dramas his mother loves to watch. *Aieesh*. "Auntie scares me."

"Try living with her."

The radio plays something by Katy Perry or Taylor Swift, sweet and saturated with a frantic rhythm and bass. I'm not fond of it, but I'm not driving, and I know Thong likes this music. It is what he calls "his form." Everything mainstream America is Thong's form.

"Cousin," he says, "are you sure of the design?"

I nod.

For the past three months I have pondered a traditional tattoo called Hah Taew, which translated means Five Rows. The tattoo is placed on the left shoulder blade on women, right on men, consisting of five vertically written Khmer lines. The first row rids malicious spirits and protects the home; the second row reverses bad fortune; the third protects you from curses; the fourth bestows good luck; the fifth row attracts the attention of the opposite sex by bestowing charm and charisma. Usually one would get the tattoo from a monk or holy person via the traditional method of a long sharp bamboo rod, *kem sak*. But I am choosing the tattoo gun and hygienic needle, the comforts of a chair and air-conditioning.

This worries my cousin. "The tattoo won't be legit," he says. "My friend is just an artist not a monk."

"Doesn't matter," I say.

"It won't be the same, Cousin. Not like Angelina Jolie's." In 2003, the actress got the Hah Taew from a tattoo master north of Bangkok. "A real one has powers," says Thong. "A friend got the same tattoo, and he was stabbed in a bar fight, but the knife broke in half and he was unscathed."

"I'm not planning to get stabbed," I say. "It's just a marker for my life."

"What do you mean?"

"A symbol."

"What's the symbol of this tattoo?"

"The end of a long year."

*

A couple of weeks before I left for Thailand, I accompanied Deedra and her oldest daughter to a tattoo parlor in Ybor City, a historical Cuban district of Tampa. Ybor is party central, much like Bourbon Street is to New Orleans. Clubs and bars, cigar shops and restaurants, line up along Seventh Avenue, which culminates at one end with a Scientology church and a Spaghetti Warehouse. Eccentric characters wander the streets, like the man who always wants to lick your shoes or the one who rollerblades in only a thong.

It was too early for the night crowd, and in the afternoon, Ybor seemed neutered.

Except for the many tattoo parlors, buzzing like a giant hive.

Mother and daughter had been planning to get matching tattoos for the past year, after Deedra's ex moved out. They wanted something small. For months, her daughter pestered her. "When are we getting one?" "I'm eighteen now. You said when I'm eighteen we'd get one." "Mother, please, please, please." Mother put it off, not wanting to commit to something so permanent. But her daughter's resolve was unshakable, and now her mother was dating a man with lots of tattoos, a man in full support and acceptance of all tattoos.

The tattoo artist at this parlor looked like a tattoo artist. He wasn't a polo wearing, neat and trimmed jock. He did not wear pastels. Who would trust a tattoo artist with that kind of curb appeal? Who would trust a tattoo artist with the name like Brandon? This tattoo artist had a name like Bark. Bark was a big man with a big voice, bald and well-inked with large gauges in his ears. There were less unfilled spaces on his body than filled, and his clothes were black with a reasonable amount of tear. On his right arm was a Kabuki mask with bloodshot eyes that seemed to follow my every move. I marveled at the level of detail, the smooth lines and crisp use of color. I marveled at all of Bark's tattoos.

Deedra's daughter described the tattoo they wanted—a circle with the Irish Triskele within a Delta symbol. Because the tattoo was small, it would take no more than ten minutes, less time than filling out forms and waivers.

"This is an awesome design," Bark said. "What does it mean?"

Mother and daughter looked at each other and smiled.

Deedra and I had been together for a couple of months, our relationship slow going, both of us wary of another heartbreak. I was married for twelve years, she for fifteen with two kids and high blood pressure and a low tolerance for bullshit. She was as jaded as I was, perhaps even more, her ex leaving her broken and angry. Unlike the amicable way Katie and I split, she resented her ex, hated the fact that he was content remaining unemployed, hated his voice that he would raise, hated how he treated her oldest who was not his. But Deedra was scared to be alone, too. To her, being with someone she didn't love was better than being without someone at all, even if she would have to sacrifice her happiness.

Her situation reminded me of Raymond Carver's short story "What We Talk About When We Talk About Love," this little piece about two couples drinking as the day dwindles down, chatting about love until they find themselves—literally and metaphorically—in the dark. One of the characters says, "My heart is broken . . . It's turned to a piece of stone. I'm no good. That's as bad as anything, that I'm no good anymore." Deedra *was* good. She brimmed with goodness, and it was this goodness that drew me in, a magnet for the presumed bad I was forming in myself. That year she had been the consistent friend, the one I found myself calling, the one I wanted to see, wanted to be near. This feeling was different from the other women I had been with; they only satiated a physical urge. What I felt for Deedra was this strong emotional tug— something internal, something akin to the sensations of a free fall, that rush of fear and adrenaline filling you up, the way the heart drops, drops, and drops, the way gravity has its way with the body.

"My mom and I got rid of an asshole," her daughter said. "And now we are in a new place."

"Badass," Bark said.

Their tattoo was quick. I held both their hands as they squeezed and said, "It hurts so, so much," and I saw their art slowly take form, the curvature of a circle, then the triangle, then the Triskele, Bark's hand steady over their skin, and I felt the turning of a page, their page, and I was part of this change, bearing witness to what they were trying to put behind them, starting a new story in their lives.

*

In the 1920s, Thai royalty vacationed in Hua Hin to escape the heat and pollution of Bangkok. The current monarch, King Bhumibol Aduyadej, lived full-time in Hua Hin until his health brought him back to the capital to be closer to his doctors. Because of its proximity to the capital, Thais often take weekend getaways or day trips there, like my cousin and I who plan to stop for seafood and enjoy the stony beaches that are reminiscent of the ones on the Maine coastline.

Thong speeds down the highway, making quick turns and quicker lane changes. I sometimes close my eyes, thinking he will clip a car or motorcycle or sun-bathing dog. He is asking me about America, asking whether the women are really as long-legged as they seem to be on TV. Everything America is from TV, and because of this, he thinks most of the country is filled with models and action stars. I don't dissuade him. I like to have him think I live my life like a *Mission Impossible* movie.

Thong pulls off the highway, onto a narrow road with sharp, ninety-degree turns. Above some intersections are round mirrors to show oncoming vehicles. Furry little chicks peck the dirt on the side of the road. Mourning doves coo on electric lines. A hairless cat balances on a stonewall.

Thong opens the window. "Smell that?"

The air is salty. Over the wind, I hear the sea.

"We're almost there," he says. "It's a secret place. The best, I assure you."

Every place in Thailand seems like a secret place. This is a country bursting with culinary goodness. Food is never far away. Because of this, good food, "the best" food, is found everywhere, like this outdoor restaurant with a dirt parking lot. The sky threatens an afternoon rain. The wind is rough on the palms, swaying and bending above us. With every gust, the restaurant groans and creaks.

"What do you want, Cousin?"

"Everything," I say.

Thong orders dish after dish. Steamed sea bass, garlic fried soft shell crab, barbecued prawns, seafood fried rice, fish cakes, clay pot vermicelli noodles and shrimp, red curry fish custard. More and more and more. Thailand is a country devoted to food and eating. A common Thai greeting is *Have you eaten?* Yet, Thais, native Thais, remain small and lithe. Like my cousin. Like my cousin vacuuming everything on the table. Like my cousin who continues to order, who says he is hungry, always hungry, who is speaking about the next meal while devouring this one.

"Cousin," Thong says, mouth sloppy with food, "why are Americans so big?" Thong's question is a familiar one. Thais marvel at the size of Westerners—their height, their girth. Friends who have vacationed in Thailand spoke of being poked and prodded like a science experiment. The body, to Thais, is public space.

I'm not fond of the question. When I am asked this, what I hear is *Why are you so big?* "Probably fast food," I say flippantly.

"You don't eat as much as me. I notice every time. And you are the most active person I know."

"I'm watching my figure." I wink.

"That's the thing, Cousin. I eat and eat and eat and never gain weight. Look at me. I'm a skeleton."

I look at him. Thong is thirty, but looks ten. He is the size of most Thai men, his arms and legs thin like pipes. He is so small I can pick him up and throw him like a football.

"The body is a mysterious thing," I say, spooning the soft flesh of the sea bass, weary of its pin-like bones.

"You are big but with purpose, like your body moves, remains active."

"What's your body's purpose?" I ask.

"To eat," he says. "Everything."

The soft shell crab melts in my mouth, followed by the crunch and taste of fried garlic that transports me to a heaven I want to exist, this place of all my favorite foods, this place of utter gluttony, free of judgment, free of stares and wide-mouthed wonderment. So free I can eat like I want to, using both hands, grease glistening my lips, my beard a collection of food detritus. So free I can forget about the body I possess, forget about the weight I carry. This is the power of food in Thailand. This is the power food sometimes has over me. A power to make me forget. Especially when I am alone. Especially when no one is watching. This heaven I imagine is a lonely heaven.

Thong and I have been quiet for some time, eating and enjoying. Rain sprinkles down, and the waiters quickly roll down a plastic shade to keep us dry. When gusts hit the shade it sounds like minor thunder.

"Some raw oysters, Cousin?"

"I'm full," I say. In front of me is a massacre of cracked shells and fish bones.

"Oysters are good for sex," he says, his eyebrows perking up.

"No one to sex here."

"You're in Thailand," he says. "Everywhere is sex."

I laugh.

"I just read *Fifty Shades of Grey*, Cousin. Do you know this book?"

I nod, though I have never read it.

"It's now my favorite. Bye-bye, J. K. Rowling. Hello, E. L. James."

"You are sex crazed, Thong."

"I want to write a book like that. Chains and whips."

"Go for it."

"I want a Red Room," Thong says, "like in the book."

I do not need to know what the Red Room is to know what the Red Room is. "What does your wife say about that?"

He smiles sheepishly. "She thinks I'm crazy."

I clean my hands with a wet napkin. "Tell me the plot of your book."

Thong's hands jerk this way and that, excitement making him speak without breath, unrolling this story about the taking of a sweet and demure woman who works at an ad agency. This woman wears the uniform of the sheltered—big glasses and oversize dresses that hide the curves of her body, blouses buttoned to the top of her neck. She is a ghost. No one sees her. No one cares about her. She is the rug everyone steps on. And in enters the suave millionaire, slick and cocksure of all things. He drives the fanciest cars. He owns homes in Berlin, Paris, London, New York City. He has a reputation, this man. Every week another woman on his arms. Every weekend his private jet takes him somewhere exotic so he can erotic whomever he is with.

"How do they come together?" I ask.

He owns a perfumery and has hired her company to do commercials. He takes a liking to her, dotes on her. Buys her clothes whose fabric comes from endangered silk worms. He accessorizes her with rare diamonds and pearls. They skip around the world together, from one exotic place to the next, and she realizes this other side of her, this . . .

"Animal side, Cousin, you know what I mean?"

I do know. The suave millionaire knows. Knows the kind of power he has over her. Knows the power of bodies, the power of touch, the power of losing oneself to desire, the power one can possess over the powerless. The man is drawn to the powerless. Drawn to the weak. Drawn to the helpless. He is . . .

"A tiger, Cousin, you know what I mean?"

I do know. This tiger has spotted his prey, this succulent gazelle, ripe for the taking. Except for one thing, the thing that becomes his undoing. In the unlocking of her desire, she unlocks something in him, something he never knew ever existed. A heart. His heart. His heart blossoming with intrepid love. Sentimental, overbearing love. The kind that makes you do stupid shit. Like stumble over words. Like tripping over a minuscule crack on a sidewalk. Like overcompensating for your every insecurity by putting on this tough bravado, while inside you are screaming *fake, fake, fake!* The kind of love that begins to gnaw on you. That leaves scars, deep below the epidermis, etched into muscle, inked into blood. And despite how hard you try to hold on to that facade of suave, you begin to crumble, you begin to fracture in unpredictable ways, and you begin to want more than a body, more than physical intimacy, more than a fast fuck, more than what any Red Room can offer. You begin to want. Again.

"Do you know what I mean?" Thong says.

"I do."

"Does the story sound good?"

"Sounds great."

"More oysters then?"

"Bring them."

*

The earth is scarred. It leaves its history in the soil, the waters, in the valleys and hills, in crags and sediment that layer the land, in the bodies we bury in its depths and the smoke and ash we burn and release into the atmosphere. This history is in the sand sifting between my toes now. In the waves that crash on the shore and then the suck and pull of the current reclaiming what once was, like a memory, like a marriage, like a metaphor.

You can turn anything into metaphor.

The tattoo is a metaphor. All tattoos are. What we etch into our bodies is a representation of who we are. Or what we were. Or what we wish to be.

The beach makes me introspective.

Thong has gone to the bathroom, but our conversation about food and sex sticks with me. I can't seem to shake images of the past year out of my head, and with that comes shame and disgust that makes me light-headed and dizzy. And then I think of Deedra and I waver on unsteady legs.

It could be the food coma I'm still experiencing.

Or the last lingering effects of jet lag.

Or the sound of the sea and its lulling properties.

Whatever it is, I don't feel right. I feel untethered, a balloon that escapes the grasp of a boy's hand and is at the whim of the wind. Whatever it is makes me find a seat on one of the many boulders on the beach. Makes me close my eyes to try to right myself. Makes me think in metaphors.

I get this way. My mind wanders off. It takes a sojourn into the surreal. The seagulls that hover, the pockets of tourists taking endless photos, the sun beginning its slant down the horizon—all of this becomes peripheral.

"Where are you?" Deedra would say. "You look like a codfish."

When I leave this world, I leave it with my mouth hanging open, my eyes vacant, like earthy pebbles. I leave it because my physical body does not matter, because my interior life never equates size as a distinguishing characteristic of who I am. My interior life concerns itself with imagination and the fluidity of thought that can turn a scream red. Sometimes, I like that space. Sometimes, I spend too much time there, reliving and retelling and reshaping. Sometimes, I get lost.

"Cousin," Thong says. He has rolled up his jeans, his sandals in his right hand, the ocean foaming at his feet. "Food goes in, food goes out."

I shake my head. "Gross."

"You feeling okay?"

"Okay," I say, but my muscles are melting.

"You're sweating. A lot."

"It's hot."

"True." He looks out at the ocean. Smiles. When he smiles, he is a boy with cavernous dimples, and I remember when he was three clinging to his older American cousin, the two of us still fascinated with robots and remote-controlled cars, the thought of women and the pleasure of the body in some distant future.

*

Once, in Thailand, I started a fight. I was at my largest, and my diabetes was sending me into moments of detachment. The stares, the clips of dialogue I caught about my size—*look at that sumo wrestler, look at the enormity of that one*—chipped away at my tolerance. The word *owan*, fat, the only moniker I possessed in this country, reverberated in my brain, this endless echo of insult. I was tired the way a wounded animal is tired, desperate the way a wounded animal is desperate. All of this culminated into a cloud of rage.

Katie and I were walking through a street festival in Chiang Mai. I do not remember what the day was like, but it was probably hot and over-cast because of the rainy season. I remember endless tables of goods for sale—Thai fabric and wood-carved figurines, scented oils and incense, teak and rosewood chopsticks. I remember the mass of people around us, so many people closing in on me, making me even more aware of myself and the space I occupied. And there were many voices, and it was as if I had turned into a superhero and was able to hear what everyone was saying, thousands of voices, all of them talking about me.

This was the delusional mind at work. Deep down I knew that. Deep down, the rational Ira was screaming that this was in my head, no one is saying anything about me, and if they were, to let it go. But my body, my hatred of my body, was louder. It was foaming.

This. Rage.

I believe what I was feeling was similar to what James Baldwin writes about in "Notes of a Native Son," that rage he felt when a waitress denied him service at a diner because he was Black. "This made me colder and more murderous than ever. I felt I had to do something with my hands. I wanted her to come close enough for me to get her neck between my hands." It was my hands clenching into fists. Katie clung to my arm. She was saying something I did not hear, about something I did not care about. The only thought I had was to hurt. It was then I saw him, this Thai man, heading in my direction. Everything tunneled onto him. And his face. And his voice. I recognized the look. *Fuck that look*. That look that said, *Oh look at that fatty. Look at this body out of control.* I could see the word form on his lips, delivered in slow motion. O-o-o-o-o-o-o-w-w-w-w-w-a-a-a-n.

Fuck that word. Fuck him.

So when he was a foot away, I revved up my voice. I said in the clearest, toughest South Side Chicago vernacular I could muster, "What the fuck are you looking at?"

I puffed out my chest. Made myself even bigger. I said the sentence in English—the clearest English I have ever spoken—because I wasn't Thai. If they were going to cast me as other then I'll be other. I'll be the other side of other, motherfucker.

I said it again, "What are you looking at?"

I took a step forward.

I felt my right arm raise. I felt it coil back.

And then I was pulled away. And then I said, "Stop looking at me. Stop fuckin' looking at me," over my shoulder. And then I was shuddering, shaking. And then that rage dissipated and what was left was a sorrow so deep, so low that I found myself unable to breathe, found myself hunched over, hands on my knees, trying to catch my breath.

I don't remember anyone's reaction, whether a crowd formed like the beginning of a schoolyard fight. I don't remember whose eyes directed themselves to the fat man speaking crazy English and his white wife, who might have looked lost and confused, her brow wrinkling into waves. I don't remember what the man said if anything or whether he flinched or got tough himself. I don't remember him because he didn't matter. He was just a person I wanted to inflict pain on, physical and brutal pain. He was a symbol of all the ugliness I felt in myself.

I was not a violent man. I captured wasps and flies and let them go instead of using the swatter. But that day, I wasn't rational. Rationality was the air I couldn't breathe. I understand the cliché—*I was not myself.* I was not. Or perhaps I was, in the deepest depths of me, this ugliness that we all possess.

When I got myself together, when my breathing slowed and the veil of pity and anger lifted, Katie's hand touched my back. I felt hesitancy in her fingers, the pause, the hover. "Are you okay?"

I nodded.

"What the hell was . . . ?"

I shook my head.

"You can't do that."

I didn't respond.

"You can't do that," she said again.

I nodded.

"Don't do that again."

Another nod.

We didn't say anything after that. We didn't say anything about the situation any time afterward either. We buried it, as if it never happened. But it haunts me. I play the movie in my mind. I play it through. I play it in different versions. Like hitting the man. Bludgeoning him. Like the shame that I would have caused, the trouble I would have gotten myself into, the honor I would have stripped away from my family, the violent fear that would enter the marriage. Or what if he fought back? Despite my size, despite my overwhelming strength, he beat me into a pulp, made my face into a badly bruised peach. Just fucked me up. Or perhaps the man pulled out a gun and shot me. Right then and there. My life ended. At one point, I considered this the best-case scenario. To be ended.

I couldn't let go of the moment; it came in a wave of guilt. After this, the lowest point in my life—I knew I had to change. I could not keep going like this.

The next year I had a dragon tattoo. The year after that I began working on my body.

*

In the last two years of my marriage, I went through a major body transformation, believing what might save this relationship, what might save me, was a new and slight version of myself. Ira 2.0. I exercised. I entered 5Ks and 10Ks and mud races. I fuckin' hate running, but did it anyway. Most of my days were spent at the gym. Everything else took a backseat to my body—my job, my writing, everything. I counted calories. I measured serving sizes. I subscribed to every health magazine, tried every new health supplement. If I traveled, I made sure to find a gym. If I could not find a gym, I always brought with me resistance bands.

A little over a year, I had lost one hundred pounds. Three months later, I had lost fifty more. Gone were my chins. Gone were my behemoth saggy arms. Gone were my audible breaths. Gone was my sleep apnea and snores. And now there was muscle. Muscle that made the turtle tattoo on my arm nod.

I had shed a person but gained all this excess skin. I did not have a muscular and toned body, like the pictures in the magazines I was reading. I was a skin demon. Skin around my pubic area. Skin under my arms. Skin on my chest. It looked as if my body was made of wax and slowly melting away.

None of this mattered.

I was skinny.

Or skinnier.

Vanity made me look in every mirror, made me take countless pictures of myself, made me spend thousands of dollars on new clothes, clothes I did not have to order from the internet. I walked with a strut. I felt good, probably the best I had ever felt in my life. Katie would come into the bathroom and find me flexing into the mirror and shake her head.

This change, however, did nothing to rectify the marriage. It further distanced us. The time I should have spent on us, I was working on me. This transformation was necessary. My body had created a shortened life span. My body was terribly diabetic. I couldn't do the things I wanted to do or have the energy to do them. The concentration on myself saved my life, but crumbled the most important relationship in my life.

"I do not love you because of your body," Katie used to say and kept saying until the end of us. For this I am forever grateful.

But.

There was something missing, something that irked me, something that I believe was the serpent of selfishness. It slithered into my brain, coiled around the collection of all my insecure thoughts. I wanted Katie to love my new body, the way I loved my new body. I wanted her to see what she had, this skinnier me, this me that was beautiful on the inside and outside. I wanted her to revel in my transformation, and perhaps we could look at me in the mirror, bypass all that extra skin, and marvel at this new body, this fresh butterfly out of the fat cocoon.

What I really wanted, what I needed Katie to know was this: *You cannot do any better than me.*

Once, after a particularly tense session of couples' therapy, I drove home, my hands tight around the wheel, my eyes only on the road. I did not want to turn to look at Katie, even only for a moment, because I was feeling self-righteous, and I knew the look I would have on my face would be one of an asshole. That was who she wanted. An asshole. Katie stared at her hands, then out into the Florida dark. We were speeding to meet friends for Happy Hour.

"I'm not feeling social," she said.

"We're not cancelling," I said. "They're already there."

"I'm tired."

"I'm tired. I go to the gym. I run five miles every day. I'm tired."

Katie did not say anything. Her eyes were aimed at the whirling dark world beyond the car window. Her silence infuriated me. This might have been how she felt when I retreated into myself, how silence has its own kind of power. If you do not speak, then a conversation fails to happen, the way it was failing to happen in the car.

I laughed—a snotty, snorty laugh.

"What?" Katie said.

"Nothing," I said.

"What?"

"You're not going to get anyone better than me." I regretted it as soon as the sentence ventured out of my mouth.

"Maybe," she said.

And that was it. We did not speak until we met with our friends, and then we pretended nothing had happened. We pretended to be the perfect couple, and when we returned home, she went to the bedroom and shut the door, and I went for a run, in the dark.

*

Bank Tattoos is a small shop, hidden in an alley, like a speakeasy during prohibition. Searching for it makes me feel like I am doing something wrong. Already I am working out what to say to my mother, but I know no level of logic or argument will sway her to acceptance. I'm thirty-eight, and still worry about my mother's disappointment.

Thong and I walk up and down the block, unable to find anything that looks like a tattoo shop. He calls and asks Bank to come out to get us. When Bank emerges from a small door, he is all smiles, putting his hands together to greet me formally, calling me Pe, a term used to describe someone older. His dreadlocks travel well past his waist, with streaks of dark brown emerging through thick vines of black. He has the round face of Buddha, Buddha with a goatee and what looks like a bone stuck through one of his ears.

I tell Bank to call me by my nickname, Tong, to ditch the formalities.

He smiles. "You speak Thai well," Bank says.

"Cousin is native," Thong says.

Sweat coats the underside of my arms. My shirt sticks to my back.

"Let's go inside," Bank says. "It's hot."

The air-conditioning is a welcoming kiss. I exhale and collapse on a brown leather love seat, my skin sticking to the surface of the couch. A bald boy surfs the internet at a metal desk. When he sees me, he puts his hands together and bows his head. Thong immediately goes through books of tattoos. On the walls are photos of Bank's work. One picture shows Bank accepting a trophy for an original tattoo, his hair not as long and serpentine.

"What did the winning tattoo look like?" I ask.

Bank tells the bald boy to show me. The boy rises, his black combat boots heavy on the tiled floor. He is tall, about my height but gangly, his navy Oxford hanging loose on his frame, his suspenders cinching tight at the shoulders. I guess he is about nineteen or twenty, but in this country I'm always wrong with ages. He bows his head, and what emerges is a purple *yuk* on the thickest part of the dome, a mythological giant with a gold ring in flaring nostrils, mouth filled with fangs.

"Wow," I say.

"It's like the temple guardians at Wat Phra Keow," Thong says.

Thong is referring to the giants standing at every entrance of the Temple of the Emerald Buddha, Thailand's most revered holy place.

When I was six or seven and saw the yuks for the first time, I could not get them out of my mind. "Holy protectors," my father used to say. "Guardians between heaven and hell."

"Did it hurt?" Thong says.

The boy nods. The yuk nods.

"You should get one, Thong," I say. "Join the club."

"My mom would kill me."

"It always hurts," I say.

"*Aieesh*." Thong shivers. "I hate needles."

Bank makes a stencil copy of what he will be inking onto my shoulder. He shows me various sizes of the Five Rows, with different line thicknesses and different spacing options between each line. He tells me he can do anything—larger or smaller, thinner or thicker, more space or less space. I want the longer and thicker lines and wider spaces.

"Are you sure?" Bank says.

"I have a big shoulder."

"Thong told you it won't be magical, right?"

"Right."

"Just so you know."

There is a moment of vulnerability before any tattoo, the moment when shirt or pants comes off and you bare a part of your body to someone you hardly know. But there is comfort in that, too. The comfort of a stranger like Bank and his steady hands and his artistic gaze over your epidermis, the giving over of your body, the confidence that he will take good care of you, that he will give you what you want. It is like a relationship, brief and wonderful.

Above me is a small statue of Buddha and one of Ganesha, the elephant-headed Hindu god of wisdom, the remover of obstacles. Before Bank starts on my tattoo, he prays, his head bowed to his hands, his lips moving silently. When he is done, he shows me the new needle he is putting in the tattoo gun and the new rubber gloves he slips over his hands. He lines up a small thimble of black ink and a smear of Vaseline on what looks like a small surgical tray.

"You ready?" Bank says.

"You ready, Cousin?" Thong says, standing beside me.

*

Thong drops me off at Tui's house. He does not want to come in. He does not want to be there when I tell my mother about the new addition on my body. "Cousin," he says, "tell her I had no part of this." We plan to meet up again, before I leave for the States. He promises me beer in Chiang Mai and the "best" food at secret places.

My right shoulder stings. Flashes of heat radiate from the spot.

Aunty Sue has a bowl of bean thread noodle soup waiting for me, pork meatballs floating like land mines among slivers of green onion. Rice steams in a ceramic bowl. I am still full, my body trying to digest the pounds of seafood I devoured this afternoon. I cannot cool my body, which feels like it is on fire.

The news is on—it always is—about the state of the country. It has become white noise. Like the fans spinning and cooling the dining room. Like crickets singing an evening song outside. My mother reads a book, an English one I left here last year—Jhumpa Lahiri's *The Namesake*. I remember enjoying the book; remember the protagonist, Gogol, and his search for identity. I think everything we do in this world is a search for identity.

"Professor," my mother says in Thai, "what does 'prevail' mean?"

I shrug, but the act of it rubs my T-shirt against my tattoo. I wince.

My aunt notices immediately. "What's wrong?" She points to my shoulder.

I bow my head a bit, the way dogs do when they know they have done wrong.

My mother puts down her book and lets her glasses dangle around her neck. "What?"

"Your son's shoulder," Aunty Sue says.

I take off my shirt. Show them the Five Rows.

"I knew it," Aunty Sue says. "Your cousin and you—trouble." She then disappears into the kitchen to check on the chicken and red curry.

"Let me see," my mother says.

She places her glasses back on. I can feel her fingers floating above each line, as if she is reading Braille. "Does it always look like this?"

"New ones, yes. It's brighter, slightly raised."

"The skin is really red."

I nod.

"How do you care for it?" My mother has not taken her eyes off my shoulder. She has not raised her voice, has not rolled her eyes. She is strangely calm. This calm makes me more cautious. Makes me think she will pull my earlobes or pinch my cheeks or flick my forehead at any moment.

"A&D ointment for a day or two," I say, "then lotion."

"We have A&D," she says. "I'll go get it." She leaves the dining room and returns a few seconds later. "You want me to put it on you?"

I nod.

"You know what each row means?"

I nod.

"Tell me."

I tell her.

I believe the Five Rows is magical, despite what Thong said. Bank is a holy person after all. The tattoo is fending off mad moms, because this mom is not the mom I expected. This mom does not seem put off by her son's tattoo, not like the last one where she tried to rub it off with a Brillo pad and then complained for weeks about it, her only son becoming a *jone*, miscreant.

When she is done, she says, "It looks good, I guess."

"Thank you, I guess."

"But kah tee," she says, *for the love of all that is holy*, "have this be the last one."

I smile. "Maybe."

Flesh of the Land

In this here place, we flesh;
flesh that weeps, laughs; flesh
that dances on bare feet in
grass. Love it. Love it hard.
—Toni Morrison, *Beloved*

We spend a lot time in a car, blurring through the world at eighty kilometers per hour, passing so much green. Green rice fields, green mountains, green jungles, green rivers and lakes. Green is relentless; it laces and twines around my limbs; it enters under my skin, becomes my veins. The land wants to swallow me, possess me, and now I am willing to go.

I'm trying to understand the land. To understand the land is to understand the body. I am scared of my body. To Deedra, I am a creature of paradox because I am most comfortable without clothes, stripping down to nothing as soon as I enter the door. I relish how air caresses skin, like wind through tall grasses. At the same time, I want my body to disappear, to vanish, to leave no trace of its presence.

*

I have the habit of staring at Deedra as she undresses. She is exquisite. Her shyness, her attempts to hide herself from my gaze, makes me want her even more. I lie quietly on the bed, watching her peel her clothing off. I tell her I want to trace my finger over her every curve. I love her imperfections: the small cluster of spider veins on her thigh that look like the tangled branches of a purple tree; or her stretch marks, cracks in dry earth, that trace over her stomach and hips; or the heft of her breasts and the delicate points of her nipples, like rocky crags on foothills.

"You will tire of this," she said.

"I won't," I told her.

Her body is endless with discovery. Like the land, there is more to study, more to take in.

"I'm learning you," I said. "There is so much I don't know. So much to figure out."

*

Our bodies are our first landscapes. We explore it before anything else. We look at it in the mirror. We know the places we like and the places we don't. Everything is visual. Our thoughts and criticisms are constructed on what we see and not how we feel. My beloved teacher Kent Haruf spoke of the intimacy between the land and the life on the land, the land and how it invades the mental spaces of the body, especially eastern Colorado where his novels are set. "If you've grown up there," he says, "it forces you to slow down and look at things more closely. If you don't, you'll miss it."

I missed Thailand. Missed the secrets bubbling underneath all that green. Missed where the wild vines climb. Missed the riddle of the swaying rice fields.

I've missed the problems of my marriage until it was too late. I missed the invective I carry within my body about my body. I've visited Thailand many times, driven through it like today and have seen the mountains of the North, the layered tiers of rice paddies in the central plains, the coastal beauty of the South, the abundance of green that sprouts and laces and overtakes. But I've missed it. I've missed a lot of things.

*

Thailand is my mother's home. While growing up, I never knew the intensity of this love. I never understood her devotion, her longing. I thought it was food and family she missed. But to love a place is to love the physical-ness of the place, too. To love a place is to know how it feels under the soles of your feet. My mother missed Thailand itself. The rivers that she paddled to school. The ponds she swam in. The dust and dirt that stained her hands. She missed the wind, the air, the smell of the soil. She missed the lulling quality of the central flat, the slightest undulations in the earth as one speeds by in a car, train, or motorcycle. Here, rice fields yawn and shiver.

All of this is outside the body, but it is essential in awakening inner longing, like a hug at the core of us, like the spread of warmth and comfort and contentment.

I've never experienced this feeling, never felt anything like this anywhere I've lived. Not in Chicago, not in Carbondale, not in Columbus, not in Oswego. Not in Tampa, where I live now. I wonder if this is because I was born an immigrant's son, born with a sense of placelessness. You are not of any world. This landscape is not yours, because it was not ours.

Or perhaps, the immigrant son fits anywhere, everywhere. Any place can be home. An immigrant son possesses all landscapes. He sees himself belonging to the world.

I like this state of mind, the hope that it carries.

The pessimist in me, however, thinks I haven't opened my eyes wide enough. I haven't allowed myself to give into the land, any land. There is a lyrical understanding of how to interact with landscape, and it starts, I believe, in the body, which for the longest time, I hated.

My vision of Thailand is not my mother's vision. I will never have her vision, will never know what it truly means to have left for thirty-six years, to live in place she did not much like. If she had the power to wind back time, would she have stayed in Chicago through so many frigid winters? Would she have suffered through a marriage that depleted her sense of self? Would she have remained in that suburban home, in a place more gray than green, with the heaviest of hearts?

I think she might have.

Part of loving a place is the longing to return to it, is the happiness of coming back. It feels, I imagine, like the flight of a million songbirds, all wind and song, an arpeggio of wings, the release of a breath we didn't know we were holding.

Man Baby

It happens every year. At some point during the trip, I get sick. And when I am sick I am a big baby. And when I am a baby I whine. And when I whine my mother takes care of me. And when my mother takes care of me she is no longer a mother but Mommy, and I am no longer a thirty-eight-year-old man but a five-year-old boy in a filthy white T-shirt with snot crusting my lips.

"Maaeeeeee," I say, like an irritated goat. I lie on the couch, the air conditioner blasting and two fans pointed at me. I keep saying Mae until she responds.

"What is it?"

"Feel my head."

She does.

"I don't feel good."

"Tell me what hurts."

"Everything."

"Your head?"

I nod.

"Your stomach?"

I nod.

"Are you achy?"

I nod.

She puts a cold towel on my forehead, a thermometer in my mouth. "Don't say anything."

I nod, but insist on telling her again, "I don't feel good," in case she missed it the first time.

"Mom knows," she says. "Now quiet."

She hums a Thai lullaby about Uncle Kom who had a lot of nephews, big and small. When I was a boy I used to dance to the song endlessly. Now I am covered in blankets, so only the top of my head sticks out. I am so cold. I am so hot. Cold. Hot. I do not know what I am.

My mother pulls out the thermometer. "Fever."

"I don't feel good."

"Yes, yes," she says. She gives me pink pills and water. She makes sure to dab ointment on my tattoo. When she moves to leave, I tell her not to go. I tell her to stay here with me because I am sick and when I am sick I do not like to be left alone because when I am alone I get scared.

"Oh boy," she says. "Such a baby."

"I *am* your baby."

"Did Katie take care of you when you got sick?"

"Sometimes."

"Does your new friend?"

"Sometimes."

She sighs. "Who will take care of you when you are so far away? Who will take care of you when I'm gone?"

Sleep tugs at my eyes. "Don't worry," I say. "I'm a man."

She laughs and tugs at my earlobe.

My mother turns on the TV and watches the news, her hand never leaving my shoulder. The last thing I hear before drifting off is Argentina edging out Belgium in a thriller. I hear this year's World Cup is full of surprises.

*

Sometimes, the body revolts. Sometimes, it aches and feels as if each limb is weighted down by anvils and your stomach no longer feels like your stomach, but a thing possessed by an alien, and that tiny alien inside of you will explode through the belly button, like that film, and run rampant through the Bangkok streets and temples and food carts. You will be responsible for the apocalypse.

Sometimes, my brain flies through the window, like it is doing now, flying and soaring. When I fly I am not so freaking hot, so hot my shirt is soaked through as if I have tumbled into a pool, as if the ocean's foamy tongue laps over every pore of me. The wind kisses my face, my limbs, my every extremity. A delusional calm spreads. Memories emerge without filter, bumping into one another, like in a pinball machine—that electronic collision on rails and bumpers, that ping, that tilt.

A crumpled blue dress on beige carpet.

The acidic aftertaste of a poorly made mojito.

A small tattoo of musical notes on a shoulder.

My brain is a flat rock skipping through water, propelled by motion, without logic, without direction, without an engagement with time.

Here is another memory: Salvador Dalí's *Meditative Rose*, a poster bought at the quad of my college during my freshman year, hanging it on the wall of my dorm room, next to a poster of bikini-clad bikers. A juxtaposition of desires.

And another: the Dalí museum in Saint Petersburg, Florida, the exact day Katie left the house, I am with a woman whose blond hair caressed the top of her shoulders, whose fingers hovered over a small print of Dalí's earlier works, some coastal town in France. Later, when she stuck her tongue into my mouth I forgot what tongues were made for.

One thought comes; one thought goes. One image comes; one image goes. I do not dwell. I am not constructing meaning. I simply exist.

Breathing. My brain is breathing.

At some point I grab the phone and text someone. *Parlez vous Francais? Je m'apelle Ira. Je t'aime. Mange moi. There is a gecko climbing the walls, and no one sees it. The gecko is staring at me. It's freaking me out, the gecko. Please send help.*

Everything is a Dalí dream. Colors and melting. It may be the melatonin I took. Or those two little pills my mother gave me, strangely pink, like dollops of candy. I do not know what the pills are, and I do not remember what she said they were. Sound is wind whipping the house; sound is a vacuous cave. I am on a rickety bridge of the real and unreal. My hand is a kaleidoscopic fan. My mother who checks on me is three or four mothers dabbing the sweat from my head, bringing me another glass of orange juice, which is the orange-est thing I have ever seen. The orange of the sun. The orange of burning.

I am burning.

The new tattoo burns.

A good burn. A burn when you play with candles, when you poke a campfire, when you eat a deliciously fresh-out-of-the-fryer spring roll and you have to huff and swallow to get it down.

I want a spring roll.

I ask for a spring roll.

Mae. Mae. Mae.

My moms are saying something, a chorus of mom voices.

Spring roll, please.

Drink. Drink. Drink.

A cup to lips.

Water. Water. Water.

A dribble along a cheek.

Now sleep.

*

I did not wash a plate until I was twenty. I did not do my own laundry until I was twenty-five. I did not learn how to write a check until later. When I was sick as an undergraduate, six hours away from Chicago, my mother and Aunty Sue would drive the length of the state to take care of me because I begged them to. Usually, when they arrived the following day, I felt better.

When Katie and I were together, at the end of every long-distance phone call, my mother and aunt would say, "Are you helping Katie with dishes? Are you vacuuming the house? Are you mowing the lawn?" I'd reply flippantly, *whatever*. "We've spoiled you," Aunty Sue said. "We did everything, and now, you know nothing," my mother said. "Help-less." I heard worry in their voices. A part of me was worried, too, the part that urged me to get off my ass and do something. The other part, however, clung to that spoiled child, clung hard to him because it was the only way of living I knew.

One of my best friends, someone who is not afraid to tell me the truth, once said I worked hard, harder than most, but there was this other part of me that always wanted to be taken care of. "You know, a Baby Man Child."

Baby. Man. Child.

A forever echo.

My helplessness is not something I am proud of. It stems from ingrained patriarchal expectations. That women did the domestic stuff. That men did whatever. I could hear my cousin Oil. *Stupid men.* I knew what I was doing was wrong, but knowing and doing were different matters. I needed to confront this helplessness, this Baby Man Child. When Katie left, she left me to deal with the house, the finances, and the divorce. This was her revenge, I supposed. Revenge is too unkind of a word. Maybe it was necessity. Maybe it was sanity. Maybe she was sensing that she would become like her father, always worrying about money, always thinking he would become destitute and alone. Or maybe it was a way to make me aware of all the things she had shouldered, one last lesson before leaving.

A wife should not be a teacher.

A husband should not be a student.

These roles do not make a good marriage.

I hated it. I hated sifting through old photos, old records, old letters. I hated staying up at night, filling cardboard boxes. The act of moving is also an act of remembering. Sometimes I'd find an item in the back of the closet, like a blue rubber ball, and I think about the dog that we loved and took care of, my little boy boo, and how he carried that rubber ball like it was the greatest thing in the world.

Moving is heartbreaking; moving by yourself shreds the heart.

On a daily basis, I made calls to bankers and accountants and lawyers and real estate agents. I would start every conversation the same way: "Listen, you are going to have to talk to me as if I am the dumbest person on Earth. This is all very new to me." Most of the people I talked to laughed. Some seemed taken aback. Why wouldn't they? Here before them was a grown-ass person, asking about how to open a savings account. Here was this grown-ass person doing taxes for the first time.

Nothing, as Buddha said, is permanent. A tree dies. A flower withers. A relationship ends. He also said: When there is nothing, there is you. Translation: Get your shit together.

Whatever grudge I felt for Katie, whatever resentment I held for her would slowly sift away because I had become self-reliant. Yet—

Baby. Man. Child.

He is still there.

I feel him. I hear him. He is the devil on my shoulder. *Do it. Give in. Get whatever you want because you are special. You are deserving.* Though I try to block him out, I fall for his words. I *am* special. I *am* deserving. What I forget is that he is not to be trusted. He is ugly desire. I imagine him born from the fat of my stomach—this gluttonous monster in diapers and a baby rattle and full beard and blood blisters and drool, buckets of drool. This is his true form. But do not blink. He can shape shift. He can be cute. Don't look him in the eyes. He can bat them the way sirens do. He can make them sad and helpless, like a starving puppy. He can make you to do his bidding.

Look away, friend.

*

Sometime in November last year, a cold took hold of me and stole my voice and energy. I had been traveling the South for a few weeks, going from one university to the next, doing readings from my new poetry collection. In some cities I met with women I conversed with online— Tallahassee, Atlanta, Jacksonville, Chattanooga. I was worn from the road and nights in hotels. After I was home, my immune system let down. I did not have anyone to take care of me. I did not want to bother my friends who I am sure would have come over with medicine and food. I did not want a friend. I wanted a caregiver. The violins of pity reverberated in my brain. Sadness, too. And loneliness.

That evening I was supposed to meet a woman at a local coffee shop in downtown Tampa. This would have been our second date. She was a kind woman, a stay-at-home mother. When we first met, we talked about her kids and how at one time she wanted to be a professional dancer. She showed me the extreme curvature of her small feet, which were like crescent moons. It was a good date that ended with a promise to get together again.

When I called to cancel, she said she would come over and make me chicken soup. She said she was famous for her chicken soup. She said someone sick shouldn't be alone. I should have told her no. I should have told her I didn't need her kindness. Instead, I gave her my address.

Her chicken soup was good.

Her company was good.

It was a good evening.

We watched a horror flick about a monster let loose in a museum. She left a little before eight. That was the last I saw of her. She would text a few times. *Did I do something wrong?* I didn't reply. I wish I could remember her name.

*

Later that evening, my temperature returns to normal, my appetite back. I had slept the day away. Strange dreams snaked in and out of my head—about France, about a gecko. I check my phone, finding a message. Deedra writes: *Scroll up and read what you wrote me. Go. I'll wait.*

The Talk of the Body

To chase the remnants of my fever away I visit Paan, Bee's close friend. Paan was trained to be a massage therapist at Wat Po, a prestigious Thai massage school. She runs a massage parlor a mile from Bee and Tui's house, and appointments with her are made weeks ahead of time. She is slender, in her late forties. When she smiles, her cheeks sink in, her teeth off-white. Her hands are all veins, her fingers copper pipes. Even though she's slight, she possesses a husky voice, as if she was once a deep smoker. Paan looks like someone who has lived a life of hardship. The deep creases in her face, her reserved smile, her sharpness with her workers, tell me she is not someone you trifle with.

Paan knows my body. She knows what ails it, knows how to untie all the knots I have accrued over the year. When Paan touches me, my body succumbs. It forgets its every flaw, its every insecurity. Her massages go deeper than skin, deeper than muscle and tendon. It is painful in the best of ways.

Before Paan starts, she puts her hands together and prays. The scent of lavender permeates the dark enclosure. I lie on a thin mattress pad, faceup.

"Where does it hurt, sir?" Paan asks.

"Everywhere."

In the darkened room, the shadow of her head nods. "When was your last massage, sir?"

"Last year. With you."

She makes an exasperated sound. "I can tell." She asks if she can use herbal balm on me—"it will be hot"—and I say yes. She taps the bottom of my foot, wiggles my big toe. "Are you ready?" she says. "This will hurt."

*

I hurt my back after helping Katie move into a 1910 farmhouse in southern Illinois. Our relationship was new, like the spring that brings out the first rise of daffodils. Katie suggested I see a massage therapist. I did not take to the thought of a stranger touching me. Though I craved touch, I was scared of it, too.

Katie found someone who would come to the rented farmhouse. He was slim with a high-pitched voice, always in flannel and jeans—half lumberjack, half hippy. I don't recall his name, but Stan keeps surfacing on the glass of this memory. One moment Stan would talk about shooting a buck, and the next he extolled the virtues of Mozart's quartets. He was easy to talk to, though most of the time we were silent. New age music played from the CD player, a lot of bells and electric noise. Every Wednesday, in the late afternoon, Stan set up in the middle of the kitchen, the largest room in the house, while Katie worked on poems in the upstairs attic, and the golden retrievers watched and wagged underneath the massage table.

A miracle happened in our kitchen—how this hippy lumberjack moved his hands along the ridges of my back, how his fingers squeezed and released the meaty parts of my shoulders, how his elbows glided along the contours of my body. My back had become a slippery ice rink, and the massage therapist's hands—his forearms, his fingers—were elegant figure skaters, gliding in concentric patterns. I emitted little groans, the way our dog Bonnie would when I found a particular onerous itch on her. My breath was in concert with his hands. When I flipped over, after my legs and chest were properly worked on, he placed the tips of his fingers at the base of my skull. "Cranial sacral," he called it, and it seemed like my skull lifted off my spine, independent of my body. His thumbs waltzed in long slow strokes at the base of my brain, moving in a way I never thought possible. When he was done, lightness came over me. It felt like I had been given a new body, and this body, though it looked the same, moved with oiled ease. My vision seemed sharper. Colors sharper. The pain in my back vanished.

"How was it?" Stan said. He washed his hands in the sink, drying them off with a dishtowel.

"Incredible," I said. My voice came from another world. I was naked, save for a blanket over my privates. I didn't care. What is there to care about when you are feeling this good?

Stan smiled. "The first time is always the best."

*

My first time comes in random images and phrases: Senior year. Someone's bedroom. Jon Bon Jovi poster above a desk, Jon licking a microphone. Stuffed animals staring with beady eyes. Kisses. Touches. Aggressive tongue. "You wanna?" "Yeah." Falling into her bosom. Fumbling with her bra. Kissing the nest of her hair instead of her neck. "You like Batman, huh?" Wearing Batman boxers. "I am Batman." Underwear with a lavender bow. The sight of my first down there. Overwhelming. Overwhelmed. Over. "Are you done?" "Um." "You're done." "Sorry." "Whatever."

The first time with someone you love is worse.

I was a straight-A college student and viewed my relationship with Katie as a test. I had passed many already—the small dates, the small talk, 3:00 a.m. conversations, innocent flirtations, first kiss, make out sessions, and now this, the biggest test of them all, 90 percent of my grade: my performance in bed.

Though Katie was not my first time, she was, in many ways, my first time. Though Deedra was not my first time, she was my first time. It felt like my first time. Felt like I didn't know what a penis was for, like the vagina was this mysterious planet, which for a man, it was.

Back then, I thought sex—good sex—was supposed to be like the choreographed scenes in movies, like Leo and Kate in *Titanic*, the camera capturing perfect pearls of sweat, hair impeccably sculpted and never mussed, in sync breathing, and succinct and flawless movements culminating in the ultimate joint orgasm, which, in the movie, was punctuated with a hand pressed against a steamy window. Iconic.

I'd never had this type of sex. I wanted to be able to deliver this kind of sex.

There were too many flaws in my logic. My body was not chiseled, like Leo's. There was nothing Leo about me. Shit jiggled. Shit sagged. When excess flesh collides with excess flesh what culminates is a startling slap. There were lots of startling slaps. My moves were not swift and light, not like Leo—fuckin' Leo—who was acrobatic. Sweat dripped off me like a leaky faucet. I panted like a chugging car. And my face, I imagine it wearing the same expression when I find myself disoriented in a shopping mall—mouth slightly open, eyes panicked and searching for any direction that would lead me home.

At one point, my glasses came off. My lack of vision made me self-conscious. I apologized a lot. I was naive and believed sex was about seeing, instead of the incorporation of all the other senses—sight, perhaps, the least important of them. Sight or the lack thereof made me aware of where I was—in this bedroom with green-leaf curtains, the golden retrievers at the foot of the bed, the light of candles flickering on white walls, between the legs of a woman I loved. Sight or the lack thereof stunted my movements. Without my glasses, I couldn't read Katie's face—*Is that a grimace or grin? Does she like it when I touch her here? Or here?*

I squinted to better focus.

I was not in focus.

I was not focused.

The first time sent both of us spinning about the lasting nature of our relationship. Not every moment thereafter was like that. It is ludicrous to think that that first night together was the reason Katie and I found ourselves where we were fifteen years later. Twelve years of marriage does not equate to one badly aimed penis, on one spring night. But the moment would be there, wouldn't it? in our heads, our minds, every time we stripped off our clothes; every time we entangled our bodies. The shadow of the first would hover over us. Peeking and prodding. It is here now, that memory like a shard of glass, making me cringe. It waves its hand. It smiles. It says, Remember me? It says, You really sucked.

*

Massage teaches you to let go. You close your eyes and appreciate the dark, venturing outside yourself.

Depart from the mind.

Disconnect from the world.

Here, you are not a fat. Here, you are not a bad husband. Here, you do not suck.

Give in.

Tautness releases, like the unclenching of a fist, like a held sigh. Though you are vulnerable—laid out bare, face down—this vulnerability is a type of freedom.

Shirtless. Pants-less. Stripped.

You chose to be here. You chose to have a stranger touch you. There is power in choice.

Focus.

Respond to a stranger's touch with sighs and grunts.

Kneading. Rubbing. Pressing.

A relationship forms. Between you and your body. You hear it, the talk of the body, coming in the rush and whirl of blood in the veins, the stretch and creak of muscle and bone and tendon. You feel it, too, all your muscles, even the ones you do not normally think about, like the forgotten ones in the fingers and toes where every nerve awakens, like fire.

You know your body. You know what your body wants and needs. You know, alas, that your body wants.

My body wanted.

During the hardest parts of the marriage, I scheduled massages three times a week, which was heavy on the bank account. I didn't care. I carried tension in every extremity, tension that made me into a massive knot. My shoulders were high, as if in the state of perpetual shrug. I could barely turn my neck because the cords on either side were thick and taut.

Massages were the few things I looked forward to, the one moment in my day where I let go. My want of them reflected how badly I needed to be touched, how I needed someone to know my body, feel my body, register my body, even if it was a stranger. I wasn't craving intimacy, though massages are quite intimate. I craved the simplicity of hands on a body. Even if those hands did strange things, which is to say, I have had plenty of strange massages.

Like the one in Arkansas, where an older woman played Russian military music. "You are fat because you retain water," she said. "Your ankles are bloated. We sell here a great juicer. It will solve all your problems."

Like the one in a small town in Alabama, with the massage therapist who was going through what sounded like a divorce. She muttered "asshole" a few times under her breath, and then left midway to berate her ex on the phone, returning to finish the session in tears.

Like the one in Denver. The massage therapist massaged my stomach. Round and round and round his hands went. Round and round and round my belly button. My stomach growled. It was telling him off. Then, I farted.

Like the one in Pattaya, Thailand, where the massage therapist was tiny and believed she had psychic abilities. "I can heal without touching." Her hands hovered above my body. "I can feel a lot of hurt here," she said and proceeded to do nothing about it.

Like the massage in Hong Kong, at this seedy place a friend took me to. The massage therapist found my body amusing. She pinched my nipples and giggled. She pulled chest hair. Then she offered a Happy Ending, which I politely declined.

The massages I sought out were the ones that left me in pain. I wanted a massage therapist with iron fingers, like Paan, who would dig into me, through me, make me scream and cry, sigh and pant. I wanted a massage therapist who would press me to my limits. I believed I looked for that in a partner, too.

"Is this hard enough?"

"No, harder."

Pain was punishment. It was reward. The two were interchangeable, the science of pleasure and pain nearly identical. Endorphins reshape pain into pleasure; serotonin and melatonin soothe the body; epinephrine and norepinephrine creates the "rush" we feel. But on the psychological level, the pleasures of pain allowed my brain to forget the self. In the grips of a painful massage, I do not dwell on abstraction. Rather I focus on something real, like those fingers tunneling into the flesh of my neck, or the sharp elbow scorching along a hamstring. The massages I yearn for leave me sucking in my breath, tears coalescing in at the corner of my eyes, when I am at the edge of tapping out, screaming "uncle." Pain fulfills a need. Pain breaks me in all the right ways. Pain puts me in the present moment.

"Is this hard enough?"

"No, harder."

I mentioned the idea of pain during sex therapy. One of our home-work assignments was to provide a list of things we wanted to try in the bedroom. This was the hardest assignment. I put it off until an hour before the session, but I had been thinking about it nonstop. Katie's list involved frequency ("I like to have sex twice a week") and phrases she did not want me to say ("I suck," "Thank you," "Sorry").

My list: Spanking. Striking. Binding. Blindfolding.

"I can't do that," Katie said.

I knew she couldn't.

"Is that what you really want?"

I didn't know what I really wanted. I only knew what we had was not working. I only knew I escaped into the gym where I pumped way too much iron and ran way too many miles, so my body could experience another type of pain.

"Is this hard enough?"

"No, harder."

For the past year, I let myself go into fantasy. I fulfilled what I had written on that list. I added a few items. I put myself in the state of mind similar to when I am on the massage table. I erased myself, in order to enjoy myself. Part of the thrill was the illicitness. Part of the thrill was being able to feel the things I did not feel in my marriage. Some of the women craved the same. Some were forthright with what they wanted.

"Put your hands around my throat."

"Bite me here."

"Tie me up."

Physicality.

Exertion.

Blossoming bruises on inner thighs.

Long scratches on backs.

Teeth marks on necks.

Nipples swollen and red.

No one knew this Ira. Katie would not have recognized this Ira. I felt like Clark Kent, Superman's alter ego, this nice guy who would not harm a fly by day, who said thank you too often. By night, I transformed into . . . into . . . what? A sex fiend? That wasn't right. I transformed into . . . someone I was not? That wasn't true either. I was still a nice guy. I was also the nice guy who sucked skin until it puckered and discolored, who bit to hear pleasurable screams, who enjoyed the startling sound of a slap. I was the nice guy, who allowed pain to spread and feed on every part of my body.

I was a nice guy.

Still a nice guy.

Nice guy.

Nice guy?

Do you hear me, Ira? You are nice.

"Is this hard enough?"

"No, harder."

*

Paan forces her fingers into my forearm, as if she is plucking the strings on a harp. This pain almost brings music. The tendons in my arm are overly tight, and she keeps at it. I take deep breaths; jaw tight with a prepared scream.

"Miss Katie," Paan says. "How is she doing, sir?"

"Fine." Searing breath.

"Why didn't she come with you, sir?"

"Work." Breath.

"Does she still not like having her feet touched? I remember she said, 'No feet, no feet.' She spoke Thai very well."

"Yes." Breath. "Feet." Breath. "No." Breath. "Touch." Breath.

"Miss was funny. She liked to talk."

Breath.

"Not like you. You are quiet, sir."

Breath.

"Please tell Miss to come back."

Breath.

Time passes. Time is the movement of fingers and elbows along the body.

Paan digs into the base of my skull, under it. I sit cross-legged, back bent. Her elbows work into my shoulders, her fingers my head. My muscles down my neck are nearly impenetrable. But Paan gets in. Relentless. This tightness is the reason, I believe, for my daily headaches. The reason I keep cracking my neck to release some of the stiffness, if only for a moment. Paan grunts. Occasionally, she stops to sop sweat away with a handkerchief. Her touch takes me to the threshold of what I can take. I am close to giving in. Close to saying, "Lighter, please." My breath is the sound of a sizzling pan.

"Does it hurt, sir?"

"Yes."

"Does it feel good, sir?"

"Yes."

"You carry a lot of tension."

Heat rushes to the top of my head, buzzes. For a moment my vision blurs. I get lightheaded, faint. Paan's voice is a far whisper.

"There has been a lot on your mind lately, huh?"

July 10

On this day last year, after reading Katie's email, I could not bring myself to get out of bed. The clock read 10:00 a.m. It kept reading 10:00 a.m. Everything had stopped—in that room, in that bed, in my body. I wrapped a blanket around me tight. It was my father's old blanket, a rustic orange and brown comforter that still smelled like him, old aftershave and Irish Spring soap. I wondered why my mother kept this blanket, why it had not been burned or thrown out or donated. I wondered why I thought about my father.

*

On this day last year, when I finally got myself together, I smiled when my family said, "Happy anniversary!" My mother's twin sisters danced circles around me. My uncle shook my hand. My mother and Aunty Sue said twelve years of marriage was a landmark occasion, both planting kisses on either side of my face.

"We wish Katie was here," they said. "Have you called her?"

I smiled. Her email loud in my head.

The amount of effort it took to curl my lips up, to put on a happy face that just wanted to melt, left me weary.

Eventually, I failed.

I replayed the entire marriage, the whole of our relationship.

I thought of the beginning. The quiet times, the simple memories that surfaced: searching for a wren in an Arizona bramble, a fiery sunset over Lake Ontario, the slow ease of floating along the Gunnison River in Colorado. I recalled our first kiss, in the attic of the 1910 farmhouse, the lights turned off. "If it's in the dark, it doesn't exist," Katie said. And maybe it didn't. Maybe none of it did. Maybe our relationship was one long fantasy.

When the heart breaks, it disintegrates. Every memory deteriorating, photos to fire.

In my melancholy, I forgot I was out in the world, at my favorite restaurant, Yangzi Giang, with my family who wanted to celebrate a twelfth anniversary but instead watched me poke at the shrimp dumpling, at the strands of stir-fried noodles, at the salt-crusted calamari.

What I must've looked like to them. What they must've thought.

"Are you sick?" one of the twins said.

"Is your stomach okay?" said my uncle.

I aimed my eyes at the oily swirls on my plate.

*

On this day two years ago, our eleventh anniversary, we ate at the same restaurant, with the same relatives, at the same table. Katie was with me, our last trip to Thailand together. Our relationship was fraying, though we didn't let on to our unhappiness.

Throughout the trip my relatives made sure Katie was satiated. That day was no different. They chopstick-ed noodles and dumplings onto her plate. They ordered nearly everything from the menu, telling her to try this and this. My family loved Katie. She loved them. They showed their love with food. It was one of the ways they communicated, the appetite a powerful language. If Katie liked a piece of cake, the next day the refrigerator would be filled with that cake. She reciprocated their love by eating as much as she could, but was always astounded by the amount Thais ate throughout the day. "Like hobbits," she would say.

"Is the food good?" my family asked.

"Very," Katie said in her best Thai, clumsy with chopsticks. A dumpling splashed into a puddle of soy sauce and speckled her shirt.

"Your Thai is so clear," they said. "You want a fork?"

"No thank you," Katie said. "Ira teaches me only the bad words."

My mother pinched my ear. "Not nice," she said.

The wait staff skipped around the table, refilling our chrysanthemum tea, responding to our every whim, and bringing out platters of food and steaming baskets of dumplings. In Chiang Mai, everyone is welcomed, the reason I am so fond of this place, why I consider it my second home. Peace pervades the city. "It's like another Illinois," Katie would say. "But with lots of Thais."

But it wasn't Illinois. Far from Illinois. Would never be Illinois.

Katie and I had talked about the possibility of getting a small condo in Chiang Mai. I wanted to make another home for us here, even after my mother and aunt passing on. I feared Thailand would disappear when they did. A home would anchor me.

But there was another reason.

I wanted to keep Katie to myself. Guard her from the world that seemed to increasingly tug and take her further and further away from me. For Katie, living in Chiang Mai would never be an option. It would be hard for her to be without her family, which was her heart. It would be hard to be away from Illinois and all that it represented in her life. Though she liked Thailand—loved it—she could only stay for two weeks at a time, the magnetic pull of home too strong.

"How much do condos cost?" I said.

"What?" said one of the twins.

"Just thinking," I said.

Katie ate a dumpling whole.

My mother raised an eyebrow.

"This is a great idea," said the other twin.

"You guys can teach at an international school."

"We can have you near us forever."

"Then we can feed you all the time! Right, Big Sis?"

Big Sis, my mother, smiled. This was her dream. She wanted nothing more than to have her son near. When I was a young, my mother always said, "You will marry someone Thai and take care of your momma, okay? This is your duty." But she recognized the impossibility of this, sensing Katie's reluctance.

"Your life is in America," my mother said. "What's here for you?"

"Family," I said.

"You have family there, too," said my mother. "They take good care of you."

"But who will take care of you. And Aunty Sue."

"I'm okay," my mother said. "We are okay."

Only the sounds of nervous rustling penetrated the quiet. The twins wanted to speak against my mother, to convince her that moving to Chiang Mai would be a good idea, her son and daughter-in-law close by, but they could tell it was not the time to cross their elder sister.

"What do you think, Katie?" my mother asked.

Katie straightened in her chair and wiped her mouth with a napkin. She was forever proper. "I love it here, but it would be hard for me."

My mother nodded. "You see."

I would be asking for too much. To uproot and move to a country where Katie could not speak the language, save for a few words. To leave friends and family. To be alone, far from home, with a husband she was not sure she wanted to be with.

I also saw it as a slight—a rejection of my family, my culture. I saw it as a dismissal of what I held close to the bone. I saw it as a rejection of me.

I shoveled a mound of noodles in my mouth.

"Happy anniversary!" the twins said, trying to alleviate the tension. "More food, Katie?"

Katie showed them the flat of her palm. "Eem," she said. *I've had enough.*

VI

Monarchs and Memory

In the fifth year of our marriage, Katie and I walked a trail around the backside of a famous golf course in Maui. We dipped into hills and canyons, taking us farther away from the overly chemical-ed fairways and greens. After a trek in a small canyon, we climbed up a muddy embankment and arrived in a meadow of prairie grass and wild flowers. Also in this meadow: millions of monarchs. It was as if our arrival had awakened an entire planet of butterflies. Katie and I were alone—only us and the remnants of fallen trees, stripped of their bark, lying silver in the sun; only us and the frangipani tree with vivid red blooms. Only us. I had the impulse to spin, like Maria in *The Sound of Music*, but was afraid I'd step on or hit a monarch out of flight; there were that many. This was their world, and we were their guests. A few settled onto our shoulders. One perched on the brim of Katie's hat. The closer we looked—on park benches, on quivering leaves—we noticed thousands of green chrysalises, thousands of caterpillars climbing up long strands of grass and trees, preparing for their next incarnation. When I turned to tell Katie the obvious—that this was beautiful, amazing, paradise—I found her moved into silently crying. I decided to say nothing but watch her and the hovering monarchs haloing her head.

When a marriage ends it doesn't erase these moments. Now, every monarch I see harkens to those fields in Maui. And in those fields are all the other joyous moments of our relationship. I want to keep them there. Call upon them when I need.

I wonder if this is the same impulse as the collecting of butterflies, pinning them under a pane of glass. Part of me wishes to let them free, have air pass through their paper wings again. But this would be impossible. What was gone is gone. Part of me wants to possess the unpossessable. Though stilled behind glass, my imagination makes them flutter and flit, makes me trail their every movement. That's part of the enchantment of a butterfly. Or a memory. It's hypnotic, the way our eyes move, the way they follow flight, as if being taken by the hand to a mythical world of the impossible.

This field in Maui is a mythical world of the impossible.

The good of the marriage exists there.

The Broken Hearts Club

When I was young, trips to Thailand were about my cousins. It does not feel like that long ago I was playing video games or throwing Chinese stars against palm trees or finding mischief in empty fields. Now we have all grown up, some have married and divorced, gone through relationships like toilet paper. This gathering—we like to call it—is the Broken Hearts Club.

I meet them at CentralWorld Mall in the busiest district of Bangkok, at a Chinese restaurant that has received a Michelin star. When I walk into the restaurant, the workers clap. They are famous for their *xiao long bao*, soup-filled dumplings, and the servers wear white hats like old-fashioned nurses. It is fancier than the establishments my mother and Aunty Sue take me to, which are usually street-side, which usually cost no more than five dollars for three people.

I hadn't talked to Oil, since she came for a day in Chiang Mai. Now with her brothers she's even livelier. "I really hate your tattoos," Oil says. Her hair is frayed at the edges; she walked from work in the heat. She makes a move toward my legs. "I'm going to rub them off."

"I have a new one," I say. "On my shoulder."

"I'm going to kill you." She threatens to hit the top of my head.

Across from me is Oat, Oil's older brother and the oldest of the cousins. When he was younger, everyone called him "Pig Legs" because of his thick thighs. Now, he has slimmed up and tries to resist age with weekly Botox shots and skin-whitening procedures. He was married ten years ago, but was soon divorced because he spent too much time on the golf course. He has a girlfriend no one's met.

"How many tattoos do you have?" Oat asks.

"Six," I say and point to those places.

"What do your students think?"

"That I'm the raddest professor in town."

And then there is Ant. When we were boys, we drove my mother mad with mischief. We played tricks on Oil, like spraying her with water or hiding her schoolbag. We lobbed pebbles at the ornery old neighbor until he chased us with his walking stick. Ant grew to be handsome, always wearing the trendiest clothes. His hair looks like it belongs in a Japanese cartoon. I wonder how many cans of hairspray he uses to keep his floppy bangs up. He has never been married and does not look like he ever will.

"Ant, how's your girlfriend?" I ask.

He smiles, his braces make him look younger that the forty-two he is.

"He has a new one," Oil says.

"Another one?" The last one I met a year ago was a bikini model for motorcycles. I don't remember her name, but I remember her bosoms because she wore a top that V-ed deep down her chest. My mother said they were like two bowling balls ready to roll out.

"What does she do?" I ask.

The table goes quiet. The cousins stare at one another, smirking.

"Well," Ant says, "she's a go-go dancer."

"In America," I say, "you are what we call a 'player.'"

When the food arrives, I dig in. Oil orders almost the entire menu, but as usual she will not eat much of anything. We mix pepper sauce and soy into little bowls and dip our dumplings in them. Our table is filled with dumplings—crab, pork, shrimp, like pristine white seashells. There are also fried wontons filled with scallops and chives. Steamed Chinese broccoli with oyster sauce. Sesame oil jellyfish. My cousins notice their American relative likes his food spicy like them.

We eat and laugh. They ask about work and writing. They ask how my father is. They want to know what my days are like in America.

After a bit Oat says, "What happened with Katie?"

I shrug, mouth full of dumpling. "We wanted different things."

"I had a feeling," Ant says.

"And now we hear you have a new friend," Oil says. "The one with the hard name."

The thought of Deedra brings a joy I had not expected, a warmth that spreads inside of me like the soup dumplings that burst and steam in my mouth. I want to share her with my cousins in a way I had not wanted to with my aunt and mother. I want to tell them everything. How we met. Who made the first move. What her kisses feel like. The obstacles that are and were in the way, yet somehow we are still together. I do not know whether this will last. I don't care. "One day at a time," we keep telling each other.

"Do you have a picture?" Oat says.

I show them the ones on my phone. They ooh and ahh. They say she is gorgeous. They love how dark her hair is, and her eyes remind them of flecked jade.

"You're the player," Ant says.

"Were you heartbroken?" asks Oat.

"Very," I say.

"That's a dumb question," Oil says. "Weren't you?"

Oat nods and smiles. "But I had friends and they took me out every night. To strip clubs. And they wanted me to give the dancers tips, but you had to put the money in their underwear. I was so shy I couldn't look. But after a few weeks . . ."

"And a lot of whiskey," Ant says.

"And a lot of whiskey," says Oat, "it got easier."

Oil rolls her eyes. Shakes her head. "Boys."

Boys. We do stupid things.

When I came back to the States last year, I didn't want to be around anyone. Katie was packing her things to leave for Illinois, and because I could not be in the house, I went out on my own—to bars, to coffee shops, to malls. Friends would call to check in, but I never answered. They would try to reach me, leaving messages and emails I would never reply to. The thought of seeing them filled me with a dread I couldn't explain. I felt like I had failed them, too. I convinced myself that I didn't want anyone anymore anyway. I didn't need them. Like my father, perhaps I was meant to be alone. Perhaps it was my lot in life.

But no matter how hard I tried to hide, my friends found me. Dee-dra found me. And despite my resistance, love found me. "The world becomes problematic when you hesitate to love." I read that somewhere, in a Buddhist magazine, I believe. It's what I carry with me. It's what my cousins carry with them, how they keep going despite their broken hearts, how they believe in their existence in the world.

"I'm full," Oil says.

"Me too," Oat says.

Ant nods.

Full. Brimming. Overflowing.

To Have, to Hold

Holding Deedra's hand is the thought that weaves in and out of my day the way her fingers do. I thought about her hands at the *talad*, as a woman wearing a hairnet deep-fried chicken drumsticks. I thought about them as Tui weaved through Bangkok traffic, asking me how much gas is in America. I thought about her hands when I put mine together and paid my respects to a statue of Guanyin—goddess of compassion—at the entrance of Tui's street.

It was her fingers I imagined running through my hair when I showered this morning. It was her fingers I imagined digging into my skin, leaving crescent-shaped indentations. It was her fingers I imagined kneading the fears I'd gathered in my shoulders the night I left. How slender they are. How each one contains willowy constellations of freckles. When we are together, she takes pleasure in playing with my calluses at the base of my ring and middle fingers—"dude," she says, "moisturize"—or how she squeezes my hand like a heartbeat. She laces and interlaces her fingers around mine, searching for the most comfortable position, searching until she is satisfied. I think about our laughter when we compare hands, how mine swallows hers. Or, after making love, how her hand in mine seems a natural and perfect place to be.

"I miss holding your hand," she says on the phone this morning. "It brings me peace."

*

The day goes by slowly. It is like this when I am with my mother and aunt, who are older and less active. It is like this when we stay at Tui

195

and Bee's house with no transportation, when they spend most of their days at work. But where would we go anyway? Bangkok traffic is sludge through a rusted pipe.

Days like this I spend most of the time holding my mother's hand. When I am back in the States, especially this last year, I work so hard I forget my other life across the ocean. Sometimes I don't call as often. Weeks go by, months.

Before my mother moved back to Thailand, when she and Aunty Sue lived and worked in Chicago, she would call at the exact time every evening, 9:00 p.m. When the phone rang Katie would say, "It's for you," without having to answer, chuckling at my mother's routine. Those 9:00 p.m. calls were a comfort, even when we made fun of them, even when Katie called me Mama's Boy. Those 9:00 p.m. calls, the vibrato of the ringing phone, was an indication that my mother was doing well, that she was thinking of me, that I was loved. It was similar to Pavlov's bell. When I heard the phone, I would get a mom treat. I didn't realize how much I would miss the sound of a phone, any phone, when evening came. It was like a kiss goodnight, a reassuring hand from across state lines, an *I love you* in repetitious ringing.

That year when I tried to distract myself with everything—work and sex and working out—I still could not stave off loneliness. It was during these moments I was acutely aware what it meant to be an immigrant's son, a boy whose entire family existed over a wide ocean. And then it would happen, this sudden surge of sadness, this sudden realization of how alone I was, without mother or wife or even dogs, in an empty house of packed boxes, and how it made me clench and unclench my hands, as if I were trying to grasp something, hold something. And then, in the midst of this sadness, I would go out to the local bar. Drink and flirt. Find someone to touch.

What I craved most was a hand on my hand, on my leg, on the back of my neck. A squeeze. Fingers doing the job of fingers. There is something about a hand that makes me realize how utterly human we are, how alive, how blood rushes through us, how we are meant to connect, how our first impulse when we emerge into the world is to cling to something so desperately with these curious things we call fingers. Montaigne said:

"Behold the hands, how they promise, conjure, appeal, menace, pray, supplicate, refuse, beckon, interrogate, admire, confess, cringe, instruct, command, mock and what not besides, with a variation and multiplication of variation which makes the tongue envious."

My mother does not know Montaigne, but she does know my hands, knows them better than I do, knows them the way a mother knows them. She knew them from infancy, and she knew them even before that, when I lived in the water world of her womb, pushing and prodding from within. And she knows them now, holding my hand and bouncing it in her own like a beanbag or ball.

"So heavy," she says. We are outside, on the marble porch, the sun hot on our skin, the marble cool on our feet.

"Look." I point to the veins on my hand, like thick worms, a new development since I started lifting weights. Even more than my weight loss, I am proud of these veins under my skin that run and disappear into the apex of my knuckles. They instill in me a sense of masculinity, as do the calluses at the base of all my fingers. These are hands like my father's. When I was a boy, I marveled at their strength, at their ability to open any bottle, fix any car.

"I have them, too," she says. She does, thick, bluish green, snaking under paper skin. I know my mother's hands, too, and each year I visit her hands change, the look of them, the feel of them. They have become thinner, lighter, more bone than flesh. Not until she grabs and holds and squeezes my hand do I register familiarity.

This, I hope, will never change.

*

It is ten at night. Bee is driving us home from a twenty-four-hour grocery store after an unsuccessful search for lychee-flavored ice cream, something I was jonesing for. Traffic is stop and go, so I take in the city after the sun goes down.

At night, Bangkok comes alive in a different way. Neon lights brighten up the dark. Bars are open, and leggy Thai women sit at round tables, waiting for paying men. Food vendors crowd the sidewalks—noodles, boiled rice, hot and spicy stir-fries. Each stall is lit up with fluorescents. Patrons sit at fold-up tables, on plastic chairs.

Bee points to a crowd of university students gathered around a noodle shop. "It's one of the best in city," she says. The vendor works like a machine, moving quickly and diligently. Straining noodles, ladling broth, spooning fried garlic, cilantro and scallions. Each bowl of noodles takes about seven seconds to complete, fast food at its fastest. A line forms around her. She's popular because of the food, yes, but also because of her precision. What she offers is more than sustenance, but a supreme artistry of food, the ultimate example of how culinary preparation is paramount in this country.

I notice Bee's eyes traveling to a couple. They stand hand in hand. The girl leans her ponytailed head on her boyfriend's shoulder. The boyfriend kisses the top of her head. I watch their hands, how tightly they hold onto each other, how I can see the outlined bone structure of each finger. They hold on, as if they are afraid some invisible force will come and pry them apart.

"But a man reached for a woman's hand and she reached for his hand and they leaped out the window holding hands," wrote Brian Doyle in his essay "Leap," the startling image of two people plummeting out of the south tower of the World Trade Center; their last act of life, love.

It is love, isn't it? Love in the simplest of forms. It is instinctive. Flesh against flesh. Doyle again: "His hand and her hand nestled in each other with such succinct ancient naked stunning perfect simple ferocious love."

Bee sighs. "Kids nowadays. So much sweet." In her voice is envy, thick like syrup.

Flowers

Aunty Sue used to grow jasmine in a plastic green pot when we lived in Chicago. She put the jasmine plant in the front bay windows of our home, so it would catch the rays of the rising sun. At night, she aimed a few plant lights onto it. There was a science to her watering. She would pinch a finger full of soil and rub it in her palms. If the soil smeared like paint, then a little water was necessary; if it spread like dust, a bit more. My aunt loved this plant, more than the Thai peppers she grew, or the holy basil, or the bitter melons and cucumbers. When the jasmine bloomed, there was a noticeable difference in the house. When my father lived with us, before the divorce, he would bounce down the stairs and take an exaggerated breath. "It smells like home," he would say, and both my mother and Aunty Sue would concur with laughter. For this reason I think of the jasmine as the family I once had. The same way I think of hyacinths as the first years of my marriage, when Katie and I lived in central New York, crazy for color after a long winter. When the hyacinths bloomed, we cut and put them all over the house, breathing in an air so sweet, a marriage even sweeter.

I am back in Chiang Mai, stuck at a traffic light. A woman goes between cars selling jasmine garlands. They are typically used as offerings to sprit houses and statues of Buddha, but I like to hang them on the posts of my bed, their fragrance sweet and delicious. There is nothing like waking to the smell of jasmine; it is as if you've discovered heaven, as if you've been born into a world of flowers.

I can't keep my eyes off the woman selling jasmine garlands in the middle of the street. She is here every day at this intersection, across from Chiang Mai University and a dental practice, wearing the same withered straw hat, selling the same white garlands. The woman's face is dark like bark, lines deep around her eyes and the sides of her mouth. She wears no expression. She extends her right hand and ten garlands hang off her wrists and arms.

I have been coming to Chiang Mai for over ten years, and it is this same woman I have seen since then. I wonder what it is like to live the life of flowers. What is it like to make these garlands day in, day out? What is it like to walk the centerline of the street peddling art in the form of blooms? Sometimes we purchase garlands from her, especially on Buddhist holidays. My aunt rolls down the window, asks for six of the freshest, and the woman smiles and tells us the price. It is a brief exchange, no more than a couple of seconds.

Today, we speed by, late for my mother's doctor's appointment, a routine checkup. I turn to watch the woman, her body becoming smaller and smaller, her arm stretched out like a branch with hanging white moss.

Some things remain constant.

Night then day. Day then night.

Somewhere a flower is in bloom.

*

At the flirting stage of the relationship, Deedra gave me a list of things I should never get her: expensive jewelry, chocolates, a shopping spree in a crowded mall. "And don't send me flowers," she said. "I'm not a flower girl."

"What about pictures of flowers?" I said.

She never said no.

Now, I'm obsessed. I have risked my life to stand in the median of a busy highway to snap a picture of a lone cosmos. I have stopped in the middle of the sidewalk to zoom in on a snapdragon. In the States, my friends think I have gone batty, pausing at every flower I encounter. "Jesus," they'd say. "Let's go." Even here, I have made my uncles and aunts stop the car so I can jump out and snap a picture of something I don't know the name of; once on a small road up a mountain, I burst out the door to capture a firework of blood red petals, the car still moving.

"You almost gave me a heart attack," my mother said and pinched my nose until I teared up.

The world is covered with flowers. I don't have to travel far to find one. Even in the most unpleasant of places, even in the urban sprawls of cities where the color of concrete seems to suffocate everything and litter floats and clots the veins of sewers, I find flora. One of my best friends, Claire, tells me that this might be the most romantic thing she has ever heard someone doing. Claire's a tall sunflower; she drinks up life everywhere she goes.

When you search for flowers, you see people as them too. The twins, my mother's youngest sisters, are sweet-smelling honeysuckle. Bee, a chocolate orchid. Aunty Sue, a hungry-mouthed hibiscus. And my mother is a star-shaped purple lotus that blooms everywhere in Thailand.

Every day I send a picture of a flower to Deedra. It does strike me as childish. I laugh at the lengths I go to get a picture. It reminds me of when I was twelve, trying to win the hand of Brenna Murphy with a bouquet of dandelions, or when I was eighteen secretly sending a dozen roses to Christine Glader, or all the hundreds of blooms and blossoms I have given Katie.

"Don't forget my flower," Deedra says on the phone.

I want to open my chest and show her the blooming of my heart.

Michael Chang

It was not always bad. It was almost all good. Katie and I went the world together. We enjoyed each other's company, each other's conversation. So many nights we would stay up and just talk, about anything and everything. It is these moments I miss most, when one thought passes from mouth to ear carried by the bridge of mutual understanding. It was the intimacy of words that brought us together, words that created in me a vessel of love because I was loved.

Once, when the winter in Oswego, New York, our first home, was particularly horrendous, when the spring came, Katie and I cultivated a large garden in a space where an above ground pool used to be. This garden was our summer backyard project. Because of the long winter, the two of us planned the garden, imagining splashes of colors once the weather warmed. I drew plans like an architect. Katie picked out color combinations. We ordered bulbs from bulb catalogues. Each week, our mailman would traverse our slick and icy driveway to deliver a box of something we would put in the garden; this was why we believed our mailman had a severe dislike of us, the interracial couple who received too many packages. But Katie and I were obsessed. We subscribed to gardening magazines. Our favorite channel on TV was the Home and Garden network.

When the first thaw happened, we went into the backyard and began our work. At the end of the day, we were covered in dirt, our faces streaked with sweat and grime, but we were proud of what we were creating, this rectangle garden filled with snapdragons, sunflowers, dahlias, hyacinths, tulips, peonies, roses, and so much more.

In the early spring, Katie and I went to a tree nursery for a Japanese maple. I had always wanted one, enamored with their delicate leaves, their twisting trunks. We reserved a spot in the garden for the maple we named Michael Chang, after my favorite professional tennis player, who was small in stature yet mighty. We placed two Adirondack chairs beside Michael Chang, and most of that summer—most of every summer in Oswego—we read in that garden, read and sipped tea and enjoyed the flora world we created.

After we separated, on one lonely night, I called Katie. That night was particularly difficult. I had come home after an evening with a woman who was everything Katie wasn't, and because Katie had been gone for about a month, this woman, who was pleasant, who had three kids and taught yoga on the weekends, who touched when she talked—my arm, my leg, my cheek—this woman in her inverse of Katie made me think of Katie. It was the beginning of October, near Katie's birthday, and she was on my mind. Deep down I knew our time as a married couple was over, but I held on to the thought that maybe it wasn't.

When she picked up the phone, I pretended to have a normal conversation. She listened. She laughed. She must've heard something in my voice. I don't remember much of what we talked about, but we ended up talking about the garden in New York.

"I wonder how Michael Chang is doing," she said.

"I was thinking about him the other day."

"He was getting big when we left."

"Spreading like a red cloud."

"Remember the ice storm?"

"It cracked two branches."

"I almost cried," she said.

"But he came back."

"He's strong."

"I wonder."

"Me too."

Michael Chang was those years in central New York, the weight of the snow he held each winter, his greed to grow and spread to other parts of the garden, pushing the heads of the *Echinacea* off to the side, becoming a beautiful obstruction on the garden path. We wanted him to continue to grow. We were growing with him. We wanted him to take over the garden, the house, then the world. Michael Chang was a world. Under him bunnies rested. Cardinals sang on the tip of his limbs. Robins pecked worms from his ground. Our dogs napped under his shadow. He never grew over four feet tall, but he spread, each year wider and wider.

"I hope he is being taken care of," Katie said.

"I hope no one cut him down," I said.

Signs

Before Katie and I moved to Florida, we were invaded by turtles. They were everywhere. We'd see them perched on logs at the edges of ponds. When we went to meet with our real estate agent, the wallpaper in her remodeled office was a pastel collage of turtles. My old friend from the Chicago 'hood, David "Turtle" Martinez, contacted me out of the blue to catch up on life. It seemed we couldn't rid ourselves of turtles.

I had accepted a job in Florida that would start in the beginning of August, and Katie and I were busy getting our log cabin ready to sell. Our married life began in Oswego, New York, and for six years we had lived and loved each other during the long stretches of winter.

It had been a difficult year. Katie's mother passed away, and her father was battling dementia. To compound things, Katie and I lived three hours apart. She had accepted a teaching position at a small college in northern New York, coming home on weekends. That winter was harsh. Winters in central New York were always brutal, the lake-effect snow heavy and deep, the wind always whipping the skin raw.

After the death of her mother, Katie entered a dark depression. No matter what I did or said, I couldn't reach her. Daily, after the school year ended, I would find her crying outside in the garden, our two cocker spaniels snuggled at her feet. Meanwhile, I wasn't faring any better, becoming more and more sedentary, never wanting to leave the house except for work. Anxiety attacks revved my heart, keeping me sleepless for days. Everything kept me on edge and made me too aware of my body and its flaws. Most days I found myself on the couch, in my head, spinning my brain into a rut.

This would be the first rift in our lives. It wasn't caused by an argument, and it wasn't because of what the other could not provide. It was our own suffering, our ghosts come to smother us, like the thick blankets of snow that whitewashed the world.

Every day that summer, someone came to fix something. Every day, we saw a turtle of some sort. In early June, Katie noticed swirls in the gravel of the driveway. The driveway was long, about two hundred feet, and we hired a truck to unload new gravel to cover the deep ruts caused by a muddy spring. These swirls Katie discovered were like crop circles—the wavy movement of water, the concentric spirals of galaxies. "Aliens," I said. "I think we are going to be abducted."

One night, Katie knocked on the front window and waved me outside. She was refilling the bird feeders, the cardinals singing their complaints, the finches flitting over empty feeders.

"You won't believe it," she said. "Come."

Katie led the way. There was a skip in her step. I hadn't seen this childlike excitement in a while. The hickories along the driveway were thick with leaves, and when the wind blew through them, the air carried a hum.

"There," Katie said. She pointed to the middle of the driveway, about thirty feet ahead of us.

I followed Katie's finger to two round lumps. They moved. They shivered. Then the sound of smothered pebbles.

"Turtles," Katie said. "They want to nest in the driveway."

We didn't go any further. It was evening, and the last drop of sun was casting the world into perpetual gray. It felt like I had entered a black-and-white movie, like I had somehow wandered into a place where time stopped.

"I think we should chase them across the way," I said.

Katie nodded.

"I think there might be something for them in the woods," I said.

Another nod.

A driveway was not a place to nest, I wanted to say, but I kept still and quiet because Katie kept still and quiet. We watched the business of turtles—how they rotated, how they tossed back gravel with their front flippers. They were digging, but with little success, the ground underneath still thawing from that cold winter. This didn't matter. They kept at it, kept trying to make a home.

But their future would not reside here. Our futures would not reside here. Katie and I had begun our move, physically and metaphorically, in different directions, to different destinations. We didn't know any of this yet. We knew only that we had each other. For the time being this was enough.

In the gray of evening, Katie smiled. "This is a gift," she said, "before we move on."

*

My family is on the lookout for signs wherever they go. If they see a car with a uniquely numbered license plate they write it down. They count how many doves are resting on the electrical lines outside the house each morning. They are always on the lookout for cats with strangely colored eyes. In the tourist district, they take note of the backpackers—who has blond or brown hair, who are wearing bandannas, and if there is a redhead among them then it is a sure sign to buy lottery tickets.

Today, they encounter a mango with two pits.

"Oh God," says Aunt Jeem, one of the twins. "Look at this." She thrusts the two-pitted mango at us, and my mother and Aunty Sue ohhhh and ahhhh. Juicy pulp hangs on the two pits, glistening. Aunt Jeem was midway into slicing it when she discovered the abnormality.

We sit outside on the porch. The sky is clear, the sun hot. I find myself in one of those moods—more contemplative, more reserved, most likely feeling the effects of spending my days with women over sixty-five for the past few weeks. I wear a hoodie, the hood over my head, even when the temperature is tipping into the high nineties.

"What does it mean?" my mother says.

"I don't know," Aunt Jeem says.

"Don't eat it," Aunty Sue says. "Give it to Buddha."

"No. Eat it," says my mother. "You can get pregnant again."

Aunt Jeem is the only one of the sisters still married. She has two sons, Thong, my partner in crime, one of them. She swats at my mother and makes a puffing sound. "It's all dried up down there, dear."

The three of them laugh. They go back and forth about down there. I recede deeper into my hood.

"If you plant this mango," Aunty Sue says, "the planet would be covered in mango trees."

"Too many flies then," my mother says, scrunching up her face. "If we eat it, good fortune comes our way."

Aunt Jeem nods. She cuts the mango into slices, quick with the knife. Juices run down her hands. She takes a quick slurp and says it is viscously sweet. She leaves no fruit on both of the pits. They are coral white. When she is done, she tells us to eat. "Good luck for everyone," she says.

"May we win the lottery," says my mother. "And maybe you," she nods at Aunty Sue, "will be less gassy."

"Probably not," Aunty Sue says.

"Tong," my mother says to me, "don't be sullen. Have a taste."

I'm not sullen, I tell her. Mangos make me go the bathroom. "Like almost immediately."

"Not this one," she says. "This one is special. Do you see? Do you see the seeds?"

They are smaller than usual, which makes me think it is one pit, but broken in half. But I don't say anything.

"He probably misses his honey," Aunt Jeem says.

"How do you say her name again?" My mother repeats Deedra's name over and over incorrectly. It has become the game of the trip.

"Does she like mango?" Aunt Jeem says.

"She loves mango."

"She hasn't had a mango until she comes to Thailand," Aunty Sue says.

"Will she come to Thailand?" says my mother.

"I hope so," I say. "If you say her name right."

Aunty Sue, ever knowledgeable, tells us the mango originated here in Thailand, millions of years ago, and a mango tree can live on for centuries, bearing fruit. It is why in India mango trees are used in wedding ceremonies, to bless the new couple with a future of many kids. "True story," she says. She takes a piece off of the plate and shoves it in my mouth. "Eat," she says. "It will make your boys swim faster."

*

Amid packing, Katie spent time researching turtles. We had seen so many that we couldn't chalk it up to coincidence. Or rather, we didn't want to. In our sadness, we were looking for some type of answer, a sign that our lives would get better, that this move was the right one. We had purchased a home in Tampa, which included a pool and hot tub and loads of space. The house was beautiful, set on a steep incline. Though it was located in a subdivision, our new home was elevated, higher than our neighbors', which seemed to isolate us from the neighborhood. We joked that the house was on the only hill in Florida.

Katie and I began to imagine our lives there. Spatially we already existed in that house, walking those rooms, swimming in that caged pool. We knew which direction the bed would face, where the leather sofa would sit, and what drawers our kitchen stuff would go in. We were there, and for me, a charge of excitement propelled me to work harder. I couldn't get out of New York fast enough. Katie shared that excitement, too, but she harbored many fears, fears that made her withdraw into her office, into herself.

"Turtles are about self-protection," she said one day. She had spent a couple of hours in her office, tapping away at the computer. "I looked it up."

I painted the front door a vivid red, a smudge of paint staining my cheek. "Hence the shell?"

"Turtles also mean taking a journey."

"We are about to go on one."

"But not only a physical one. A spiritual journey, too."

"This sounds new-agey," I said.

"We're talking signs and symbols," she said.

"Everything is going as it should then," I said.

"Seems that way."

"Seems this was meant to be."

"I hope so."

"The turtles are leading the way," I said.

Right before the job interview, Katie and I were in Maui, our second trip there. We had saved up so we could leave the gray of New York and spend our days on the beach. Both of us were enamored with snorkeling. Exploring the underwater world made me see how immense this planet was. Made me aware there was more to this earth than the ground I stood on, that I should not only aim my eyes skyward but also underneath beneath my feet.

Black Lava Rock was a popular snorkeling spot. Katie followed schools of rainbow fish. I marveled at the glowing coral. Then he came. A sea turtle. He emerged out of nowhere, swimming slowly through the haze of the ocean. He headed directly for me, swerving when he was only a few feet away. Katie took photos with an underwater camera, but I remained as still as possible. The turtle swam back and forth, as if doing figure eights around me. His shell was chipped at the edges, and there were long gashes from what I assumed were made by the blades of a motorboat. His aged face contained the wisdom of the planet, all the answers of the world gathered into those round, onyx eyes. I reached out, but then I feared my touch would scare it away. The turtle moved with little effort, his flippers propelling him through the water in short bursts. My eyes never left his. His never left mine. We had connected, like all those stories my mother used to tell me about Buddha and his ability to find companionship with any animal. I knew the turtle. The turtle knew me. We were interchangeable, the two of us. All my hopes, all my past lives, all my fears were under this great shell. If I stayed with him, I would be safe. I would not be so afraid of this future that seemed looming and uncertain. My biggest worry was the future. Years from now. Decades. Death. My worries were about the things that have not happened, might not happen. I dwelled in the *what if* for long stretches of time—witnessing catastrophes, failure, unhappiness. I saw myself alone. Which was illogical. Because I would have Katie. I would have friends. I would have family. This frightened me most of all. Being alone in the world. The turtle knew that. The turtle knew aloneness. He spent most of his life alone. And yet, he was content. Or seemed content. What does turtle contentment feel like? What does contentment feel like? He swam between my legs, grazing my calf, looking back at me once more, before disappearing in a few quick thrusts. I started to follow. I could still see the trail of bubbles the turtle left in its wake. Katie tugged at my swimming trunks, the strands of her hair billowing like sea grass. We were already far out, and I wasn't a good swimmer. It took a lot for me to turn away. The turtle wanted to tell me something, I was sure of it, lead me somewhere, I was sure of it.

I would tell a friend this later, and she said what I was doing was a type of suicide. To abandon logic and safety. To believe a sea turtle would guide me to some sort of understanding. But I truly believed. The way Katie and I believed in all turtles thereafter. They were telling us something. They were leading us somewhere. We needed to believe this.

*

I look for symbols everywhere I go. The shape of the clouds, like the ones above me, look like lips. Or the river stones on the ground are in the milky shade of Deedra's skin. Or the small baby in a basket at the market, anklet bells chiming when he tosses in his sleep, a reminder of the temple bells I fell in love with a few years ago on a deserted mountaintop.

My mother and aunts, however, are looking for something they can carry over into the next life. They believe that after sixty, the world is whispering messages to them, secrets they need to retain into their next incarnation.

I've always been drawn to the connectedness of all things, Jung's idea of synchronicity. What we think and do ripples out into every facet of our day. Like the strange orange cat in Florida. Like the strange conversation with Deedra about the orange cat in the neighborhood, the one we've named Thomas, who greets us every night with his melodic meows. Like orange cats suddenly creeping up in the writings of my students, cats peeking behind sentences, rubbing their flanks around the pillar of metaphor and the crumbles of a comma splice. Like the orange cat I saw a few hours later, walking a lonely wooded road near a marsh I'm sure is infested with gators. This has been happening with more frequency, this interconnectedness of all things. Aunty Sue engrained this idea over and over in my head: Poke a spider web and everything shivers. Here's another: The air we breathe is breathed by everyone.

There have been too many coincidences I can't overlook.

Like the orange cat. Like the turtles.

Or rather, my eyes are ever open to them, searching for what stands out, that harkens perhaps to a time long ago, a past where I was not a divorced English professor in love again, but a soldier riding an elephant into war. My brain makes meaning out of everything. Or tries to. It is no different from what my father does when he is staring at grids and telling his clients their fortune.

"Do you want a baby now?" my mother says. We wait for her prescriptions to be filled at the pharmacy. She says this in a public space, where patrons are all around us, a knack she possesses, like asking whether I still had diarrhea at a crowded food court. A few schoolgirls giggle and go about their business. The pharmacist smiles and quickly disappears to the back to fill my mother's order. "You might be too old. Maybe you should think hard about it." She's staving off disappointment. My mother has become accustomed to this. Wanting and not receiving. She does not want to hope too much. Nor does she want me to believe that this is expected of me.

"I'm happy," she says. "With the way things are."

*

A day before our drive to Florida, something was ambling across an isolated road. A turtle. I didn't want the turtle to be crushed under the wheels of oncoming traffic. I had seen too many crushed turtles in the last few weeks. The image of a shattered shell in a pool of pink came to me in nightmares.

I pulled the car over into some tall grass. The turtle was large, the size of a hubcap. It moved like it didn't have a care in the world—one slow, wobbly, step at a time. I approached it and said, "Hey guy." I didn't know why I spoke to the turtle. "Hey, I'm here to help you across, okay?"

My shadow fell over the turtle, and it shrunk into its shell, backing away.

The wind was loud that day, and the sun was bright. Summer came into full bloom in central New York, the leaves in the trees a crisp shade of green. Far down the road, a pickup truck was making its way toward me.

"I'm going to pick you up now, guy."

I bent down. The turtle hissed. I didn't know turtles hissed.

"I'm only here to serve," I said.

I put my hands along either side of its shell and hefted it up. It was a heavy sucker, like the can of paint I'd been hauling all over the house, touching up the walls. Before I could walk the turtle to the side of the road, its head curled around the shell, its neck long and wrinkly. It snapped at my fingers. The snap sounded like the crunch of dry wood.

I dropped him.

The turtle landed on its back.

I noticed my right hand wet.

A puddle formed around the upended turtle.

"You peed on me."

The turtle had peed on me. Its legs flailed helplessly. It hissed even louder.

I righted the turtle, flipping him over with my foot, while wiping my hand on my pants. The turtle didn't back down, his beaked mouth going for my big toe.

"Chill, guy," I said. "Go on."

The turtle didn't go on. He lunged at me once more, his head coming out like a jack in the box. The pickup was getting closer. Only a block away. It slowed.

I shooed the turtle.

"Shoo, guy, shoo."

The turtle didn't shoo.

I rounded the turtle as the turtle rounded me, like boxers in a ring. Only we weren't in a ring but in the middle of the road with a pickup that was sidling up the side of me to a stop.

Two white men sat in the truck, both with baseball caps and flannels though it was warm. They were in their mid-twenties, unshaven and expressionless. Not a smile. Not a scowl.

"Hey," I said.

They didn't say anything.

I pointed to the turtle. "Turtle," I said.

Not one word.

"Trying to help it along."

Nothing. They never looked at the turtle, still hissing. They kept their gaze on me, like dead-eyed mannequins.

Then they sped off, wheels screeching, leaving a long skid in the road and the smell of burnt rubber.

I stood and stared at the back of the truck. The turtle finally lost interest in me, making its way toward a flooded drainage ditch.

When I told Katie about it later, she laughed. She said I was lucky. It was probably a snapping turtle, she told me, and snapping turtles can extend their neck a foot out of their shells. "You could've lost a finger," she said.

What I didn't tell Katie was the danger I felt when the pickup neared. What I didn't tell her was the ghostly look on those two men's faces, who didn't register me as human. What I didn't tell her was I thought I could've died, could've been murdered, in the middle of nowhere, my body abandoned on that isolated road. In those slow seconds, I had imagined it all.

This was my anxiety talking.

But it was also a sign.

We needed to get the hell out of here. We needed to move as fast as we could. This I was certain of: we weren't going to survive here.

*

After the pharmacy, my uncle drives my mother and me out of the city and into the natural world. We were meeting the aunts at a small restaurant in the middle of nowhere that served the best fried tofu. "It was on TV," says my uncle. I say I'd go anywhere that was on TV.

We speed by empty fields at the foot of the mountains. I keep my eyes aimed out the window, hypnotized by the lulling land, going into a strange trance.

"Look," my mother says. "Do you see?"

On a dead rubber tree, in the middle of a green field, stood twenty storks. All of them facing a single direction.

"What does it mean?" I say, though I knew what they meant, how a new bundle came delivered on the wings of a stork. But I don't say anything.

My mother smiles and chuckles to herself. "We are buying lottery tickets today," she says.

July 10

On this day, for twelve years, I was married to one person, believing I was strong enough to make it work, believing divorce happened to weak people, like my father, who was weak, like my mother, who was weak. Weakness does not destroy marriages. Sometimes it is time that divides and cleaves. Sometimes it is desire and want. Sometimes you find yourself two different people, and the person you once were is no longer there. Sometimes it is love and its brutality. Sometimes.

*

On this day a year ago, in the evening, I began a reply to Katie's email. I couldn't get past the first line. I filled the page with beginnings.

Dear Katie, Happy anniversary . . .

Dear Katie, You are selfish

Dear Katie, You are heartless . . .

Dear Katie, How are you . . .

Dear Katie, I can change . . .

Dear Katie, What do you want from me . . .

Dear Katie, I hope this reply finds you well . . .

Dear Katie, Did you send this on our anniversary on purpose . . .

Dear Katie, I miss the dogs . . .

Dear Katie, I reject your request . . .

Dear Katie, I've done everything for you . . .

Dear Katie, Fuckin' shit motherfucker . . .

Dear Katie, My parents don't know what's wrong with me . . .

Dear Katie, Do whatever you want . . .

Dear Katie, I don't deserve you . . .
Dear Katie, I don't deserve this . . .
Dear Katie, You are right . . .
Dear Katie, You are so fuckin' wrong . . .
Dear Katie, This is stupid . . .
Dear Katie, I'm sorry . . .
Dear Katie, Dear Katie, Dear Katie. . . .

*

On this day a year ago, I turned the TV on loud, because the birds outside distracted me. I wanted them to shut the fuck up. To take their song elsewhere. Everything was too loud. Too fuckin' loud. Because to hear that a world was happening around me hurt too much. Everything had to stop and observe my suffering. I hated this thought. Fuckin' selfish. Melodramatic, like the soaps my mother and aunt gather to watch in the evenings, like the high school boy I once was, all angsty and emo, mourning the unrequited love of all my crushes. Once, I flipped a couch and raged my bedroom into a wreck. Once, I threw my algebra I book against the classroom chalkboard.

But in the cold of the room, I was without energy, without strength.

Outside birds sang. Outside the hacking cough of the neighbor. Outside the rapid ascent of a lizard in a tree.

The world was moving.

VII

At the Border

A few years ago, on a trip through Ayutthaya, Aunty Sue started to cry. I had never experienced this before. It happened without warning. One moment she was talking about the good old Chicago days as an ICU nurse, and the next she was all tears and snot. Because the day had been long and hot, because I was in a bad mood for a reason I don't recall, all I could think of was how ugly she was. Aunty Sue was an ugly crier. The ugliest. Throughout her life, she has been a handsome tomboy. She keeps her hair short. She never wears makeup. Her ears are not pierced. On the rare occasion she has worn a dress—like on my wedding day—it looks odd on her, like finding a starfish in a desert. She is the opposite of feminine, the opposite of my mother and her sisters who are ever aware of their appearance. So when she cried in the car that day, loud and messy, the only thing I could say was, "Stop crying. It's gross."

"I can't help it," she said. She pointed to the crumbling ruins outside the car window. We cruised by them every block or so. "It's so sad."

I never know what to say when someone cries, especially someone who never cries, especially someone who spent her years consoling me when I have cried. Stupidity spilled out of my mouth. "You're such a baby. Yuck."

"Why were they so ruthless?" Aunty Sue patted her eyes with Kleenex, blew her nose that sounded like a muffled horn.

"The Burmese?"

"Sut," she said, *Animals.*

"They're people, too," I said.

"People don't do this."

It was so unlike my aunt to be unreasonable. That characteristic belonged to my mother, who opted to stay behind on this trip because of a headache. Aunty Sue has always been the paragon of reason. She was the person who brought my mother and me back to center.

"The past is the past," I said, borrowing my mother's favorite phrase.

"The past is our present," she said. "Sometimes we can't let go."

Sometimes we can't. Sometimes there are images and memories that keep haunting, that stick to the core of us. Sometimes we go over them again and again and shiver. Five, ten, fifteen years later these memories echo back. Reverberate in our skulls. Freezes us up.

Many of my memories did not circle around what I did, but rather what I did not do. The moments I remained stagnant, like the evening in my father's minivan with Tracy Pine, and I was sixteen, and she waited for me to lean in and kiss her, but I kept both hands on the steering wheel. Or the times I watched my mother rail on my father, her voice high-pitched and cracking, her hands hitting his chest and face. Or all the times Katie wanted me to go on a walk with her, but instead I opted to sit and watch TV. Sometimes we suffer over what we do not do, what we should have done.

Aunty Sue shook her head. "They were close to taking our country."

"Why do you care?"

"When Thailand is scarred, my heart is scarred."

"But Thailand is no longer scarred."

"Scars never go away." Another ruin passed, a stunted pagoda, a Buddha charred and stripped of color.

"What about forgiveness?" I said.

"Never," she said. "I will always hate them."

Aunty Sue was resolute. I was tired. "You're such an ugly crier."

"Quiet." She threw her dirty Kleenex at my head.

I carry this moment with me as we are near the Myanmar border, Mae Sai, to shop for jade. En route, I call Deedra. Most of our conversations have been brief, about five minutes long. We either catch each other while one is going to sleep or has just woken up. Hearing her voice, no matter what time of day, sends a charge in me, like the sugar rush from the most decadent of chocolates. Our conversation makes Aunty Sue pucker her lips and say, jube, jube, *kiss, kiss*. Makes my mother say, "So sweet." Makes the twins talk about the splendor of young love.

On the phone, I tell Deedra I am entering the deep jungles of Burma to get her a gift. I say that I might not return, that a Burmese python might eat me whole. I could be like Jim Thompson, I tell her, the American who revitalized the Thai silk trade in the '40s and '50s, then mysteriously disappeared one day in the jungles of Malaysia.

"Are you kidding?" she says.

"The things I do for love," I say.

We arrive at Mai Sai in three hours, taking roads that wind and curve through the mountains. A stone's throw away is the country formerly known as Burma. Hundreds of markets cluster on either side of the border. The irony: the Thai side is known for jade, but most of it comes from Myanmar, while the Myanmar side is known for cheap DVDs and electronics from Thailand.

The land on either side of the border looks no different from the other—hilly, green, filled with vans and cars. Each side speaks a mixture of both languages; each side is busy selling, selling, selling. If you got rid of the border no one would know the difference, the same way Iowa bleeds into Nebraska seamlessly. It is hard to believe that in this cordial atmosphere of commerce the two countries have been mortal enemies, that three major wars have been fought since 1548, that kingdoms have been laid to waste, that the mention of Burma to someone Thai, like Aunty Sue, more often than not will get you a look of pure disdain.

But here, Thailand and Burma have put aside differences, united by commerce. Peace via currency.

We travel from shop to shop. My mother and her sisters are a hurricane, six women wanting what they want, for the price they want it at. They ask vendors how much items cost and shake their heads and counteroffer at half the price. Then the game begins. Numbers sling back and forth until they reach a fair arrangement. If not, the aunts walk away, say out loud that there is another vendor across the street who will see them eye-to-eye. This tactic usually works, the vendor acquiescing to their price.

I have a particular fondness for jade. It reminds me of the green lollipops I enjoyed as a child, tilting them into the light and looking through them at a green world. Jade, like any other stone, however, appears the same to me. I am quickly overwhelmed, so many settings and so many stones, not knowing whether or not I am being swindled.

The vendors in Mai Sai swarm. They thrust jade in my face and hard-sell me on everything. *Sir, I have the best price. Sir, I have what you are looking for. Sir, the best quality, I assure you. Sir, trust me.* Because I do not possess the same tenacity as my family, the vendors look at me as prey, salivating at my slouching presence, my timid demeanor. Usually, I flee as fast as I can.

"Sir, I have the perfect stone for you," a vendor says. She is about eighteen, face round and white, hair with streaks of red in it. She wears a T-shirt that reads Made in America.

I shake my head. This doesn't stop her. She shadows my every step, shoving a ring into my face, a large gaudy one that would sit heavy on a finger. The setting looks like a spacecraft, something from *Star Wars*, the Millennium Falcon with loopy ears. She gives every little detail of the ring pinched between her fingers, speaking in rapid-fire Thai, with a slight northern dialect, which makes me think she is from the other side of the border, like many of the vendors here.

"This stone is rare. Look at its color. It came from a cave with little moisture, so the green is greener. You will not find a stone like this anywhere, only here, in my store. Only in my hand right now."

In America, it would be easy to say, "I'm just looking." Here, that doesn't work. Here, despite my size, I shrivel into a husk of myself. For this reason I have accrued many useless and garish souvenirs over the years. "Remember that black velvet painting," Katie would say. "Remember the weird purses, the chubby monk dolls, the back scratcher shaped like a naked woman? What were you thinking?"

"Sir," the vendor says, "this ring is one hundred percent white gold, handmade. I know the family who made this. They are wonderful people. Very attentive. Best in Thailand. In Burma, too. Your sweetie will love it. You have a sweetie, yes? Of course you have a sweetie. You are big and handsome, like a *farang*. And you have a nice smile. Your sweetie is very lucky."

My sweetie would despise this ring. My sweetie would take one look at this ring and think I know nothing about her. This ring will dispel all this young love we have accrued over the months of being together. This ring is like the cursed rings I used to read about in the fantasy books of my youth, rings that bring about leprosy, rings that steal all fortune, rings that shatter the heart. This ring is the epitome of flamboyant, like the other jade figurines all over the store, priced at thousands of dollars, like the jade pickup truck or the jade motorcycle.

Ah, to be a rare stone chiseled into a Harley.

"Sir, this ring is not expensive. I'll give you a special price, only 136,000 baht."

My eyes widen. The ring costs almost four thousand dollars. I shake my head and pucker my lips. I tell her I don't have that much.

"Discount," she says. "Give me your price."

In one of the showcases is a tray of inexpensive rings, thrown into a disorganized pile. In the pile is a small ring, with a dark green stone. The silver is tarnished, like smoke. The shape of the stone, however, captivates me. It is looks like an ever-watchful eye.

"What about this ring?" I say. I point into the showcase.

The vendor sucks in her lips. "You don't want that ring, sir."

"I want to see it."

The vendor sighs and puts the tray of rings on the showcase. I pick out the ring, turning it in my fingers, raising it up to the overcast sky. Against the gray it looks like a mysterious green sun.

"This ring is machine made," the vendor says. "The stone is too dark. I don't want to sell it to you."

"How much?" I say.

"Sir, this is a better ring." She thrusts the spaceship ring in my face.

Confidence builds in me, a rush, a surge. I wonder if this is what my family feels like when they barter, this sense of invincibility. Like my mother with fruit, wanting what she wants.

"How much?" I say again. I straighten and stick my chest out. My shadow falls over her, or I want to imagine my shadow falling over her. I don't think there was enough light for a shadow.

The vendor pouts. Her brow furrows. "Sir, I don't want to give you a bad ring."

"I want this ring," I say. "How much?"

She shakes her head but I stand resolute.

"Tell me," I say.

"Fine. For you, fifteen hundred baht."

"Three fifty," I say.

"Sir, you are killing me. You don't buy the better ring. You want junk, and still you want to lowball me."

"If it's junk, I will take it off your hands," I say. "If it is junk, you can part with it at my price."

"Six hundred, then."

"Three fifty."

"Sir, please."

"Three fifty or I leave and buy nothing from you. And . . ." I point to my family two stores over, haggling over a jade tree, "I will tell the women over there to not buy anything from you either, and they love to buy."

The vendor crosses her arms. "Sir doesn't play fair," she says. She is thinking of her next move, perhaps her next sale. Then she sighs. "Fine. You win."

*

I find a coffee shop and sit and read a romance, *Eleanor and Park*, a strange little novel about two unlikely teenagers who fall for each other. The shop is connected to an old hotel—the lobby walls and floors constructed from teak wood, lacquered and shiny. All this wood makes me feel like I'm in Colorado instead of near the Myanmar border.

On the TV above the barista, the news replays highlights of Germany demolishing Brazil, 7–1. The Germans are now in the finals of the World Cup, awaiting the winner of Argentina and the Netherlands.

Aunt Jume finds me. She's the other half of Aunt Jeem, her twin, the youngest of the sisters. Throughout the visit, Aunt Jume has been bringing out old photos of herself and her sister, when they were babies, teenagers, and young adults working as flight attendants for Thai Airlines. She asks if I can tell them apart. I can, easily, even when my mother can't. The twins are amazed. They sometimes don't know who is who. What is it that distinguishes them? they want to know. "Admit it," says one of them, "I'm prettier." I laugh. The fact is I don't know what it is that sets them apart. Physically they are identical. I think it's posture and smile, or perhaps Aunt Jume looks deeper in thought, a bit more ponderous. It's this virtue that makes me fond of her. When I was young, I clung to her; "my little orangutan," she used to call me. She was married for thirty years until she found out her husband had another family in Bangkok. "She couldn't give him kids," my mother told me, "so he found someone who could." Aunt Jume remains friends with him, however, and he calls and sends her money every month.

"You look tired," Aunt Jume says.

"Jade is hard work," I say.

"Ah," she says, "I'm an expert."

Aunt Jume explains jade like a science teacher. Jade comes in different colors—lavender, yellow, even black—depending on what gasses and light the stones are exposed to. Green is the most common. One way to find out if a stone is real is to hold it. Jade is cool to the touch. No two stones should be alike. Real expensive jade possesses clouds of white, yet retains its transparency. It's like you are looking through a window and seeing a world that's similar to your own but the edges are dulled, the lights dimmed, and everything is ghostly green.

"Is there something you're looking for?" Aunt Jume says. "For someone special?"

I take out the ring I bought and show her. "Is this good?"

Aunt Jume squints to better focus. She comments on the silver, "good quality," which would shine like new with a little polish. She says the stone holds positive energy. She can feel it vibrate in her hand. She says the cut is very unique, like a teardrop. I don't know if what she tells me is true, but I didn't buy the ring because of its quality. I bought it because it was what I thought Deedra would like. I bought it because, among all the other rings in that store, this was the one that stood out.

"This is for your girlfriend?" Aunt Jume says.

I nod.

Aunt Jume leans in and lowers her voice. "Can we speak seriously?"

"Of course, Auntie."

"Your new girlfriend? Is this a brief thing? People your age have brief things."

I choke on my coffee.

"I'm very sorry about Katie," she says. "We all are. I love her. I want to send gifts. Can you take them to her?"

I nod, wiping my mouth.

"And you're still friends. That's good. Not like your mom and dad. Not healthy. Your mom, she gets so mad at the mention of him."

I laugh into my hand.

"They're old now—your mom and dad. They share you. They should be cordial. More years have passed than their marriage."

What Aunt Jume speaks of is true, but a friendship between my mother and father will never happen. That bridge has already burned. That bridge nuclear-ly exploded into a million slivers and what is left is radioactive space. Their relationship remains in the realm of the unforgiving, like many things in the world—this country and its opposing sides, this past of war and destruction.

Aunt Jume wipes a bit of sweat from her forehead with a handkerchief. "Look at me and my ex-husband. We speak every week. We love each other, but in a different way. Yes, he has another family. Yes, he has another wife. Yes, he has a son. But what can I do? In this life, I am dealt with what I am dealt."

"Mom is stubborn," I say.

"Oh my God," Aunt Jume says in exasperated English. "Your mom is the most stubborn person in the world."

On the TV are the faces of crying and dejected Brazilian fans. They look like someone has killed their beloved dog. The news anchors have a good laugh.

"All of us want you happy," Aunt Jume says. "Are you happy?"

I had forgotten what that felt like, happiness. I knew I could play the role of a happy person. I knew I could go to work, like I did this year, and smile and laugh and crack jokes and appear to be in complete joy. I knew I could be in conversation with someone, but inside, wanting to flee. I contemplated never returning to the States. I contemplated teaching English in Asia and living without needing others, not even my family. I imagined this other life, this hermit life. I romanticized it, being alone, making my own way in this world. It sounded impossibly plausible. But I didn't do it. I came home. Part of me thought myself a coward for not going through with my plan. The other part said it was much more difficult to come home and face life. That other part knew that healing, bad or good, would have to happen here.

So I let go.

And in that I found a bit of myself, just a bit. I can't pinpoint the time or place this happened. I can't even tell you what letting go feels like. It wasn't dramatic. It wasn't a sudden epiphany. But it happened. Gradually. Day by day.

I did miss the pain. I won't lie. It's the reason, I believe, people remain static in their lives. The reason why people stay in unhappy marriages. The reason we cannot soften ourselves to forgive. We become comfortable with suffering. To think of another way of living scares the ever-living shit out of us.

"I am happy," I say.

"Does this new friend make you happy?"

"Very much."

"Then that's all we want."

Deedra makes me happy. A happiness that scares me. A happiness that scares her. This fear is necessary. This fear makes us want to never let go of this feeling we share.

"Listen," my aunt says, "I want to give your new friend gifts, too, but I don't know what she likes. Tell me about her."

"She loves all living things," I say. "Except fruit flies."

Aunt Jume laughs. "I'll buy her what I would like then. How does that sound?"

"Great," I say.

"Let's go then," Aunt Jume says. "There's a lot to buy."

Balance

Today we go to an unfinished temple in the mountains of Phrae, where Aunty Sue was born and raised. Phrae is a small town. Time has stopped here. Much of the downtown district retains the look of the '40s and '50s. Building-front shops with signs made of wood hang on rusted chains. Ponies with carriages wait at intersections. Old-fashioned steel tubs on wooden carts carry fresh coconut ice cream. Some houses—like Aunty Sue's—were built in the 1900s, in the traditional way, elevated off the ground in case of flooding, completely made of teak. Now, Aunty Sue's home has Wi-Fi, a fact she is proud of. "I can look up Chinese food recipes on Google," she says, "and play games. Do you know Candy Crush?"

I love Aunty Sue's house, despite its age, despite cringing whenever I step on the floorboards, creaking and cracking, despite my fear that I will break through the house. I love the house and Phrae because this was what the country used to look like, in a time when water buffalo tilled fields and horses were the only mode of transportation. Phrae's town symbol is a horse. Now everywhere I go harkens to a modern age, with modern conveniences. Fast food chains like McDonald's and Burger King sprout like daisies. Starbucks has invaded. The malls have become larger and larger, the movie theaters louder and louder. Cell phones are prevalent, even among monks, who tuck them in the sleeve of their robes. Thailand has learned from the West and taken it to another level. Several astronomical levels. But Phrae resists. It holds onto what Thailand once was, a disappearing Thailand.

Aunty Sue splits her time in three places: by herself in Phrae, with my mother in Chiang Mai, and with Tui and Bee in Bangkok. Though she is a social person, she likes doing things her way, and the older she becomes the more she seems to seek time alone. About once a day, Aunty Sue disappears. Most of the time, she is outside cooking or preparing to cook, a type of meditation for her. Sometimes, she's in the bathroom, and when I inquire whether she's sick, my mother says, "Just sick of me." This need for solitude is what I've inherited from her. She has taught me how to see the world, to keep my eyes open, to look for the idiosyncrasies in life. In many ways, her introspection, her sense of being, has trained me to be a writer. It is what I carry onto the page. I seldom write about my aunt, however, my mother and father having usurped the stage. I seldom write about her because she's always there, the balance I seek in life.

We make a quick stop so Aunty Sue can check on the house. When she exits the car, baby chickens follow her, pecking at the dry grass. "Are you hungry, my little chickens?" my aunt says. She throws them leftover rice and they greedily dart for the grains. The rest of us—the twins, my mother, and the hired driver—wait in the car.

The twins begin to talk, like parakeets, their voices squeaking and squawking over each other. It's hard to know who's saying what.

"She should sell the house."

"She would get a lot for it."

"Look at all the land."

"It's wild."

"The trees are heavy with leaves."

"Sagging to the ground."

"So many trees."

"So much fruit."

"Unpicked."

"And look."

"The vines are climbing."

"And lacing."

"So much green."

"She has mango, longan, and banana trees."

"Like an orchard."

"The bananas are perfect."

"And the house."

"So old."

"But look at it."

"The wood is good."

"Beautiful."

"I can't believe it's still standing."

"It won't fall for a hundred more years."

"They built them to last."

"But what's to do here?"

"Phrae is nowhere."

"Phrae is lonely."

"Phrae is boring."

"What if she gets sick?"

"She's not steady anymore."

"Sometimes she sleeps for hours."

"Too old."

"She can't stay here forever."

"Didn't one of her sisters just die?"

"Yes."

"In the house?"

"Last year."

"Ghost."

"Older sister," the twins say in unison, "you should encourage Sue to sell."

My mother is quiet. She smiles at her sisters. Even in their sixties they chatter like children, and I wonder if this is what my mother had to deal with when she was a teenager, the oldest daughter, helping her parents wrangle the younger ones. My mother holds my hand. She watches the baby chicks eat the rice, the mother hen a distance away purveying. My mother likes this house, too. She occasionally hops on a bus and makes the two-hour trek to be with Aunty Sue for a few weeks. She tells me about the breeze that passes through all the windows, and the rooster that climbs atop the concrete wall and wakes up the town in the morning.

"It's her home, little ones," she says. "It's hard to get rid of your home."

*

My cousin Oat has planned the new temple ceremony. He works with Ant to fill ninety-nine buckets with young banana trees to be planted around the grounds. For him to organize such a ceremony means he wants to accrue plenty of karma and luck in his life. Means he has big plans, which he has not told anyone. Means, I speculate, that he is preparing to ask the woman he is seeing to marry him soon. Ceremonies like this are only for big-ticket items like marriage and pregnancy and death.

It is bizarre to witness an unfinished temple. The walls are without color or jewels or gold. The temple lions that stand guard in front of the doors look like lumpy, featureless clouds. The slithering serpent that serves as the handrail for stairs is denuded of scales and fangs. The grand Buddha that resides on the mountaintop remains unfinished, bamboo scaffolding running up the front and back of the statue. His face is blank—no eyes, no mouth—just the point of a nose, making him look like something from a horror film. The entire temple is a blank canvas.

When we arrive, we scatter into different areas of the temple to help. I stuff ninety-nine plastic bags with uncooked jasmine rice and place the bags into the buckets with the trees. My mother and aunts fill ninety-nine envelopes with money, which I again place into the buckets with the trees. Ant sticks money trees into the soil of the bucket, long sticks that I tape small bills to. Ninety-nine small bills on ninety-nine money trees with ninety-nine banana trees in ninety-nine buckets.

I drip with sweat. My back hurts from bending and lifting. I have dirt stains on my white dress shirt and khakis. I've inhaled several flies and gnats. I wonder why this hasn't been done already. Why we haven't been preparing for this the last few days, weeks? Ninety-nine buckets is a lot of fuckin' buckets. Ninety-nine banana trees are a lot of fuckin' trees. I whisper this to my mother, minus the "fuckin'." She nods. Says in a quiet voice that some people are not very good at planning. Says some people are kind of dumb about it. Says some people are kind of dumb. She's prickly, too, and I know whom it is she is referring to, Oat and Ant. I love them both, but organizing is not their strong suit.

Aunty Sue feels faint, so she sits on a plastic chair under an awning. I find her a cool bottle of water and fan her with the book I'm reading.

She comments on the cover, the naked back of a woman with a tattoo on the shoulder.

"You like women like this?"

"What women?"

"White women," she says, taking deep breaths. "With tattoos."

"I like all women."

"Don't be like your father."

I laugh so hard the sparrows flit away, a dog lifts his head up from slumber, and people working on the temple stop and stare.

"Does your new friend have a tattoo?" Aunty Sue says.

"No." A lie.

"Does your new friend have crazy piercings?"

"No."

"Does your new friend make you pay for everything?"

"No."

"Does your new friend make you happy?"

"Yes."

"I like her then."

She takes a drink. I keep fanning her. Sweat beads on her forehead and runs down her cheek onto the maroon top my mother sewed for her. Most of my aunt's clothes are made by my mother or bought on clearance at Big C, the Thai version of Walmart.

"Too hot today," she says.

"Too boring," I say.

"That's been your favorite word since you were six. That and stupid and whatever."

"Whatever," I say. "This is stupid."

She laughs.

"Why the number ninety-nine?" I ask.

"In China," my aunt says, "the number nine means longevity. If you love someone you send nine, ninety-nine, or 999 roses. The forbidden city has 9,999 rooms." She goes on and says that *gow*, nine, is not only a number but it also means to step forward, as in *gow nah*.

"We could have done this with nine buckets?"

"Probably," she says.

"So stupid," I say.

I grab my aunt's hand. It is light, her dark skin like thin silk, her fingers tough. The tips of them are callused from too many times cutting herself with a kitchen knife, from her daily routine of taking her blood sugar. I've always been a mama's boy, always overly affectionate with my mother. But never my aunt. Even when I was younger, she said my mother and father should come first in my life, then Buddha, then the country, and then her. After the divorce, she dropped my father, but the rest stayed the same. Aunty Sue, however, is close to my heart, before Buddha and Thailand. She is my father and mother and friend. I love her with a ferocity that no one can rival, but I don't show it enough, like an adolescent who doesn't want his friends to see how mushy he can be.

She squeezes my hand. "I feel like this year you've become an adult."

"You say that a lot."

"But this time I mean it."

"Because I've failed at marriage?"

"I sense something has changed in you," she says. "I'm glad to see this before I die."

"You won't die."

"Dream on," she says. "Everyone dies."

I usually dissuade her when she talks of death. She does this often. Every year when I leave to go back to the States, she says, "If I'm alive, I'll see you next year," and I usually tell her to shut up. But the truth is: Aunty Sue is getting older. Her health fluctuates. She has her good days and bad days, and now the bad days are adding up, the bad days come on more frequently.

We sit quietly, hand in hand, and watch my mother and the twins finish the preparations for the ceremony. Parishioners from town join in and donate their own money. Some have brought the monks everyday essentials, like soap and toothpaste and toilet paper. Some of Oat's beauty store clients attend and thank him for putting together such a wonderful event. Oat and Ant have laid out the buckets into four rows, their faces slick with sweat. The buckets sit on long strips of yellow cloth. When it is time, everyone will place a hand on the cloth and present the buckets to the head monk who accepts the offering.

Nine monks sit on aluminum folding chairs. When the ceremony starts, the monks begin their prayers that echo throughout mountain.

Aunty Sue keeps holding my hand even when we are supposed to put them together. She squeezes hard. She puts her other hand over the top of mine. We remain that way well into the prayer before she gives one last squeeze and lets go.

*

Germany wins the World Cup, the news says. It also says elections for a new government will happen in a year. My mother is asleep on the couch, mouth open, catching flies. Aunty Sue is passed out on the cool marble floor, her stomach exposed. I change the channel and find a Thai soap opera to watch, about love and how it hurts.

Lesbians

When Ellen DeGeneres came out in 1997 on the Oprah Winfrey Show, I received a call at my apartment in Carbondale, Illinois. My mother told me that Ellen was a man. "She said she was gay," my mother said in Thai. She believed the term "gay" referred to only men. Ellen, to her, must be a man. I tried to explain to her that gay meant having a preference for the same sex and was not gender-specific. "You are wrong," she said. "I watched it on Oprah."

How we arrive years later on the topic, I do not know. One moment we are sitting in the middle of a botanical garden at Doi Ang Khang's Royal Agricultural Station, surrounded by an eruption of flowers, and the next my mother says, "We are not lesbians!"

The Royal Garden is tiered, ascending a hill toward a skinny evergreen that rockets into the sky like a green finger. The workers—all from hill tribes in the area—work diligently to keep weeds out and pluck the dead heads off petunias. The king developed the Royal Agricultural Station in 1969, to provide jobs for the local people and to cultivate the land with wintering flowers, fruits, and plants. At Doi Ang Khang, the temperature is twenty to thirty degrees cooler than it is in Chiang Mai, the humidity lifting its oppressive blanket. The weather stays consistent throughout the year, which is why so many of the flowers here are ones I've grown when I've lived in New York and Illinois—marigolds, pansies, dahlias, alliums, hyacinths. Because of the weather, my mother wears a thick coat with a stocking cap, Aunty Sue is in layers of sweaters. It is as if we are elsewhere, not in a tropical country. It is the reason Doi Ang Khang is also called "Little Switzerland."

"We are not lesbians!" my mother says again.

"We are best friends," Aunty Sue says. She takes a picture of a pansy with her new Leica camera.

"Has someone called you lesbians?" I say.

"People say things they don't understand," Aunty Sue says, her eyes in the viewfinder.

"People talk too much," says my mother.

"Who are these people?"

"People," my mother says. "We're not having sex. We're not kissy kissy. We're not anything."

"Being intimate doesn't define being a lesbian." I say.

My mother rolls her eyes and tilts her head into the clear sky. I know what's she thinking. There he goes again, my smart professor son, trying to civilize his crazy, irrational mother.

"We don't love each other like that," Aunty Sue says and captures a large-fisted pink peony.

"I don't understand why two women who love each other have to be called lesbians."

"It's not a bad thing," I say.

My mother swats a hand in the air.

In the past, my friends and I have discussed whether my mother and aunt are lesbians. Many of my friends teach queer and gender studies. They tell me sexual intimacy is not the only thing that defines same-sex relationships. "It's a trust we have for one another that we do not and cannot have with a man," says a friend. "Being a lesbian is not a male's wet dream," says another. "We are not always in each other's crotches."

Friends have asked whether my father moved out because of my mother and Aunty Sue's relationship. It's a question that always catches me off guard. It's a question that makes me stammer. But the truth is: Perhaps. Perhaps my father thought he had to compete for my mother's attention. I already sucked onto her like a leech, and now there was this woman who lived in the house, too, a woman who incidentally was there before he came onto the scene. And perhaps that was what drove him into the arms of another.

I've never thought of my mother and aunt's relationship as peculiar. I've thought of it as normal. I've thought of it as two Thai women who came to America and met in 1968 in a nurses' dormitory in Chicago and have been inseparable since.

Bamboos knock against one another like hollow chimes. The sun slants against the hill, lighting the flowers in an avalanche of brilliant hues. A breeze blows across the garden, and the flowers nod and sway. The sun feels good on my skin, warms it.

"They don't understand the Thai way." My mother's voice rises. When she's worked up, she believes the louder she is the more convincing she sounds. "Thai woman stick together."

"Like sisters," Aunty Sue says. She snaps a photo of a vine twining a light pole.

"Yes, like sisters."

"Why stick together?" I ask.

"Who can trust a Thai man?" they both say.

"True dat," I say. My use of slang goes over them.

Aunty Sue looks through the viewfinder of her camera. She clicks pictures here and there. Click, click, click. "When women get old," she says, "when their husbands have disappeared, we seek each other." She aims the camera at my mother and me. Click.

"Who will take care of us but us?" my mother says.

This question transcends sexuality. It's a question that many of us have pondered, regardless of being gay or straight. Who will care for us when our children have gone to live separate lives? Who will be beside us, as our joints and muscle grow weak, our minds becoming dull? Who will feed us soft foods when our teeth are gone?

"We love each other," my mother says. "But we're not lesbians."

*

Later, when we are at a hill tribe village, I buy a few homemade bracelets from a little girl. She has a bowl cut and addresses me in English, but I respond in Thai. The girl is maybe eight or nine. She looks over my shoulder at my mother and Aunty Sue, haggling over prices for dried apricots and plums. My mother and aunt are the same size, though my aunt's hair is close to the base of her neck, while my mother's is long, stopping at her shoulders. An argument starts. Aunty Sue wants more apricots; my mother wants more plums. They say sharp words to each other. It happens at least three times a day, Aunty Sue expressing her annoyance in sighs. My mother pouts. In seconds, the argument ends. They don't make up. An argument is an argument. An argument is part of their language. To them, there is no winning or losing. They know no one will leave. No one will want a divorce. Nearing eighty, they know they are in it together, to the end.

The sun settles into my eyes, and for a moment, they merge into one, and I can't distinguish them.

Invisible Partners

On my mother's refrigerator are pictures from my high school dances—
homecoming, the Sweetheart's Dance, prom. My mother magnets so
many photos of me to the refrigerator you can barely see the surface, just
hundreds of different Iras sporting different facial hair. But those dance
photos—there is something missing in each one of them.

My mother has cut out my dates.

It is me, in suspenders and hunter green slacks, half an arm around
no one. It is me, wearing contacts for the one and only time in my life,
and part of my hand is on the hip of no one's waist. It is me, in a tux and
sequined teal vest, cheek-to-cheek with no one.

"Why did you cut my dates?"

Aunty Sue, shaving carrots at the dinner table, laughs.

My mother sews together the pants I ripped earlier in the day. I was
kowtowing to Buddha at Wat Chedi Luang in the center of town when
I heard the rip. My mother laughed so hard her dentures popped out.
Aunty Sue had to rush to a bathroom so she wouldn't pee herself. I, on
the other hand, pulled my shirt down and refused to go anywhere else
the rest of the day.

"I save only what I want to remember," my mother says. "Those
white girls, I do not want to remember."

"Ask her what she did to other photos," Aunty Sue says.

"What photos?"

"Old photos with your father in them."

"What did you do?"

My mother shrugs, but does not lift an eye off the needle. Her fingers work quickly.

"What did she do?" I ask my aunt.

Aunty Sue smiles. "She cut him out."

My mother's glasses are thick. When she looks up, they enlarge her eyes, like a bug. "I want to remember what I remember."

*

They have been relegated—my dates—to the void where all halved pictures go. I imagine a planet of them. So many lost partners, so many severed parts. There they mingle, in a two-dimensional world, like a pop-up book. There they try to find a fit to complete the photo. But no cut fits flawlessly, an imperfect puzzle.

Those dates—Becky, Sharon, Vicky—find a table in the corner of a coffee shop. They are beautiful in their dresses, their hair primped and pampered, their nails painted vivid red. Vicky's spaghetti straps make boys in the coffee shop look on with lust. Becky's lips stand out from the pale of her skin. And Sharon's blond hair feels soft like the strands of fine yarn. In this world, they are the best of friends, though in real life they ran in different circles. In this world they play one role, and it is the one role they share: Ira's date. The night comes early here, but the sky never darkens. Lights swirl like a perpetual disco ball. They tell one another stories of the dance.

"Ira, he could move, couldn't he?"

"I didn't know a Thai guy could James Brown like that."

"Did he do the running man for you?"

They comment on how he was the perfect gentleman, except for Becky, who found him dancing with Tanya Tallon, his senior year crush. They went as friends anyway, so it didn't matter.

"And when a slow dance came on, he'd pull you close to him and you could feel the warmth of his torso."

"And he had shoulders you could rest your head on."

"You felt other things, too."

They laugh and laugh and laugh. There was so much about Ira that was entertaining, how he went to the bathroom every fifteen minutes to check on his hair, how he was paranoid there was a booger in his nose, how he insisted on opening every door and saying in a lousy English accent, "After you, madam." They agreed he was such a boy, but different from the others, respectful, thinking about them before anything else.

"He let me wear his jacket when we were on an after-dance cruise on Lake Michigan and it was thirty degrees out."

"It rained hard, so he gave me his umbrella and carried me to the car so my dress didn't drag."

"He was so shy when he kissed me."

A melancholy settles among them, those three dressed-up girls. This happens a lot in the world of halved pictures. They wish their other half was there, their versions of Ira, asking them to the dance floor, holding them tight, singing in their ear how beautiful they are, how this song is theirs, how this night is theirs, how they do not have to fear anything, not other lurking pictures, not a pair of scissors come to sever them.

*

There is one photo my mother hasn't cut: Katie and me on our wedding day. She used to keep it in the dining room, the most public place in the house. Now, it resides in her room, next to her bed. It is the same one in my father's house where we are dressed in traditional Thai garb—Katie in burnt orange, me in emerald green. Our hands are joined at the center, our heads leaning toward each other. Behind us is the blurred hotel pool. Our smiles brim with happiness, stilled by a photographer who kept instructing us to get closer. And though the day had been long, and you could see the fatigue in our faces, at that moment, captured in that picture, is us and the life that will happen thereafter.

My mother will not sever this photo. She will look at it and think, Once upon a time, my son was married. Once upon a time, I had a daughter, and despite how blindingly white she was, I loved her with my entirety.

July 10

On this day a year ago, near midnight, I looked in the bathroom mirror. What stared back was not me. What stared back was the person I most hated, the one I wanted to destroy. Pathetic fuck. I punched my face. Again. Again. I slapped my chest, my stomach. Over and over. Slapped hard, the sound of it echoing in the small bathroom. My mother and aunt were asleep. Mosquitoes buzzed my naked body. I did not swat them away. I welcomed their greed. I wanted them to suck all the blood out of me, like in a horror movie, leaving me a dried and shriveled husk. My body glistened with sweat in the bathroom's fluorescents. I never took my eyes off of my reflection. Fuckin' loser. Ugly fuck. Fuckin' failure. I let loose my fists. Again and again. Over and over. I wanted to feel. I wanted to hurt. I hurt. Red emerged on my skin, fist-sized. Red welts on my stomach and chest. My chin swelled. My lips cracked. Blood dripped from my upper lip and from a cut inside my mouth. I spit into the sink and took joy in the red that swirled down the drain.

*

On this day a year ago, I thought about taking my life.

*

Today, I call Deedra. In a few days, I tell her, I will be home. In a few days we will be together. I do not want to hang up, fearing in that single action, she may disappear and all that I thought I had learned and understood would vanish. I would be lost again. I ask her about her day. I ask about the girls and the dogs and the cat and the bird and the guinea pig. I ask if she got rid of the plague of fruit flies that invaded her home. She knows what today is. She knows like my family knows, who did not mention Katie or anything about Katie, who took me to lunch at the Sizzler because they wanted something American. They know. Deedra knows. She does not pry. She does not push. She does not say "How are you?" in an overly concerned voice, or "Do you want to talk about it?" I love her more for not asking. But it is in the mundaneness of the conversation. It is in every little question we ask. Every little detail we share. "Tell me what you cooked today." "Describe those noodles you had?" "How did the cat torture the bird again?" "You gave the guinea pig your leftover salad? Fascinating." "Tell me more. Tell me everything."

Before we hang up, I say, "Thank you for finding me."

VIII

Okay

One morning, I woke in tears. Katie and I were living in Oswego, and the winter brought about a heaviness that settled for months. To compound the winter, Katie's mother, Dinny, passed away in late November.

It was a dream that had caused the tears, a dream that faded the way dreams do. But images stuck. Lines stuck. I didn't want to lose them, so I whispered out loud incoherent details to make them real, to make them stick. I wasn't sure if these were tears of waking or tears from the dream I carried with me into the awake world. I was certain I had been crying there, too. There: a crisp green place, filled with dogs. There: the sun, an orange globe that lit a prairie on fire. One moment, I was asleep, and the next I was sniffling into the back of Katie's neck.

"What is it?" Katie said, sleep tugging at her voice.

"Dream," I said.

"About?"

"I'm not sure."

"I'm sorry." She turned to kiss my forehead.

"For what?"

"For the dream."

"I think it was good," I said.

"Was it?"

I nodded and wiped my eyes with the pillowcase.

"You're crying."

"I am."

"You don't cry."

"I know."

"Remember any of it?"

I nodded.

"Tell me," she said.

In the morning light, she looked stunning, though saliva clung to the corners of her mouth, though the outlines of the pillowcase dented her face. Our dogs were curled in round balls at the foot of the bed.

"I dreamed of Mom," I said.

It was not the Mom before she left us. I dreamed of the way Dinny was before cancer and age stripped the body bare. In my dream she possessed the fullness of her hips again and the rose of her cheeks. She did not have bad knees, did not limp around with a walking stick.

"How is she?" Katie said.

"She's with dogs."

Katie pulled me closer to her. "I bet it's all our dogs," and she began to list the canines in her life that had passed away, all of those four-legged creatures she'd loved and lost—Amber and Sergeant, Mick and Bonny—dogs and dogs and more dogs.

For a while we didn't speak. For a while, we let ourselves remember, and I could tell Katie was getting weepy herself. She missed her mother, her compass through life, and now her mother was gone. Now her father's mind was gone, believing the phone repairman across the street was tapping the lines, was breaking in to steal money from his wallet. Now Katie was fearing she might be gone, too, a darkness coming over her like a winter storm.

"Anything else?" Katie said.

There was.

In the dream that was becoming a distant murmur, I remember Dinny's voice, which sounded as if it was syphoned through a tube or connected via string and cans.

"She said everything will be okay."

"Will it?"

"I don't know," I said.

"I don't either."

"If Mom says so," I said, "why should we believe otherwise."

Katie nodded.

For the longest time, I thought the dream meant we would heal from her loss; we would find a way to live without her presence in our lives, that Katie's father would find clarity again before passing on himself not long after. But I had heard that line before, uttered in almost identical fashion. It was years earlier, when Katie and I first dated and we fought over every little thing, when there was doubt we'd even make it one year, let alone fifteen. I vacationed with her family in Colorado, and a thunderstorm passed through the mountains. I was in the car with Dinny, driving back from a grocery store. Around us, the gray sky deepened the level of the green in the trees, in the leaves, in the grasses that spread in stretches of valleys. Dinny knew Katie and I were still learning each other; she witnessed our arguments in the small cabin, but never judged, never took sides. "You'll be okay, Ira," she said. "No matter what happens with my daughter." I nodded because I was twenty-one and did not know how to respond, and because gusts of wind pushed the car onto the dirt shoulder and lightning jagged in the distance.

"We'll be okay," Katie said, years later, when the car was full of her belongings and the dogs, when she was about to pull out of the driveway and into a new phase of her life.

I think of this dream because of its premonition-like quality. I think of this dream because I feel Dinny was talking to us now. I think she knew, even then, the troubles heading our way, knew when our marriage wouldn't be good, and that perhaps we would have to figure out our lives separate from each other. That's the thing with dreams: We can make them say whatever we want. We can manipulate them into fortunes.

That day, however, Katie and I held each other and cried, we held each other as if our lives depended on it, we held each other even when the snow outside began to fall, heavy and thick, blanketing the world in white.

That Long Couch

The worst days were when I did nothing. When I sat for too long on the couch and didn't move. On those days I went into myself. Going inward. I retreated into the squall William Styron spoke of in his memoir on depression, *Darkness Visible*. "It is a storm indeed, a storm of murk." On these days, Katie would find me and know I couldn't be reached because inside I went. Inside I stayed.

I wonder if this is what Buddha felt on his way toward enlightenment. Whether he had days of doubt, whether he wondered if the pain he suffered from would ever end, whether he would find what he was looking for. His life—all our lives—is about hard decisions. When Siddhartha decided to seek the life of a holy man, he abandoned his home, his duties as the crowned prince, his wife and child. He took to the woods, cut his luscious hair, and there, among the trees, he devoted his life to meditation. When I was in my moody twenties, I thought his choices were irresponsible. I was the worst Buddhist, a Buddhist who didn't believe in Buddhism, a Buddhist who didn't want to be Buddhist but was afraid to be nothing. I thought Buddha took the easiest path. *Yes, yes, go be deep and contemplative in the woods. Don't worry about your grieving wife or anything. Oh, and you decided to leave on the day your son was born? Nice. Seriously, what kinda dude does that?* Part of me still believes this.

But now, it's complicated. I think it would've been easier for him to stay. To continue living and suffering and not knowing how to alleviate what was ailing the mind. To be unhappy and unfulfilled. That unhappiness would seep into the marriage, would seep into the life of his child, his wife, his kingdom. He would spend the rest of his life wondering if there was a better path.

Doubt crawled into mind on those long days after Katie left. It made me question the entirety of my marriage, my choices, my sadness, my happiness, my anger. What happened, on that long couch, was I spun my wheels. I thought myself into a rut, and that rut cleaved my self-esteem, cleaved it into ribbons. To defend against this, I couldn't remain still. I was in a state of constantly doing. I concentrated only on the present. The present was elusive, like mist on the northern mountains, like smoke from candles at temples. I took to reading street signs out loud or singing songs obnoxiously. If not, I'd be gone. Delving headfirst into past regrets that scarred and scared. It didn't take much to slip, and suddenly, I was there. Laid out before me were the wrongs in my marriage. My stumbles since the divorce. My failed love life of the past. I compiled these into a melodramatic anthology of heartbreak entitled *My Life Sucks Because I Suck*. It was a bad book. Lots of violins of pity played in it. On that couch, I said, "I hate myself." On that couch, I said, "I'm such a loser." On that couch, I said, "No one loves me." The illogic poisoned me. There was no room for logic, no room for reason.

"We love you," my friends said. "Everyone loves you." I didn't hear them.

That long couch swallowed me whole. I plummeted down, like Alice, plummeting and plummeting, and the longer I descended, the less hope I had.

It's easy to compare my year between visits to a child's tale of mayhem. But it also seems apropos. Alice needed to save Wonderland, rid the land of the Queen of Hearts. I needed to save myself, rid the part of me that was wounded, or at least, see it for what it was: a lie.

*

It was not an easy decision, I'm sure, to send that letter. Katie must've ached. She must've doubted sending it. She most likely drafted it over and over, choosing the right words and phrases to awaken something in me, to make me really understand how unhappy she was. Unhappy we were. For that I'm eternally grateful, though at the time it tore me in two.

Sometimes the right path is the hardest one.

In November, Katie came back for a visit. We had agreed to see each other every two months before making a final decision about us. I picked her up at the airport and drove to a café where we sat outside in the cool Tampa winter, the temperature in the seventies. We ordered sandwiches, Katie a chocolate chip cookie she ate first. There was little talk between us, but it felt comfortable. We were two friends enjoying lunch, enjoying each other's company without the interruption of words.

"I think this should be permanent," I said.

"Me, too," she said.

"I think I'm learning a lot about me."

"Me, too." A piece of shredded lettuce clung to her mouth.

"I think we had a good run."

"We did."

"You're my best friend."

"You're mine."

"You have lettuce on your mouth," I said.

We had become different people. You could see it in the way we held ourselves, the confidence we possessed as we ate our sandwiches that afternoon. We didn't talk about what we had been doing while apart, or who we were seeing. We didn't talk about the sudden rushes of loneliness and doubt that crept up on us. We didn't talk about divorce or who would get what or any of the other business of breaking up. That would be settled in a couple of months. That was the easiest part of ending a marriage. Signatures and forms. We celebrated with more sandwiches when the divorce was final, calling each other ex-wife and ex-husband. "Is your sandwich good, Ex-wife?" "Delicious, Ex-husband."

That day in November, we simply enjoyed each other's company.

"I love you," she said.

I rolled my eyes at her sentimentality, like I rolled my eyes at all sentimentality. "I love you, too, I guess."

And I did.

I do.

In a different form, a form that didn't hurt us, didn't bring the worst out of us, didn't push us into the folds of a couch.

*

On this lazy day before I leave for the States, I find myself on a couch
my mother shipped from Chicago to Chiang Mai, a black leather couch
she bought before I was born, cushions held together by electric tape; a
couch my mother can't let go of. On this couch were too many memories.
So she kept it, though her sisters complained about how ugly it looked,
how no one wanted to sit on it, how she kept spending money to restuff
the cushions. She kept it like she kept all the other remnants of her prior
life—the magnets on the fridge, the sewing machine, all the suitcases on
top of her dresser, her dresser.

Strangely, I have never seen her sit on the couch, and I don't recall
her sitting on it when it resided in our home in Chicago. To her it
seemed the couch was like a piece of art, something the eye can gaze at
and transport you elsewhere.

There are things in life we keep, no matter how ugly. Like that couch.

When we climb out of a hole, we arrive at the same opening. I wasn't
surprised the couch was where I loved again. Wasn't surprised Deedra's
and my relationship began on a couch. How she sat at the very edge,
farthest away from me, afraid what might happen if we got closer. How
I kissed her for the first time on a couch, late into the early morning, and
when we were done we stared at each other, wondering what line we had
crossed and whether there was such thing as a line. How Deedra said
one day on the couch, "You forgive too easy," and I thought, I haven't
forgiven enough.

Not the trees, not the birds, not the persistent mosquitoes.

I forgive.

Not a past, not a marriage.

I forgive.

Not a father.

I forgive.

Not a mother or an aunt.

I forgive.

Not an ex-wife.

I forgive.

I forgive myself.

Goodbye

Sometimes I think whatever happiness I have found in the past year won't last. I've inherited my mother's jadedness. I have the family curse. I am incapable of finding and holding on to love. I think—no, sometimes, I'm sure—I will lose all that I cherish—Deedra, Katie, my friendships, my sense of self—all of it washed away in some wild flood, and what resurfaces, what keeps popping up, is the detritus of my inadequacies. No matter how hard I tell myself to occupy the here and now, I'm years ahead of myself, bounding in time, witnessing what I'll do wrong, creating—in a sense—a bad memory that has not yet happened.

Sometimes, I foresee myself alone.

Sometimes I am that boy—awkward and shy, pudgy and pale—hiding behind his mother's leg, or clutching at the back of his father's shirt, or needing Aunty Sue's voice to settle down the anxiety he carries in him like sodden rags. I am that boy, forever that boy, and his hands won't still, so he shoves them in his pockets, but then his legs won't still, so he crosses them, but then he rocks, slamming his back against a wall. I am that boy, that stupid boy, who believes his fist could go through walls, that when the universe cracks, he could stave off sorrow with pain. Pain, for this boy, feels better than this unknowable ache. Pain, physical pain, has a source; it is locatable. He puts his hand in fire; it is the fire that scalds him. He cracks a beer bottle in his hands; it is the glass that cuts him. He pulls out one leg hair at a time; it is his fingers that pluck. He likes to control his pain. He likes control, because sometimes he feels as if the earth were a rickety swing bridge about to heave him over the edge. I am that boy, the heartbroken one, in ripped jeans and a T-shirt and heavy Doc Martens, wondering if his father will return after driving off that winter night, wondering if his parents will forgive each other but knowing they never will. This is the thought the boy carries with him: love is not enough. It is engrained in the back of his mind. He hates it, so he pushes it down, throws quilts and pillows and books and anything over it, anything to dissuade him of this truth. Love is not enough. When the boy grows up and marries a poet, a woman who seems to emerge from the rich Illinois soil itself, he will convince himself that their love is impervious to whatever pitfalls await them in the future. He believes their marriage will remain a wonderful one. And for most of it, it was. It was a melodic birdsong. It was hundreds of tulips blossoming. It was a field of monarchs. But it ended. It ended because things end. And because the boy was prone to melodramatics, he thought everything would end with it.

That boy, that dumb boy.

Now, he finds himself here. In this world ever turning, ever blooming, ever evolving. Like him. He has changed, though he makes no promises that the clouds won't gather again or that he has fixed all the fractures within him. He hasn't. Some are so deep he doesn't know where to start. But he knows they are there. He knows. This is his first step.

*

Last year, I did not want to leave Thailand. Last year, the thought of returning home filled me with a dread that made my insides quiver. But I did. I returned. Waiting for me was Katie, who looked wrecked, who began boxing up things in the house. As she drove from the airport she cried and I looked out the window at the dark Tampa sky, at the haze of polluted pink that hovered above the city. Last year, before I boarded the plane back to the States, my mother and Aunty Sue said everything would be okay though their faces were full of worry. I nodded and said I would miss them. I said I loved them. I said that I'd see them in a year.

"Have you prayed yet?" my mother says.

My luggage is gathered around the living room floor. The twins busy themselves with getting the car ready to go to the airport. Aunty Sue tries to find some American dollars to give me.

"I haven't," I say.

"Sit with me," my mother says.

We kneel in front of a Buddha on a small shelf above us. It is a replica of the Emerald Buddha, the original residing in Bangkok near the Royal Palace. In 1434 lightning struck a pagoda in Chiang Rai, and a monk discovered a Buddha made of stucco that flaked like sunburned skin. The monk began removing the stucco, his fingers and hands caked in dirt and grit. What he found was a green Buddha that was not emerald but solid jade.

Underneath all of us is a precious stone, bright and beautiful, a true self. I think it's there. I think we spend most of our lives trying to find it, and when we do, we hold on tight. We never want to lose something in us that special.

"Pray with me," my mother says.

We put our hands together and recite prayers I learned when I was three, words spilling forth like holy water. I am a child again, praying every morning to the Buddha in Chicago, leaning against my mother's torso, needing the warmth of her, watching her squeeze her eyes tight, mouth silently moving.

"Ask Buddha for a safe trip," she says.

I do.

"Ask Buddha for a safe life."

I do.

"Ask Buddha for guidance in every step you take."

I do.

We kowtow three times, my forehead kissing the cool tiled floor.

Aunty Sue says it's time to go. I rise and pull my mother up, her knees cracking like stuck gears. "I have a good son," she says in Thai, then in English, "a good boy."

*

Geoff Schmidt wrote at the end of his essay "Otis and Jake," "Why do we take things close to our hearts, why do we love? . . . Why do we marry, why do we have children? Why do we love at all? When you lose love it mauls your heart. It bloodies you. And yet, again and again, we choose to love. Again and again. Why do we choose to love, again and again and again?"

Because.

To love is instinctual, no matter how scared we are of it. No matter how hard we protect ourselves from it. Despite our overemotional remarks about love, like "I'm never loving again." Or "Love is for wimps." Or the infamous one, "Love sucks." We believe what Tina sang, "What's love but a secondhand emotion?"

But in the end, we come back.

I feel this love. It is a warmth that spreads throughout all of me. It is a warmth that is different from the outside heat and humidity, but more akin to sipping warm tea and allowing it to travel to the core of you.

In the plane, taking off, I feel it coursing through me, this love. There is love in this plane. In the atmosphere we are cutting through. There is so much love—a water rush of petals—in this small country, my second home. There is love waiting when I arrive eight thousand miles later, a love that will run in my arms and take my face and kiss my very chapped lips, hold my very stiff body.

Love.

I go through my goodbyes, as the plane climbs higher and higher, like when I was a child and my mother and I would say our goodbyes to everything in Thailand. Goodbye trees, goodbye flowers, goodbye butterflies, goodbye temples and hills and mountains. Goodbye aunties and uncles and cousins. Goodbye dogs and cats and birds.

Goodbye, goodbye, goodbye.

Below me, the land yawns in green, endless green, layers of green, a green that extends to the horizon, to the slight curve of the earth, until it disappears under layers of clouds. This green life. This jade world.

IX

The Next Life

I walk hand in hand with a boy. He's my boy. He's mine. He has the name of a tree that Buddha was born under, gained enlightenment under, and died under; and a middle name of a tiny bird with a beautiful song. His hand is soft. It contains need. This boy needs me. Wants me. He is barely two. When he calls for me—wherever I am: toilet, office, kitchen—I say, *I'm here, I'm here*, and run to him as quick as I can. My wife Deedra says I spoil this boy. My wife says this boy will never want.

But he will. Everyone wants.

His emergence into the world came after a storm. For a while the midwife could not locate a heartbeat, and my wife was screaming in a way I never knew possible, this woman who nearly chopped her finger off but finished making dinner anyway. My wife is a badass, but the sounds coming out of her mouth made me grab her hands tighter. Made me fear like I have never feared before. Made me question, in the minutes before delivery, whether it was all worth it. Whether I made right decision to get here—in a delivery room in Tampa, Florida, married to a woman whose name rhymes with mine, who offered me this possibility.

And then the boy arrived. And he let out his first cry. And my next life began.

I called my mother and aunt. Told them he was here. Nothing could deter their joy. Not even eight thousand miles. When I relayed how he came into this life, with the umbilical cord wrapped twice around his neck, they said this was how I arrived. In the same way. In such a rush to greet the world that I had tangled myself up. And then I called my father and he laughed and it was so loud I held the phone away from my ear. "Be better," he said. "Be the best."

"Daddy, Daddy," the boy says, tugging my hand.

"I'm here," I say.

Here: In a world that gives as much as it takes away.

I squeeze his hand, a heartbeat, a reminder that this is real; he is real. It is how my mother holds my hand, squeezing as if to remember everything before she passes into the next life.

Every day I fear I am waking up to an illusion. One that will evaporate. Will vanish. But the boy looks up at me. I look down at him and his small round face, which is my face and his mother's and the history of countries. He says, "Daddy." I say, "Yes." He says, "I want," and in that slight pause, the milliseconds for the brain to find the right word for his young mouth, I fill that gap with all my wants, and all of them for him. I want you to live a beautiful life. I want you to have everything you need. I want you to find that special one. I want you to be strong when the world breaks its word. I want you to know happiness.

"I want," the boy says, "french fries."

"Okay," I say.

I don't say what else I would give him. I don't tell him how I want to wrap up all this green in the world and put it in a box and when he is older, when I am gone, he will open it and out will blossom his wishes, in every leaf and tendril, in every growing limb. This gift is my heart, son. How it spreads, this lushness.

"Do you like french fries?" I say.

"And ice cream."

"What kind?"

"Chocolate," he says. "Can I have french fries and chocolate?"

Son, you can have anything. Son, you are every possibility.

To order or obtain more information on these or other University
of Nebraska Press titles, visit nebraskapress.unl.edu.

CPSIA information can be obtained
at www.ICGtesting.com
Printed in the USA
LVHW030200211221
706761LV00003BA/442

9 781496 226013